IARIA

AA004377

GEOProcessing 2017

The Ninth International Conference on Advanced Geographic Information Systems, Applications, and Services

March 19 – 23, 2017

Nice, France

GEOProcessing 2017 Editors

Claus-Peter Rückemann, Leibniz Universität Hannover / Westfälische Wilhelms-Universität Münster /North-German Supercomputing Alliance (HLRN), Germany

Yerach Doytsher, Technion - Israel Institute of Technology, Haifa, Israel

Jianhong Cecilia Xia, Curtin University, Australia

Fernando José Braz, Federal Institute of Education, Science and Technology Catarinense - Brasil, Brazil

Printed from e-media with permission by:

Curran Associates, Inc.
57 Morehouse Lane
Red Hook, NY 12571

Some format issues inherent in the e-media version may also appear in this print version.

Printed by Curran Associates, Inc. (2017)

International Academy, Research, and Industry Association (IARIA)
412 Derby Way
Wilmington, DE 19810

Phone: (408) 893-6407
Fax: (408) 527-6351

petre@iaria.org

Additional copies of this publication are available from:

Curran Associates, Inc.
57 Morehouse Lane
Red Hook, NY 12571 USA
Phone: 845-758-0400
Fax: 845-758-2633
Email: curran@proceedings.com
Web: www.proceedings.com

Table of Contents

GEOProcessing 2017

Forward

The ninth edition of The International Conference on Advanced Geographic Information Systems, Applications, and Services (GEOProcessing 2017), held in Nice, France, March 19 - 23, 2017, addressed the aspects of managing geographical information and web services.

The goal of the GEOProcessing 2017 conference was to bring together researchers from the academia and practitioners from the industry in order to address fundamentals of advances in geographic information systems and the new applications related to them using the Web Services. Such systems can be used for assessment, modeling and prognosis of emergencies

GEOProcessing 2017 provided a forum where researchers were able to present recent research results and new research problems and directions related to them. The topics covered aspects from fundamentals to more specialized topics such as 2D & 3D information visualization, web services and geospatial systems, geoinformation processing, and spatial data infrastructure.

We take this opportunity to thank all the members of the GEOProcessing 2017 Technical Program Committee as well as the numerous reviewers. The creation of such a broad and high-quality conference program would not have been possible without their involvement. We also kindly thank all the authors who dedicated much of their time and efforts to contribute to the GEOProcessing 2017. We truly believe that, thanks to all these efforts, the final conference program consists of top quality contributions.

This event could also not have been a reality without the support of many individuals, organizations, and sponsors. We are grateful to the members of the GEOProcessing 2017 organizing committee for their help in handling the logistics and for their work to make this professional meeting a success.

We hope that GEOProcessing 2017 was a successful international forum for the exchange of ideas and results between academia and industry and for the promotion of progress in geographic information research.

We also hope that Nice provided a pleasant environment during the conference and everyone saved some time for exploring this beautiful city.

GEOProcessing 2017 Chairs

GEOProcessing Steering Committee

Claus-Peter Rückemann, Leibniz Universität Hannover / Westfälische Wilhelms-Universität

GEOPROCESSING 2017

COMMITTEE

GEOProcessing Steering Committee

Claus-Peter Rückemann, Leibniz Universität Hannover / Westfälische Wilhelms-Universität Münster / North-German Supercomputing Alliance (HLRN), Germany [Chair]
Yerach Doytsher, Technion - Israel Institute of Technology, Haifa, Israel
Monica De Martino, Consiglio Nazionale delle Ricerche - Genova, Italy
Thierry Badard, Centre for Research in Geomatics - Laval University, Quebec, Canada
Jianhong Cecilia Xia, Curtin University, Australia
Timofey Samsonov, Lomonosov Moscow State University, Russia
Thomas Ritz, FH Aachen, Germany

GEOProcessing Industry/Research Advisory Committee

Mete Celik, Erciyes University, Turkey
Katia Stankov, Synodon Inc., Canada
Lena Noack, Royal Observatory of Belgium (ROB), Belgium
Bariś M. Kazar, Oracle America Inc., USA
Petko Bakalov, Environmental Systems Research Institute (ESRI), USA
Olivier Dubois, OSCAR, France
Albert Godfrind, Geospatial technologies/Oracle Server Technologies - Sophia Antipolis, France

GEOProcessing 2017 Technical Program Committee

Mohd Helmy Abd Wahab, Universiti Tun Hussein Onm Malaysia, Malaysia
Al Abdelmoty, Cardiff University, Wales, UK
Diana F. Adamatti, Universidade Federal do Rio Grande, Brazil
Ayman Ahmed, GIS unit Kuwait Oil Company, Kuwait
Nuhcan Akçit, Middle East Technical University, Turkey
Zaher Al Aghbari, University of Sharjah, UAE
Rafal A. Angryk, Georgia State University, USA
Thierry Badard, Centre for Research in Geomatics - Laval University, Quebec, Canada
Petko Bakalov, Environmental Systems Research Institute (ESRI), USA
Fabiano Baldo, Santa Catarina State University, Brazil
Fabian D. Barbato, ORT University - Montevideo, Uruguay
Michela Bertolotto, University College Dublin, Ireland
Mehul Bhatt, University of Bremen, Germany
David Brosset, Naval Academy Research Institute, France
Benedicte Bucher, French National Institute of Geographic and Forest Information (IGN), France
Mete Celik, Erciyes University, Turkey
Yao-Yi Chiang, Spatial Sciences Institute | University of Southern California, USA
Dickson K.W. Chiu, University of Hong Kong, Hong Kong
Sidonie Christophe, IGN/LaSTIG/COGIT, France
Christophe Claramunt, Naval Academy Research Institute, France
Konstantin Clemens, Technical University in Berlin, Germany
Ana Cristina Costa, NOVA IMS - Universidade Nova de Lisboa, Portugal

Christophe Cruz, Université de Bourgogne, France
Monica De Martino, Consiglio Nazionale delle Ricerche - Genova, Italy
Anselmo C. de Paiva, Universidade Federal do Maranhão, Brazil
Mahmoud R. Delavar, University of Tehran, Iran
Jean-Paul Donnay, University of Liege, Belgium
Yerach Doytsher, Technion - Israel Institute of Technology, Haifa, Israel
Suzana Dragicevic, Simon Fraser University, Canada
Olivier Dubois, OSCAR, France
Süleyman Eken, Kocaeli University, Turkey
Javier Estornell, Universitat Politècnica de València, Spain
Nazli Farajidavar, University of Surrey, UK
Marin Ferecatu, Conservatoire National des Arts et Metiers, France
Mauro Gaio, LIUPPA - University of Pau, France
Zdravko Galić, University of Zagreb, Croatia
Georg Gartner, Vienna University of Technology, Austria
Birgit Gersbeck-Schierholz, Leibniz Universität Hannover, Germany
Albert Godfrind, Geospatial technologies/Oracle Server Technologies - Sophia Antipolis, France
Enguerran Grandchamp, Université des Antilles – LAMIA, France, Guadeloupe
Amy Griffin, University of New South Wales | Australian Defence Force Academy, Australia
William Grosky, University of Michigan, USA
Erik Hoel, Esri, USA
Yan Huang, University of North Texas, USA
Sergio Ilarri, University of Zaragoza, Spain
Xunfei Jiang, Earlham College, USA
Shuanggen Jin, Shanghai Astronomical Observatory, China
Katerina Kabassi, TEI of Ionian Islands, Greece
Hassan A. Karimi, University of Pittsburgh, USA
Izabela Karsznia, University of Warsaw, Poland
Jean-Paul Kasprzyk, University of Liège, Belgium
Baris M. Kazar, Oracle America Inc., USA
Margarita Kokla, National Technical University of Athens, Greece
Robert Laurini, INSA de Lyon - Villeurbanne, France
Dan Lee, Esri, USA
Lassi Lehto, Finnish Geospatial Research Institute (FGI) | National Land Survey of Finland, Finland
Thomas Liebig, TU Dortmund University, Germany
Jugurta Lisboa Filho, Universidade Federal de Viçosa, Brazil
Zhi Liu, University of North Texas, USA
Cheng Long, Queen's University Belfast, UK
Qifeng (Luke) Lu, Sapient, USA
Jesús Martí, Universitat Politècnica de València, Spain
Michael P. McGuire, Towson University, USA
Grant McKenzie, University of Maryland, College Park, USA
Beniamino Murgante, University of Basilicata, Italy
Alan Murray, University of California at Santa Barbara, USA
Ahmed Mustafa, LEMA (ArGEnCo) | University of Liège, Belgium / Purdue University, West Lafayette, USA
Lena Noack, Royal Observatory of Belgium (ROB), Belgium
Daniel Orellana, Universidad de Cuenca, Ecuador

Kostas Patroumpas, Athena Research Center, Greece
Thomas Ritz, FH Aachen, Germany
Armanda Rodrigues, NOVA LINCS | Universidade NOVA de Lisboa, Portugal
Ricardo Rodrigues Ciferri, Federal University of São Carlos (UFSCar), Brazil
Claus-Peter Rückemann, Westfälische Wilhelms-Universität Münster / Leibniz Universität Hannover / North-German Supercomputing Alliance, Germany
Timofey Samsonov, Lomonosov Moscow State University, Russia
Markus Schneider, University of Florida, USA
Spiros Skiadopoulos, University of the Peloponnese, Greece
Francesco Soldovieri, Istituto per il Rilevamento Elettromagnetico dell'Ambiente - Consiglio Nazionale delle Ricerche (CNR), Italy
Mudhakar Srivatsa, IBM T. J. Watson Research Center, USA
Cristian Stanciu, University Politehnica of Bucharest, Romania
Katia Stankov, Synodon Inc., Canada
Leon Stenneth, HERE (BMW, Audi, Daimler), USA
Kazutoshi Sumiya, Kwansei Gakuin University, Japan
Ruby Y. Tahboub, Purdue University, USA
Muhammad Ali Tahir, Institute of Geographical Information Systems (IGIS) - National University of Sciences and Technology (NUST), Islamabad, Pakistan
Ergin Tari, Istanbul Technical University, Turkey
Maristela Terto de Holanda, University of Brasilia (UnB), Brazil
Taketoshi Ushiama, Kyushu University, Japan
Michael Vassilakopoulos, University of Thessaly, Greece
Caixia Wang, University of Alaska Anchorage, USA
Fusheng Wang, Stony Brook University, USA
Jue Wang, Washington University in St. Louis, USA
June Wang, Washington University in St. Louis, USA
John P. Wilson, University of Southern California, USA
Ouri Wolfson, University of Illinois, USA
Jianhong Cecilia Xia, Curtin University, Australia
Ningchuan Xiao, The Ohio State University, USA
Xiaojun Yang, Florida State University, USA
Demetris Zeinalipour, University of Cyprus, Cyprus
Chuanrong (Cindy) Zhang, University of Connecticut, USA
Wenbing Zhao, Cleveland State University, USA
Xun Zhou, University of Iowa, USA
Qiang Zhu, University of Michigan, Dearborn, USA

Semi-automatic Oil Spill Detection in Sentinel-1 SAR Images at Brazil's Coast

Alexandre Corrêa da Silva[1], William Gomes de Branco[1], Dagnaldo Penha Torquato da Silva[1], Lui Txai Calvoso Habl[1], Thaise Rachel Sarmento[1] and Mariano Federico Pascual[1]
[1]HEX Informatica Ltda (HEXGIS)
Brasilia, Brazil
e-mail: {alexandre.silva, william.branco, dagnaldo.silva, lui.habl, thaise.sarmento, mariano.pascual}@hexgis.com

***Abstract*— This paper reports a methodology proposed on the matter of semi-automatic detection of oil spills using Sentinel-1 Synthetic Aperture Radar (SAR) images to improve the capability of management of government agencies for oil spills incidents over the seas. This is an initiative to create a semi-automated system of detection based on free images of Sentinel-1 using an intelligent database of samples statistics of oils, confirmed by vessels or airplanes and photo-interpreted, and oceanographic features that continues improving itself over time. The results indicate that both the VV and HH polarizations of the Sentinel-1 detected probable oil-spills and look-alikes, however, the utility of the Sentinel-1 cross-polarizations (VH and HV) in oil-spill detection could not be discarded. Other parameters will be improved and included in this study, as parameters of segmentation, besides process of data mining.**

Keywords-semi-automatic; sentinel-1; sar; oil spill; seas monitoring.

I. INTRODUCTION

One of the challenges that the oil and gas industries face is the management of oil spills at seas. Brazil has a huge coastal zone with over 7,000 kilometers of extension and with many activities of offshore oil exploitation, oil transportation and a constant high vessels traffic. Monitoring constantly such an extensive area with the existing paid Synthetic Aperture Radar (SAR) increases substantially the costs of any projects in this area, making most of them inviable. As a low-cost alternative, the Sentinel-1 Satellite radar images are made available by the European Space Agency (ESA) free of charge on the Sentinel data hub. However, this is a recent technology (launch year 2014 for satellite 1-A and 2016 for satellite 1-B), and the revisit time is of 12 days for most Brazil's areas, thus, one of the project problems to solve is the shortage of oil spill samples. Other difficulties are the needs of a valid compatible database with spills and look-alikes for algorithms improvement [8].

The SAR monitoring of the oil spills over the oceans had proved its efficacy during daytime, nighttime, and any kind of weather. In the last decade, a lot of researches on automatic and semiautomatic methods of oil spill detections have been documented [2][6], and they provided a lot of knowledge for the creation of a methodology with the usage of Sentinel-1 satellite images.

The main objective of the proposed methodology is to create a semi-automated process capable of helping the interpretation of oil spills using Sentinel-1 SAR images as a primary input.

This work is presented in four sections, as follows: Section II presents the methodological approach initially adopted to solve the problems mentioned in the introduction, including information about the studied area, the statistics used, the processes applied to the images and the digital resources used. Section III presents the preliminary results, since this work is under implementation now, and a discussion about these results. Section IV exposes the conclusions that could be obtained, so far in the research process.

II. METHODOLOGICAL APPROACH

This proposal was initially inspired by the methodology for automatic oil spills detection in Envisat, Radarsat and ERS SAR images, as described in [1] and adapted to work with Sentinel-1 images. Most of the adaptations were made by: (a) using sensor specific modules; (b) generating the wind data from the input image; (c) including combined filters before segmentation and; (d) including specialists control of classification quality, alerts and warning reports through the interface of the system.

A. General explanation

The SAR images chosen to work with in this project were Sentinel-1A and 1B with the beam mode of Interferometric Wide and the polarization VV. After the availability of the image on the ESA website, Ground Range Detected (GRD) data are downloaded and passed through seven preprocessing/processing steps consisting of: (a) Orbit corrections and radiometric calibration to sigma naught to generate the Normalized Radar Cross Section (NRCS) values; (b) The direction of the wind for the image is estimated through frequency domain method and the speed is estimated through C-band Geophysical Model 5 (CMOD5); (c) The image is resampled to 40 meters and then filtered with Median Filter followed by a Low-Pass Filter as suggested [4] for better results in suppressing the speckle noise; (d) The land parts of the images, if there are any, are masked and the dark spot segmentation step is applied through a process of Adaptive Threshold as described [2]; (e) The object resulting of the segmentation has its statistics calculated and the more significant samples are chosen to fill the samples database in order to improve continually the process. (f) The statistics of the new objects area compared with those of the database and through Support Vector Machine (SVM) classification returns a percentage to the object to be in the class of oil spill; (g) Through a web interface the users of different agencies can decide the importance of the dark spot visualized, if it is a case of oil spill verification or alert, this information also returns to the database of samples, helping to improve the classification.

B. Information About the Statistics

The statistical analysis was based on researches like [7]; however, those which were tested in this work are:

- Area of the object in square kilometers.
- Length of the border of the object in kilometers.
- Perimeter to Area ratio.
- Object complexity [10].
- Object mean value.
- Object standard deviation.
- Object power to mean ratio.
- Background mean value.
- Background Standard Deviation.
- Background power to mean ratio.
- Ratio of the power to mean ratios.
- Mean contrast.
- Max contrast.
- Mean contrast ratio.
- Standard deviation contrast ratio.

Also, three additional statistics were added to the previous list to complement the attributes of the dark spots polygons:

- Area in pixels
- Minimum value
- Mean wind field intensity.

C. Representation of the processes

In Figs. 1-4 it is possible to visualize the whole process and the decisions associated with the automatic part and the user decision part.

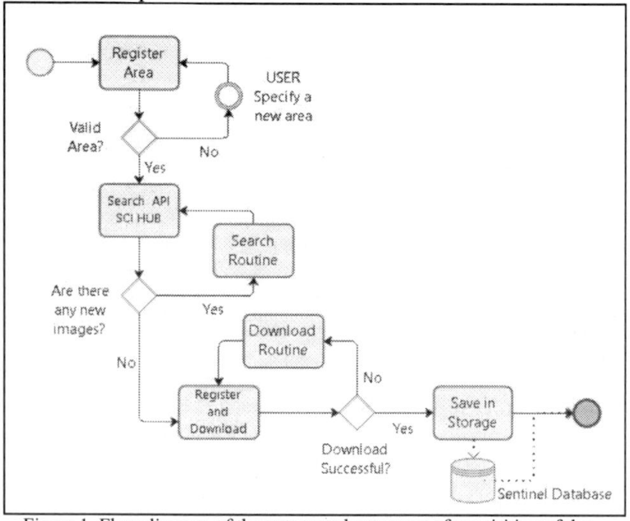

Figure 1. Flow diagram of the automated processes of acquisition of the proposed semi-automatic oil spill detection.

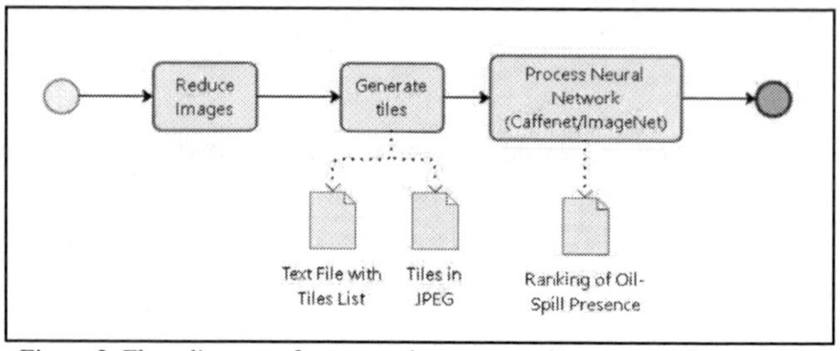

Figure 2. Flow diagram of automated processes of image qualification of the proposed semi-automatic oil spill detection.

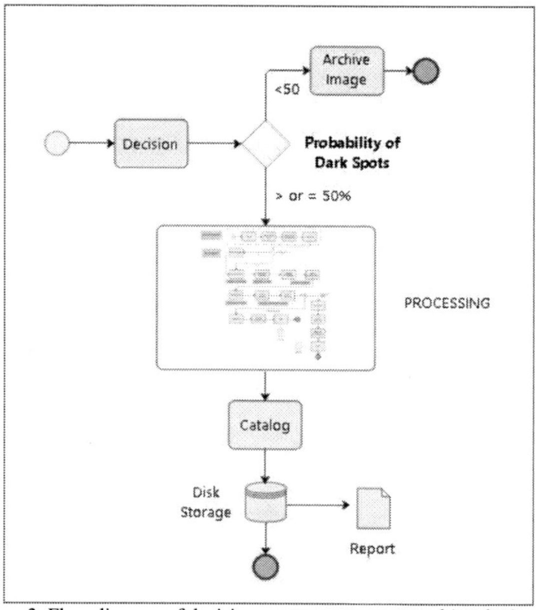

Figure 3. Flow diagram of decisions to processes or to archive the images of the proposed semi-automatic oil spill detection.

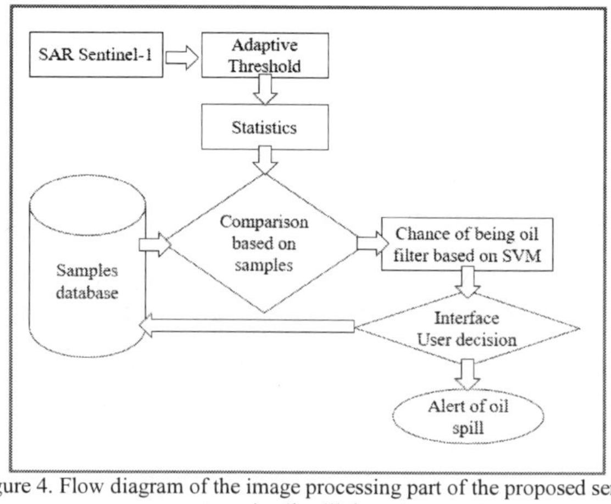

Figure 4. Flow diagram of the image processing part of the proposed semi-automatic oil spill detection.

Figure 4 presents the image processing methodology based on [8] adding an extra part at the end for the user interaction and decision.

D. Development

All processes are already automated using python scripts together with the modules of the open source software and extensions: (a) SNAP (Sentinel Application Platform); (b) S1TBX (Sentinel-1 Toolbox); (c) QGIS; (d) GDAL (Geospatial Data Abstraction Library) and; (e) PostGIS.

E. SAR Images and Study Area

One hundred Sentinel-1 images were analyzed, most of them over the Campos sedimentary basin, located on the coast of the states of Rio de Janeiro and Espírito Santo - Brazil, one of the most relevant regions for oil exploitation and with a great volume of vessels traffic. Fig. 5 shows the location map of Campos basin and the research area.

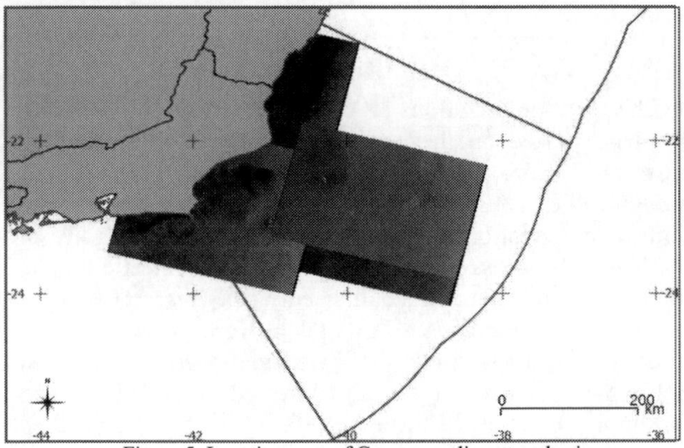

Figure 5. Location map of Campos sedimentary basin.

The Brazilian Institute of Environment and Renewable Natural Resources - IBAMA is helping the project with oil spills interpretations, reports and verified samples. Two groups of samples were created to contribute with different weights:

1) Samples photo-interpreted by speciatlists;
2) Samples confirmed with flights or other sources.

Bellow, in Figs. 6-8 are presented some of the samples with the respective delimitation generated by the Adaptive Threshold segmentation process:

Figure 6. Oil spill in proximity of a platform at Campos Basin.

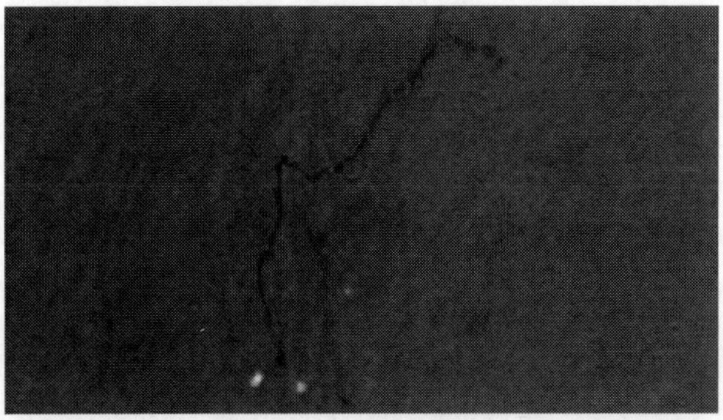
Figure 7. Oil spill in proximity with a vessel at Campos Basin.

Figure 8. Orphan possible oil spill at Campos Basin.

The statistics of the samples are weighted and then used as a data input to the Support Vector Machine Classifier - SVC to set scores for each class to each polygon generated by the Adaptive Threshold segmentation. The SVC was initially chosen for its ability to classify data that is non-linearly separable. These scores are then used to compose a filter to display only the relevant polygons to the users interact on the web interface.

III. Results and Discussions

In the scientific research mentioned in [9], it seems that using X-band SAR images can provide better results for oil-spill detection than using L-band or C-band SAR images. The Sentinel-1A and Sentinel-1B have C-band SAR sensors. Also, it is observed that many researches mention that the VV polarization gives better results for interpretation of oceanographic features. In this project using the proposed methodology we detected probable oil-spills and look-alikes in both polarizations VV and HH.

When the backscatter of the ocean reaches, or stays close to the noise floor of a SAR sensor, it may produce a non-adequate signal with limited interpretation capability reducing the utility of that data. In most cases, it is visible a stripe pattern in the parts where it stays close to the noise floor along the image; that pattern was identified along many cross-polarized Sentinel-1 images. The Sentinel-1 noise floor in sigma naught is -25dB.

In Figs. 9-12, it is possible to see the results on a prior stage with manual attribute filters, before the SVC, where the green features are selected for the interaction with the users and the red features are filtered.

Figure 9. Classification results at image 0451 on Campos Basin at 2016 January 29 on an early stage.

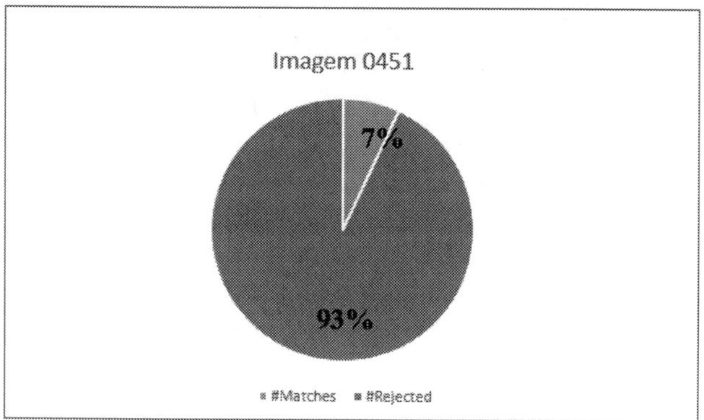

Figure 10. Graphical representation of visible features, in green, for user interaction on the web interface for the image on Figure 9.

Figure 11. Classification results at image 2D51 on Campos Basin at 2016 July 20 on an early stage.

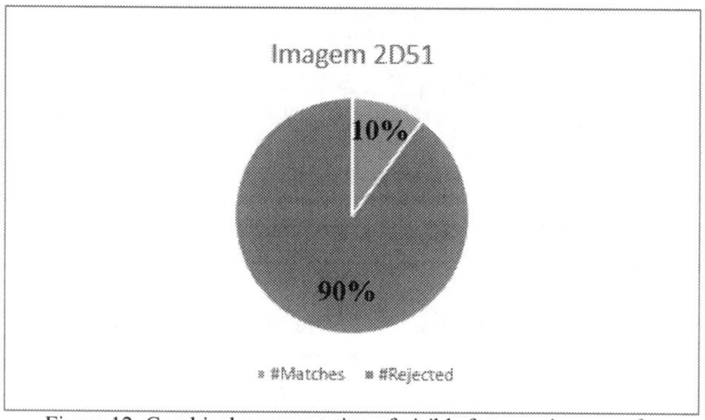

Figure 12. Graphical representation of visible features, in green, for user interaction on the web interface for the image on Figure 11.

The resample to 40 meters described in the methodology was adopted after a comparison between the segmentation results from the same images with and without resample. The comparison results were that the polygons generated had different areas, perimeter and shapes; however, the comparison between the values extracted from the features of the sample groups, the 10 meters and the 40 meters, shows that the results were very similar. More studies about these results could describe the differences more precisely with efficient comparison methodologies, and the impact that these differences can cause on the features extraction or on the results of the classification. The implementation of this resample improved the processing time of the images from 5 to 6 times and the result is clearer and with more defined bounds.

IV. Conclusions

The cross-polarizations (HV and VH) of all the Sentinel-1 images tested on the ocean areas, could be responding close to the noise floor, as the dark spots are not visible or recognizable. Thus, the entire research is being conducted with co-polarization (HH and VV). However, the utility of the Sentinel-1 cross-polarizations in oil-spill detection could not be discarded since it would need further researches.

Using as a reference a table taken from [7] with the 25 most used features for oil-spill detection, we implemented only 15 to achieve the results presented in this paper, and the implementation of the other 10 features could be used for further implementation of the processes to achieve better results. The selection and implementation of the additional features is a difficult part, since it is necessary to analyze the features that give a better separation between the samples of oil and the samples of each type of look-alikes, modifying the features set and each weight to be applied. In the current work, the 15 features listed on subsection II.B were initially selected based on the project contingency, considering: (a) the speed of the research; (b) the speed of the implementation and; (c) the influence of the feature on the results. Since the system was developed to attend a governmental necessity to speed up the manual process of generating vectors and reports, the speed was an important matter. Also, it was based on classification learning through samples and user decision. One of the main objectives of the project was to reach an operational version as soon as possible while the research continues to run in the background.

With the system implemented, the expectations are that with the increase of evaluations of the samples, the database will become more robust and reliable, with many different samples shapes in many different conditions, solving the problem of shortage of oil-spill samples. In Figs. 13-14 is possible to see the evaluation process in the application.

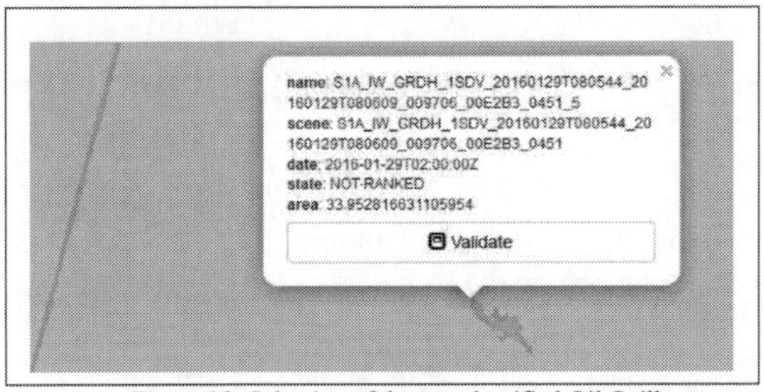

Figure 13. Selection of the pre-classified Oil-Spill.

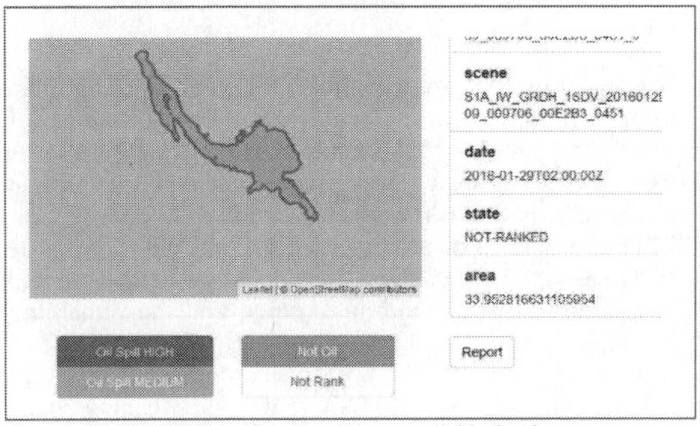

Figure 14. Classification options available for the users.

As seen in the previous figures, the user can select the dark regions in the application window or from a list and choose a predefined class to classify or reclassify them. The application also keeps record of the changes and the person who changed it.

The team is continuing analyzing Sentinel-1 images and improving the parameters of segmentation to have the best possible delimitation of the samples to extract the statistics. More statistical data could be included in the set. Once the project keeps running its development phase, the characteristics that are on the row to be included are:

- First invariant planar moment
- Slick width
- Distance to coast
- Quantity of objects in the proximity
- Proximity of big areas
- Chorophyll-a information
- Sea surface temperature information

A process of data mining is going to be applied to create the best number of classes with a good combination to be used in the SVC process. Other classifiers can also be used to compare results. Besides oil, the classes could be low wind, coastal wind shelter, upwelling, and further classes that become more suitable to improve the classification success rate. Also, more studies on the interchangeability of statistical data from another sensor could be made and an integration of the system with other sources of images will be on the schedule.

The main contribution to achieve with this project is to reach the best features set to automatically classify the oil-spills. Another contribution is the creation of a large database with the statistical characteristics of oil-spill, oceanographic and weather features derived from Sentinel-1 images. Specialists will continuously analyze and validate each pertinent dark region as the system is implemented.

ACKNOWLEDGMENT

The work described in this paper is part of a UK-Brazil cooperative project entitled *Oil & Gas Production and Operational Efficiency*, which is sponsored by the Prosperity Fund, through the British Embassy in Brazil. HEX Informática Ltda. was responsible for developing the project's component on improving the detection of oil spills in Brazilian waters. The project also counts with the technical support of the Brazilian Institute of Environment and Renewable Natural Resources - IBAMA.

REFERENCES

[1] A. S. Solberg, S. Dokken, and R. Solberg, "Automatic detection of oil spills in Envisat Radarsat and ERS SAR images," Proc. IEEE Symp. International Geoscience and Remote Sensing Symposium (IGARSS 2003), IEEE press, 2003, pp. 2747-2749 vol.4, doi: 10.1109/IGARSS.2003.1294572

[2] A. S. Solberg, C. Brekke, and R. Solberg, "Algorithms for oil spill detection in Radarsat and Envisat SAR images," IGARSS 2004. 2004 IEEE International Geoscience and Remote Sensing Symposium, Anchorage, pp. 4909-4912 vol.7, 2004.

[3] C. C. Wackerman, W. G. Pichel, and P. Clemente-Colon, "Automated estimation of wind vectors from SAR," 12th Conference on Interactions of the Sea and Atmosphere, 2003.

[4] C. Özkan and F. Sunar, "Comparisons of different semi-automated techniques for oil-spill detection: A case study in Lebanon," Proc. 27th EARSeL Symp. Symposium on GeoInformation in Europe, Millpress, 2007, pp. 463-470.

[5] H. Hersbach, "CMOD5, An Improved Geophysical Model Function for ERS C-Band Scatterometry," Report of the European Centre Medium-Range Weather Forecasts (ECMWF), 2003.

[6] K. Topouzelis, V. Karathanassi, P. Pavlakis, and D. Rokos, "Oil spill detection: SAR multiscale segmentation and object features evaluation," Proc. SPIE Vol. 4880, Remote Sensing of the Ocean and Sea Ice 2002, SPIE, 2003, pp. 77-87, doi:10.1117/12.462518; http://dx.doi.org/10.1117/12.462518

[7] K. Topouzelis, D. Stathakis, and V. Karathanassi, "Investigation of genetic algorithms contribution to feature selection for oil spill detection," International Journal of Remote Sensing, Vol. 30, No. 3, March 2009, pp. 611-625, doi: 10.1080/01431160802339456.

[8] K. Topouzelis and S. Singha, "Oil spill detection: past and future trends", Proc. Living Planet Symposium 2016, SP-740, ESA, May 2016, pp. 1-4.

[9] M. Fingas, Oil Spill Science and Technology: Prevention, Response, and Clean Up., 1st ed., Burlington, MA: Gulf Professional Pub./Elsevier, 2011, pp. 125-132.

[10] V. Karathanassi, K. Topouzelis, P. Pavlakis, and D. Rokos, "An object-oriented methodology to detect oil spills," International Journal of Remote Sensing, March 2006, Vol. 27, No. 23, pp.5235–5251, doi: 10.1080/01431160600693575.

Statistical Analysis on Sewer Pipe Characteristics and Occurrence of Ground Cave-ins

Kiyeon Kim, Joonyoung Kim, TaeYoung Kwak, and ChoongKi Chung
Dept. of Civil and Environmental Engineering
Seoul National University
Seoul, Republic of Korea
e-mail: ddolsoo@snu.ac.kr

Abstract — **A damaged sewer pipe is considered a major cause of the occurrence of urban ground cave-ins. Identifying the sewer pipe characteristics that contribute to the occurrence of ground cave-ins can be highly helpful in detecting the damaged sewer pipes and preventing ground cave-ins. To achieve this aim, Student's t-test and chi-square test were performed with all the sewer pipes in Seoul that included the ground cave-in occurrence and nonoccurrence cases.**

Keywords — ground cave-ins; damaged sewer pipe; Student's t-test; chi-square test

I. INTRODUCTION

Numerous ground cave-ins induced by a damaged sewer pipe have been reported from many urban areas in the U.S., Japan, and South Korea [1]-[3]. Japan National Institute for Land Infrastructure Management (JNILIM) reported that about 17,000 ground cave-ins occurred in Japan between 2006 and 2009 [2]. In Seoul, 3,626 cases of ground cave-ins were reported between 2011 and 2015 [3]. Extensive inspection using a video camera robot and a ground penetrating radar (GPR) is required for detecting and replacing the ruptured sewer pipes to prevent ground cave-ins [4][5], but most of the big cities in the world run thousands of sewer pipes beneath the streets. Seoul, for example, runs 370,000 sewer pipes, with a total length of approximately 10,000 km [3]. The massive number of sewer pipes running beneath the streets makes their inspection practically impossible. For their efficient inspection, suspicious sewer pipes and the surrounding area that may induce ground cave-ins should be preferentially investigated. To achieve this aim, the sewer pipe characteristics that may contribute to the occurrence of ground cave-ins need to be determined.

JNILIM and Davies et al., [2][6] investigated the relationship between the sewer pipe characteristics and the occurrence of ground cave-ins. The previous researches, however, considered only the ground cave-in occurrence cases and did not consider the ground cave-in nonoccurrence cases. But studies on nonoccurrence group, together with occurrence group, can also provide meaningful implication for ground cave-in occurrences. In this study, for the ground cave-in occurrence and nonoccurrence groups, comparative analysis (i.e., Student's t-test, chi-square test) was performed.

The statistical analysis including data acquisition and analysis method are laid out in section 2. Section 3 presents and discusses the statistical analysis results and section 4 summarizes the contributions and conclusions of this study.

II. MATERIALS AND METHODS

The sewer pipe database built by the Seoul metropolitan government provides the characteristics of each of the sewer pipes buried in Seoul (221,242 cases). Using Google map, the addresses of the ground cave-ins obtained via the ground cave-in reports (968 cases) were converted to TM coordinates. With the coordinates of ground cave-ins and the sewer pipe database, damaged sewer pipes were identified and assigned to the ground cave-in occurrence group, and the remaining sewer pipes were assigned to the ground cave-in nonoccurrence group by using nearest sample tool in QGIS 2.14.4. R, a language for data analysis was used to analyze the obtained data. Based on the previous researches, the sewer pipe characteristics that were to be tested for their contribution to the occurrence of ground cave-ins were chosen.

For the continuous variables, six sewer pipe characteristics (i.e., length, average burial elevation, average burial depth, height difference between the two ends, equivalent radius of the cross-sectional area, and operating duration of the sewer pipe) were selected. Independent Student's t-test with the null hypothesis "the means of the two groups are the same" was performed to determine if there was a significant difference between the mean of the ground cave-in occurrence group and that of the ground cave-in nonoccurrence group [7]. Applying Student's t-test, a pooled two-sample t-test was performed when the assumption of homogeneity of variances was available, whereas an unpooled two-sample t-test was performed when the assumption was not available [8]. To assess the homogeneity of variances, the Levene test was performed [9].

For the categorical variables, two sewer pipe characteristics (i.e., cross-sectional shape and material of the sewer pipe) were selected. A chi-square test with the null hypothesis "the two categorical variables are independent" was performed to determine if the explanatory and response variables were independent [10].

III. RESULTS AND DISCUSSION

Table I summarizes the results of the analyses of the Levene test for the homogeneity of variances and of the Student's t-test performed for the continuous variables. For the average burial elevation, average burial depth, and operating duration of the sewer pipes, which showed a less than 0.05 p-value in the Levene test (i.e., not available for homogeneity assumption), an unpooled two-sample t-test was performed. On the other hand, a pooled two-sample t-test was performed for the length, height difference between the two ends, and equivalent radius of the cross-sectional area of the sewer pipes, which showed a higher than 0.05 p-value in the Levene test. The length, average burial elevation, average burial depth, and operating duration of the sewer pipes showed a far lower than 0.05 p-value in the t-test, which implies that there was a highly significant difference in mean between the ground cave-in occurrence and nonoccurrence groups. On the other hand, the height difference between the two ends and the equivalent radius of the cross-sectional area of the sewer pipes showed a higher than 0.05 p-value in the Student's t-test, which implies that there was no significant difference in mean between the ground cave-in occurrence and nonoccurrence groups. Based on the results of the Student's t-test and the mean values of the ground cave-in occurrence and nonoccurrence groups, it can be concluded that the susceptibility to the occurrence of ground cave-ins increases as the length and operating duration of the sewer pipe increases and as the average burial elevation and average burial depth of the sewer pipe decrease.

Table II summarizes the results of the analysis of the chi-square test results. The equivalent radius of the cross-sectional area of the sewer pipe, whose p-value was higher than 0.05, was independent of ground cave-in occurrence. On the other hand, the material of the sewer pipe was dependent on ground cave-in occurrence because its p-value was lower than 0.05.

IV. CONCLUSIONS

This study investigated the sewer pipe characteristics that contribute to the occurrence of ground cave-ins by performing Student's t-test and a chi-square test on the ground cave-in occurrence and nonoccurrence groups. Based on the analysis results, the conclusions shown below were drawn.

(a) In the case of the continuous variables, the length, average elevation, average burial depth, and operating duration of the sewer pipes showed significant differences in mean between the ground cave-in occurrence and nonoccurrence groups. In other words, there is evidence that longer or older pipes are damaged more often, which may have contributed to ground cave-in. Additionally, the pipes with lower burial depth and lower average elevation also induce ground cave-in more frequently.

(b) In the case of the categorical variables, the material of the sewer pipe showed a significant correlation with ground cave-in occurrence, while pipe shape did not.

Student's t-test and chi-square test, however, have limitation that they only deal with mean difference independence. To find a specific correlation between the sewer pipe characteristic and the occurrence of ground cave-ins, further research including regression analysis need to be performed.

ACKNOWLEDGMENT

This work was supported by the National Research Foundation of Korea(NRF) grant funded by the Korea government (MSIP) (No. 2015R1A2A1A01007980)

REFERENCES

[1] N. R. Calrson, and S. A. Urquhart, "A sewer sinkhole study using TEM" The Leading Edge vol. 25, Issue 3, pp. 348-350, Mar. 2006 doi:10.1190/1.2184104,

[2] Japan National Institute for Land Infrastructure Management, "Current situation of ground cave-ins causes by sewer pipeline", 2012.

[3] Seoul Metropolitan Government, "Report of precise investigation about degradation sewage pipe over 30 years", 2016.

[4] E. D. Zisman, M. J. Wightman, and C. Taylor, "The effctiveness of GPR in Sinkhole Investigations", The 10th Multidisciplinary Confrence on Sinkholes and the Engineering and Enviromental Impacts of Karst, pp. 608 – 616, Sep. 2005 doi: 10.10614/40796(177)65

[5] S. S. Wilson, Laxmi Gurung, Esa Aleksi Paaso, and Jack Wallace, "Creation of robot for subsurface void detection", IEEE Conference May. 2009, doi: 10.1109/THS.2009.5168102

[6] J. P. Davies, B. A. Clarke, J. T. Whiter, and R. J. Cunnigham, "Factors influencing the structural deterioration and collapse of rigid sewer pipes.", Urban Water, 3, pp. 73-89, 2001.

[7] J. C. F. de Winter. "Using the Student's t-test with extremly small sample sizes.", Pract. Assess., Res. Eval. Vol.18, pp. 1 – 12, 2013

[8] Mouchumi Bhattacharyya, "To pool or not to pool: A comparison between two commonly used test statiscs", International Journal of Pure and Applied Mathmatics Volume 89 No.4, pp. 497-510, 2013.

[9] Levne Howard. "Robust tests for equaltiy of variances", In Ingram Olkin; Harold Hotelling; et al., Contributions to Probability and Statistics : Essay in Honor of Harold Hotelling, Stanford University, pp. 278-292, 1960.

[10] A. Agresti, and M. Kateri, "Categorical data analysis", Springer Berlin Heidelberg, 2011.

TABLE I. RESULTS OF THE LEVENE TEST AND STUDENT'S T-TEST

Variables	Mean		Std deviation		Levene test		Student's t-test	
	Non-occurrence	*Occurrence*	*Non-occurrence*	*Occurrence*	*F*	*p-value*	*t*	*p-value*
Length (m)	31.35	47.14	31.54	32.67	1.936	0.164	-15.541	1.961×10^{-54}
Operating duration of sewer pipe (year)	20.65	22.47	11.73	11.45	17.405	0.000	-4.932	9.539×10^{-7}
Average elevation (m)	26.96	24.78	18.40	14.67	31.230	0.000	4.592	5.000×10^{-6}
Average burial depth (m)	1.01	0.97	0.72	0.48	25.226	0.000	2.700	7.000×10^{-3}
Equivalent radius of cross-section (m)	0.67	0.69	0.52	0.48	0.122	0.726	-1.358	0.175
Height difference between the two ends (m)	0.30	0.32	0.60	0.53	0.411	0.522	-1.099	0.272

TABLE II. RESULTS OF THE CHI-SQUARE TEST

Variables		No. of sewer pipes		chi-square test	
		Occurrence	*Nonoccurrence*	*chi square*	*p-value*
Sewer pipe material	Hume pipe	190,349 (99.6%)	848 (0.4%)	37.980	3.800×10^{-7}
	Concrete box	16,523 (99.6%)	65 (0.4%)		
	Wrinkled tube	4,238 (99.1%)	39 (0.9%)		
	Concrete pipe	2,621 (99.8%)	6 (0.2%)		
	PE pipe	2,467 (99.9%)	3 (0.1%)		
	Other	4,076 (99.8%)	7 (0.2%)		
Sewer pipe cross-sectional shape	Circular	203,587 (99.6%)	903 (0.4%)	1.020	0.312
	Rectangular	16,687 (99.6%)	65 (0.4%)		

Towards Building Smart Maps from Heterogeneous Data Sources

Faizan Ur Rehman*, Imad Afyouni†, Ahmed Lbath‡ and Saleh Basalamah§
*‡ LIG, University of Grenoble Alpes, France
* Science and Techology Unit, Umm Al-Qura University, Saudi Arabia
† § Technology Innovation Center, Wadi Makkah, Umm Al-Qura University, Saudi Arabia
§ College of Computer Science, Umm Al-Qura University, Saudi Arabia
Email: *fsrehman@uqu.edu.sa, †iafyouni@gistic.org, ‡ahmed.lbath@imag.fr, §sbasalamah@uqu.edu.sa

***Abstract*—In today's busy world, users and authorities require better services to achieve their daily activities and tasks in a smart way by using available resources in an optimized manner. The variety of available data sources, starting from crowdsourced data, open governmental data, and other online sources can provide users with smart tools to better manage their daily activities. However, collecting and integrating this multitude of overlapping data sources is a challenging task. Particularly, digital maps are being extensively used to browse and share information about points of interest, plan trips, and to find optimized paths. Within this context, there is a real opportunity to enrich traditional maps with different knowledge-based layers extracted from the variety of available data sources. This paper introduces the concept of "*smart maps*" by collecting, managing, and integrating heterogeneous data sources in order to infer relevant knowledge-based layers. Unlike conventional maps, *smart maps* extract live events (e.g., concert, competition, incident), online offers, and statistical analysis (e.g., dangerous areas) by encapsulating incoming semi- and unstructured data into structured generic *packets*. These packets are processed to extract statistical knowledge on accident-prone and safe areas, and detect *Events of Interest* (EoI), based on a multi-dimensional clustering technique. This approach lays the ground for delivering different intelligent services and applications, such as: 1) city explorer that provides latest information collected from multiple sources about places and events; and 2) route and trip planning that leverage smart map framework to recommend safe routes.**

***Keywords*–Smart Maps; Events of Interest; Social Networks; Crowdsourcing.**

I. Introduction

Publicly available data is increasing rapidly with a rate of 30% every year and will continuously keep growing with the advancement of technologies in sensors, smartphones and the Internet of Things. Data from multiple sources can improve the coverage for providing relevant knowledge about surrounding events and points of Interest (POIs) [1]. Moreover, adding social network data can provide fruitful insights and complementary sources of information. Social data can be used in various scenarios, such as emergency situation, inferring events in cities, and showing breaking news. Meanwhile, the use of digital maps is tremendously increasing with the aim of sharing preeminent information about current locations and spatial characteristics of surroundings. Big giants including *Google*, *Yahoo*, *MapQuest* and *Bing* generate dynamic layers about traffic updates, such as traffic jams, accidents, and congestions but they still lack to provide knowledge about statistical trends, ongoing events, and POI semantics and ranking from crowdsourced data. Such knowledge can be extracted and enriched from heterogeneous available data sources. Different knowledge-based layers can enrich existing traditional maps to

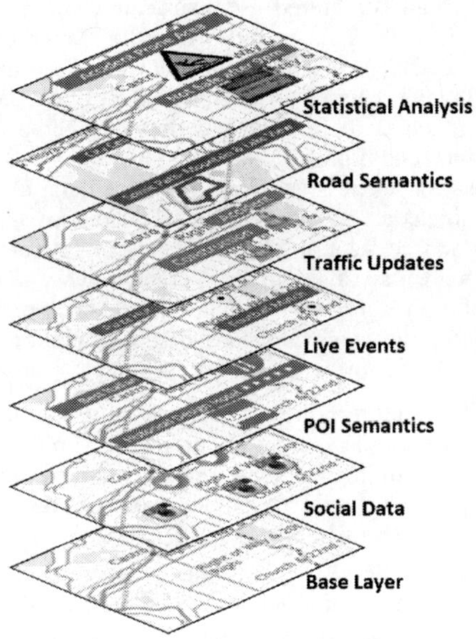

Figure 1. Dynamic layers of smart maps

know more about surroundings, and can be used to enhance existing spatio-temporal queries (see Fig. 1). In this work, we present a framework that collects and integrates data from different sources including crowdsourced data (social data including Twitter and Yelp), Open Street Map (OSM) data, and other online data (Google traffic, Open government). The system applies different mining and clustering techniques in order to convert existing digital maps into smart maps. Smart maps are maps that intelligently self-update themselves based on information extracted dynamically from heterogeneous data sources including social media streams, crowd-sourced data, sensors and online news sources. Smart maps can discover new content automatically by identifying new points of interests, events, or findings that were not specifically entered to the map. We believe that smart maps will form the next generation of digital maps by providing awareness about surroundings, such as events, traffic updates, road semantics (e.g., scenic or safe path), POI semantics (e.g., fast food restaurant), online offers, and statistical analysis (e.g., dangerous areas) as illustrated in Fig. 1.

Smart maps provide the following dynamic layers on top of existing maps: 1) *Events of Interest (EoI)*: live events in cities, such as concerts, football matches, jobs hiring and other relevant information (e.g., pizza hut discount, sales in CityMax) are displayed at different levels of abstraction; 2) *Statistical Analysis*: illustrates analysis of (un)safe areas by extracting knowledge on accident prone areas, safe or polluted areas; 3) *Traffic updates from social data*: shows information about traffic constraints, such as accidents or road blocks collected from social data; and 4) *POI Semantics*: describes semantics and ratings of geographical places from crowdsourced data (e.g., using Yelp data to judge quality of POIs, such as best Italian pizza, historical design hotel, etc.).

The contributions of this paper are manifold: a) collect, store and clean structured, semistructured or unstructured crowdsourced data. This includes digesting microblog social data (Twitter, Yelp), OSM, online data in real-time (Google Traffic APIs) and other historical open government data (Crime and accident data); b) design a common schema to resolve data conflicts and integration issues of social data, and to increase the conciseness and correctness of data; c) extracting relevant knowledge by applying state-of-the-art text mining techniques and correlation to find Events of Interest (EoI); d) visualize smart map layers in an interactive way, and f) taking leverage of *smart maps* to enhance spatio-temporal queries. The following two applications are demonstrated on top of the smart maps framework:

- City Explorer: provides latest information collected from multiple sources about historical places, touristic places, dining, ongoing and upcoming events, shops, news, live social feeds, weather updates, traffic updates, semantics of points of interest.
- Routing Service: recommends optimized trips and paths to users not only based on traditional spatial and temporal data analysis, but also by taking into account safe areas to avoid accident and crime prone places.

The remainder of this paper is as follows. Section II discusses the related work from different perspectives. Section III introduces an overview of our system architecture. Section IV highlights the implementation and map visualizations; while Section V draws conclusions and future challenges.

II. Related Work

In this section, we review relevant work on data collection and integration from smart cities, social networks mining, and events of interest detection from heterogeneous sources. We also review the existing maps and their layers and explain how smart maps can enrich current state-of-the-art of knowledge-based layers.

A. Data Collection and Integration for Smart Cities

The growth in population within cities will have an impact on transportation, city infrastructure and the global economic growth, etc. Therefore, it is suggested to convert big cities into smart cities to provide better facilities to citizens [2]. Big giants, including IBM (Smarter PlanetSmarter Cities) [3] and Microsoft (CityNext) [4], have launched several projects around the world to enhance city infrastructures and human life style. Smart cities generate multiple types of data sources which lead to the problem of data collection, cleaning, and integration [5]. Data collection and integration has been performed in the past for many applications, such as 1) analyses and extraction of points of interest from multiple web sources [6]; and 2) finding traffic flow for intelligent transportation services by using Twitter [7]. Data integration for multiple sources requires schema mapping, comparison of string resemblance, data dependency, source authenticity, and duplicate detection [5]. With this context and in order to detect live event from social data, we exploit multiple types of data sources by wrapping incoming data streams into packets, that is, a generic structured form out of semistructured or unstructured data. Like the analogy of TCP protocol, each packet has a meta-data header, containing source, location, time, type, potential event and event properties, and a payload, containing the actual content.

B. State-of-the-art mapping technologies

Today's maps are often crowd-sourced, and make use of *'Volunteered Geographic Information (VGI)'* [8], where users can enrich maps with their own information. Researchers, authorities, and industries generate thousands of interactive analytics every year to meet their social and economic needs [9]. In addition, 'Live Maps' now contain data that is updated in real-time. For example, live updates of bus schedules, traffic conditions, restaurant opening hours, and road accidents can be displayed on *Google Maps*, among others. With the wide spread of social networks, people start to post their own social contributions on live maps, such as Foursquare check-ins, Flickr images, tweets [10], Yelp reviews, and news RSS feed [11]. Moreover, natural language processing (NLP) techniques were embedded to extract spatially-referenced news from online newspapers and tweets [11]. However, Live Maps still lack intelligence in extracting knowledge about new events of interest to safe areas and other statistical analysis.

C. Events of Interest Detection from Crowdsourced Data

In the last few years, the use of social media is increasing rapidly all round the world. The number of social media users worldwide has grown to around 2.51 billion in 2017 [12]. Many real-world applications, such as for traffic updates, surveillance, and earthquake detection, continuously collect crowdsourced data including social network data to detect events of interest. Early events of interest detection can be helpful to society, users, and authorities to take proper action on time with respect to event. A few algorithms and methods are available to detect events and to discover clusters from social media or user-generated content [13] [14]. Event detection from social network data is used to: 1) detect earthquake and broadcast the alarming situation to all nearby potential users [15]; 2) extract social trends [13] and unusual activities [16] from Twitter data, and Flickr data [17]; 3) to forecast popularity for upcoming events [14]; and 4) detect traffic flow and traffic constraints including accidents, road closed or blocked [7]. In this paper, we propose a technique to take advantage of the growing set of live and historical social datasets to identify events of Interest, POI semantics, and also enhance maps with traffic updates and roads semantics from social data, and statistical analysis from open governmental data.

III. High-Level Architecture

We present a smart map building framework that retrieves data from multiple sources, processes that data in order to find knowledge-based layers and visualizes those layers on maps.

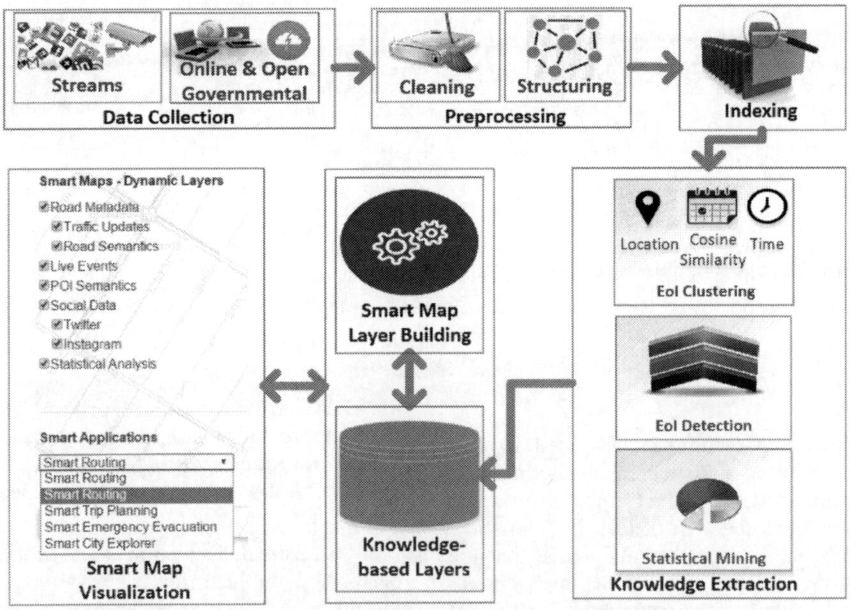

Figure 2. Architecture of the smart maps framework

This framework collects microblog social data streams, open government data, and online data under one platform in order to provide relevant knowledge to users. This helps users in understanding their surroundings, such as live or upcoming events within cities, traffic accidents, road constructions, temporarily closed paths, POI semantics, as well as offers and discounts. Fig. 2 shows an overview of our proposed smart maps architecture with the salient components.

Data Collection and Management Data is retrieved from different data streams, available APIs and online web services. Multiple techniques and policies (frequency, format, structured or unstructured) should be applied on each source of data to be collected. Following are the three ways that we used to collect disparate data from multiple sources:

- Data chunks: In data chunks mode, we download files from different source links that contain partial or full datasets. This data can then be imported or converted into another format for further processing (e.g., crime and accident statistical data). For our use case, we used datasets provided by authorities or open data for different cities, such as New York, USA (including area boundaries, transportation networks, geological data, resources etc.), and other crowdsourced data from Open Street Map and Yelp.

- Single Query: In a single query mode, we used an interface to fetch data by using a single query. This can be achieved by using Restful API to retrieve data in XML and JSON (e.g., Google Traffic and Weather API).

- Continuous Query: In a continuous query, we run crawlers that collect streams of data for each data source (i.e., Twitter and Flickr). Data in this mode is retrieved through Restful APIs of social networks. This mode requires specific handlers for each source of data.

Preprocessing: In the preprocessing step, data cleansing is required by removing noise and irrelevant fields and, in case of social data, converting semi- or unstructured data into a structured format referred to as packets. Each packet has a meta-data header, containing source, location, time, type, potential event and event properties, and a payload, containing the actual content (see Fig. 3). Based on the list of predefined event corpus database, useless data will be discarded and potential packet marked as true. For statistical data, we clean them by removing irrelevant fields. For EoI detection, we used NLP techniques for tokenization and to identify Part-of-Speech by taking into account stop words, out of vocabulary words and other abbreviations, such as '*i know you*' (*iky*).

{"**header**":{"**time**":"Fri Jan 01 00:39:11 +0000 2016","**geo**":{"**type**":"point","**coordinates**":[34.84863834,-95.54509333]}, "**source**": "twitter", "**eventType**":["Party"], "**type**":"text","**potentialEvent**":"true", "**eventname**":"Social events/party","**country**":"United States","**city**":"Oklahoma"}, "**payload**":{"**tags**":[],"**id**":"2605873770","**followers**":"581","**title**":"","**text**":"Party @ Stacey's 😊", "**viewers**":"0", "**screenName**":"TheLedgenBeare", "**language**":"en", "**displayName**":"Ledgen","**url**":null}}

Figure 3. Sample Data Packet from Twitter Streams

Indexing: Preprocessed data needs then to be stored and indexed for further data integration and clustering. Spatio-temporal indexing schemes for efficient retrieval of queries are implemented. As we are dealing with geo-tagged data for the whole world, we propose a hierarchical data structure (similar to a partial quad tree [18]) that helps in the efficient processing and clustering by comparing packets within leaf cells (i.e., nearby geotagged data packets). This approach divides the world into cells at different levels of granularity based on the number of data points. Geo-tagged streams, Yelp, OSM and statistical data pieces are tagged within a particular *cellID*. We design two types of indexers: 1) a spatial geohash indexer for spatial raw data packets; and 2) an knowledge-based indexer for extracted events and layers data.

	yelpid character varying(100)	poiname character varying(100)	twitteraccount character varying(40)
1	bryant-park-new-york-2	Bryant Park	bryantparknyc
2	red-dawn-combat-club-fresh-meadows-4	Red Dawn Combat Club	RedDawnBJJ
3	queens-botanical-garden-flushing	Queens Botanical Garden	queensbotanicl
4	harlem-yoga-studio-new-york	Harlem Yoga Studio	harlemyoga
5	gleasons-gym-brooklyn	Gleason's Gym	Gleasonsboxing
6	stone-street-tavern-new-york	Stone Street Tavern	stonesttavern
7	the-royal-palms-shuffleboard-club-brooklyn	The Royal Palms Shuffleboard Club	RoyalPalmsClub
8	the-fashion-class-manhattan-2	The Fashion Class	TheFashionClass
9	brother-jimmys-bbq-new-york	Brother Jimmy's BBQ	BrotherJimmys
10	the-bahche-brooklyn-4	The Bahche	The Bahche

Figure 4. PostGIS screenshot to demonstrate data integration of POIs from Yelp ID and Twitter Screen Name

A. Knowledge Extraction

Text mining and clustering techniques are used to find Events of Interest and to infer statistical analysis, such as accident and crime prone places. We extract time, location and identify text similarity to detect the type of EoI. For statistical analysis, we find nearby roads and points of interest that are unsafe (i.e., accident prone and hot crime zones by a certain threshold). We have also divided the knowledge extraction module into the following three levels:

- Direct Detection: In this level, data from trustworthy or authorized sources are considered. We can find authentic social accounts or feeds related to traffic, incidents, etc., in order to classify POIs and to detect social events from trustworthy sources. Most of the announcements related to EoI, such as offers, discounts, upcoming and ongoing events, are published by PoI owners, so it is important to identify authentic sources in social data so that these events can be reported. As illustrated in Fig. 4 and during the preprocessing phase, the system identifies Twitter screen names and Yelp identifiers of trustworthy sources by using location and string matching techniques between social data and POI data collected from Yelp and OSM.

- Indirect Detection and Mining: The second level is to apply mining techniques on fused data from multiple sources in order to extract EoI semantics from unspecified happenings. This level is more complex as compared to the first level, as here we need to consider a truth probability model. Our system adopts the graph analogy where each potential event stream is considered as a *node* and the value of 'cosine similarity using term frequency - inverse document frequency(TF-IDF)' between streams as a weight of the bidirectional *edge*. Data packets with a high text similarity value are clustered using the DBSCAN clustering algorithm. The DBSCAN is suitable in our approach as, unlike most of the other clustering methods, it does not require a prior knowledge of the minimum number of clusters. It will help to detect unspecified events and the hot topic detection as well.

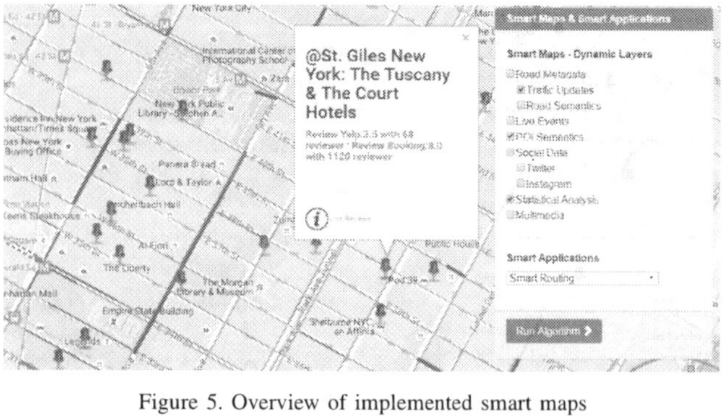

Figure 5. Overview of implemented smart maps

- Statistical Detection and Mining: The third level is performed on historical open governmental data. We apply mining and detection techniques in order to extract statistical analytics, mainly, accident prone areas and crime hotspots. Clustering of crime and accident data is performed within each cell of the hierarchical index tree, and based on a predefined threshold value, edges and POIs inside that area are marked as a crime/accident prone area. We use this approach to find safest path (see Section IV).

B. Knowledge-based Layers

Extracted knowledge will then be spatio-temporally indexed in a knowledge-based layers database. Each EoI is tagged with the cell Identifier, and pieces of statistical analysis are associated with segments or nodes of the road networks. For temporal aspects and cleaning of expired EoIs, we took two parameters: a) *'birth time'* that indicates the first existence of the event in our system, whenever we calculate the first cluster of packets related to that event; and b) *'time of occurrence'* that marks the actual happening time of the event (e.g., next Monday). We clean the EoI from our data after the *'time of occurrence'* has expired using a combination of piggy back and periodic approach. Periodic verification is used to check expired events periodically, whereas piggy back approach is to check for expired events whenever we get any new event within the same cell in the hierarchical tree.

C. Smart Map Layer Building

This component is used to fetch index events from main memory and/or disk. It has two main components; a) query optimizer and b) query engine. The main task of the query optimizer is to find the best query plan. It handles predefined queries related to existing layers displayed on map. The query engine retrieves the plan from query optimizer, so that sub-queries to fetch data from the main memory or disk can be performed. Finally, the smart map layer builder accumulates different results and sends it to the visualizer.

D. Generating and Visualizing Smart Map Layers

The visual interface provides a rich set of spatio-temporal dynamic layers on top of existing maps. The visual renderer interacts with the map building engine to run queries including range, k nearest neighbor (K_{NN}), aggregated and routing

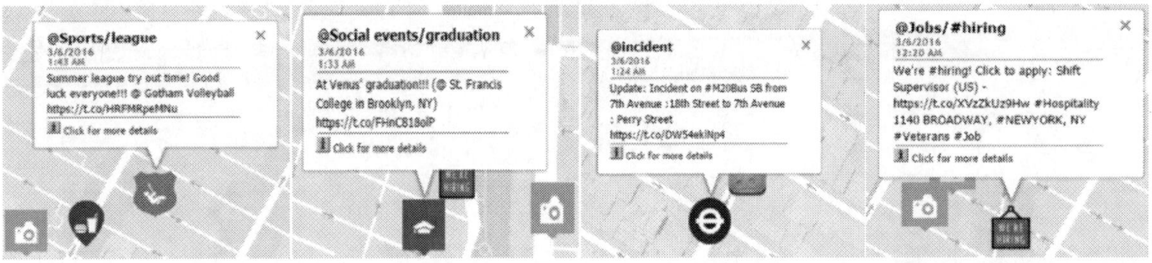

Figure 6. Enhanced city explorer on smart maps: Different type of EoIs on 3rd June: sports, graduation party, road incident, jobs hiring (from left to right)

queries. Fig. 5 Illustrates the visualization of implemented smart maps with POI semantics (displayed as marker), traffic updates and statistical information (blue and pink thick color lines demonstrating accident prone and crime prone roads)

IV. Implementation and Results

To validate our approach, we developed a prototype based on 30Million+ geotagged tweets of world and Yelp, Booking.com, Open Statistical Data from USA governmental website, OSM road network and OSM POI list of New York, USA. The front-end is a web-based application that is used to visualize *smart maps* with dynamic layers and providing a interface to perform the queries related to enhanced routing and city explorer. We are using i7-4712 HQ-CPU @ 2.30GHz with 16GB DDR-2 RAM for in the back-end for processing using the following libraries and software:

- osm2pgsql: The Open Street Map component contains planet dump data that is converted into PostGIS datasets by using the osm2pgsql (github.com/openstreetmap/osm2pgsql) tool.

- *PostGIS*: We installed PostGIS for spatial query over PostgreSQL to store road network data, POIs extracted from Yelp, Booking.com and OSM with their semantics.

- *NLP*: We used Ark-tweet-NLP [19] library for part-of-speech and annotation. This library is trained for Twitter and produce better results than Stanford NLP. It takes care of the out-of-vocabulary words, and stop words used in Twitter.

- *Clustering Algorithm*: Data packets with a high text similarity value are clustered using DBSCAN clustering algorithm. The DBSCAN is suitable in our approach as, unlike most of the other clustering methods, it does not require a prior knowledge of the minimum number of clusters.

- *Taghreed Crawler* [10]: The same crawler was used to collect geotagged tweets.

- *OsmPoisPbf*: We used OsmPoisPbf (github.com/MorbZ/OsmPoisPbf) tool to extract POIs from OSM in PBF file format.

- *Other libraries*: Apart from above, we used Jackson JSON and Yelp, and the Brezometer weather REST APIs in our system. OSMPgRouting A* algorithm used to calcuate the path and we updated edge values using google maps API in case of traffic and increase the weight of edges based on crime and accident frequencies. Back-end implementation is done in Java 1.7.

Following are the "City Explorer" and "Routing" applications as demonstrated on top of the smart maps framework:

TABLE I. RELATION BETWEEN KEYWORD OF USER'S QUERY, EOIS AND SOURCES OF DATA COLLECTION

Keywords	Layers	Sources
Safe	Accident (Prone Edges)	Open Government Data
Safe	Crime Hotspots	Open Government Data
Music Concert	Social Events	Social Data and News
Discounts	POI Announcements	Social Data

A. City Explorer

Fig. 6 illustrates an example output by showing different type of EoIs a) 'Sports League'; b) 'Graduation Party; c) 'Traffic Incident'; and d) 'Jobs Opening'. This allows us to show live events that provide latest information collected from multiple sources about historical places, touristic places, dining, events, shops, news, live tweets, weather updates, traffic updates, semantics of points of interest, and visualize multimedia information that enhance the system usability.

B. Routing

For a given spatio-temporal area, we use the *smart maps* system to enhance traditional queries. We grouped extracted EOIs including social gatherings, 'hotspots' and 'hot times' in a criminal activity, POI semantics, accident-prone roads, in order to provide enriched response of users' routing queries. For example, Consider a city dweller who is interested in current ongoing activities in her neighborhood district and she posts the following query , *"Show safe and fastest path to find the nearest music concert with some ticket discounts"*. Currently, existing maps are unable to provide answers to this type of queries. *Smart maps* framework can support such queries, by determining the relationship between the list of keywords in that query, and the corresponding layers and sources of data (cf., Table 1). Fig. 7 shows the results of the query: a) a map with crime (pink color) and accident prone (blue color) edges; b) an optimized path with respect to time between two markers (showing with red color), c) a crime free path by avoiding crime prone edges (light green color), whereas the safest path can be calculated by avoiding both accident prone and crime prone edges (showing with blue color).

V. Conclusion

This paper presents a *smart maps* framework, that adds dynamic layers to traditional maps by handling social data

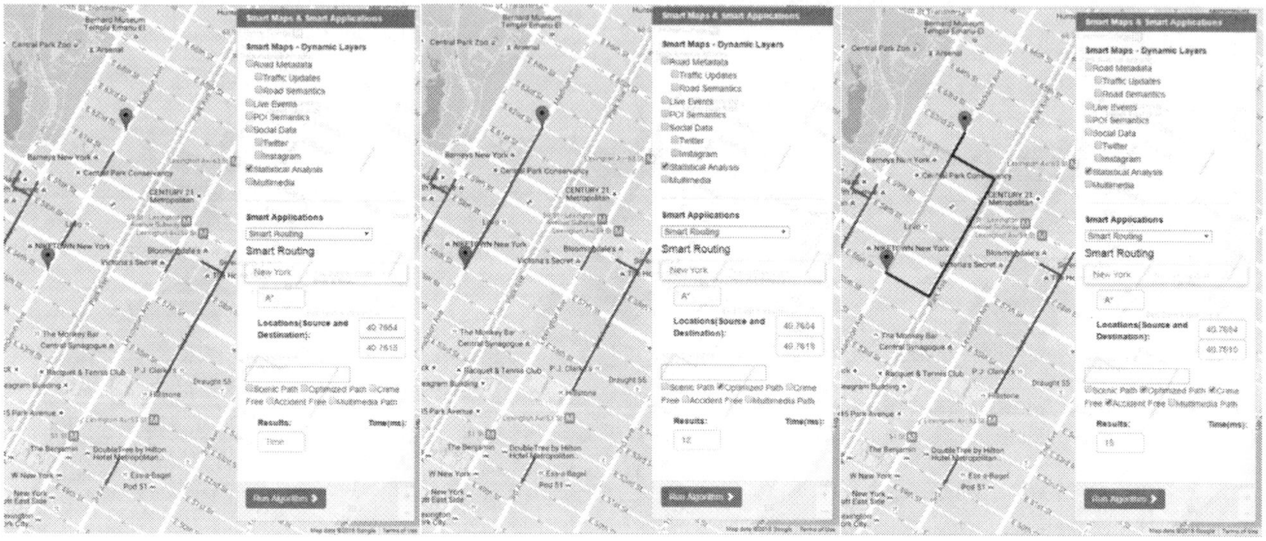

Figure 7. Enhanced routing on smart maps with different options, such as, optimized, crime free, accident free.

streams, and by developing different algorithms for the efficient extraction, clustering, and mapping of live crowd-sourced events. This framework wraps incoming unstructured data streams into data packets, that is, a generic structured format of a potential event. These packets are then processed to extract EoIs based on different dynamic layers. This framework helps in enhancing existing spatial queries including city explorer and routing using extracted knowledge of the dynamic layers. This platform can be easily enriched with new data sources, such as online newspapers. The system can provide valuable knowledge to authorities, governments, market firms, POI owners, event organizers, and end-users in decision making, thus enhancing infrastructure and human life style. Our approach is scalable but not tested for the whole world. In future, we are planning to work on a big data platform to validate scalability and performance factors. Furthermore, we plan to add more data sources to increase completeness, correctness, and conciseness of detected events.

REFERENCES

[1] A. Halevy, A. Rajaraman, and J. Ordille, "Data integration: The teenage years," in Proceedings of the 32Nd International Conference on Very Large Data Bases, ser. VLDB '06. VLDB Endowment, 2006, pp. 9–16.

[2] S. Consoli, M. Mongiovic, A. G. Nuzzolese, S. Peroni, V. Presutti, D. Reforgiato Recupero, and D. Spampinato, "A smart city data model based on semantics best practice and principles," in Proceedings of the 24th International Conference on World Wide Web, ser. WWW '15 Companion. New York, NY, USA: ACM, 2015, pp. 1395–1400.

[3] "Smarter planetsmarter cities. http://www.ibm.com/smarterplanet/us/en/smarter_cities/overview," 2016.

[4] "Citynext. https://partner.microsoft.com/en-us/solutions/citynext," 2017.

[5] X. L. Dong and F. Naumann, "Data fusion: Resolving data conflicts for integration," Proc. VLDB Endow., vol. 2, no. 2, Aug. 2009, pp. 1654–1655.

[6] G. Lamprianidis, D. Skoutas, G. Papatheodorou, and D. Pfoser, "Extraction, integration and exploration of crowdsourced geospatial content from multiple web sources," in Proceedings of the 22Nd ACM SIGSPATIAL International Conference on Advances in Geographic Information Systems, ser. SIGSPATIAL '14. New York, NY, USA: ACM, 2014, pp. 553–556.

[7] F. U. Rehman et al., "Toward dynamic path recommender system based on social network data," in Proceedings of the 7th ACM SIGSPATIAL International Workshop on Computational Transportation Science, ser. IWCTS '14. New York, NY, USA: ACM, 2014, pp. 64–69.

[8] M. F. Goodchild, "Citizens as sensors: the world of volunteered geography," GeoJournal, vol. 69, no. 4, 2007, pp. 211–221.

[9] J. Krygier and D. Wood, Making maps: a visual guide to map design for GIS. Guilford Press, 2011.

[10] A. Magdy et al., "Taghreed: a system for querying, analyzing, and visualizing geotagged microblogs," in Proceedings of the 22nd ACM SIGSPATIAL International Conference on Advances in Geographic Information Systems. ACM, 2014, pp. 163–172.

[11] H. Samet et al., "Reading news with maps by exploiting spatial synonyms," Commun. ACM, vol. 57, no. 10, Sep. 2014, pp. 64–77.

[12] "Statista: The statistics portal. http://www.statista.com/statistics/278414/number-of-worldwide-social-network-users/," 2016.

[13] S. B. Kaleel and A. Abhari, "Cluster-discovery of twitter messages for event detection and trending," J. Comput. Science, vol. 6, 2015, pp. 47–57.

[14] X. Zhang, X. Chen, Y. Chen, S. Wang, Z. Li, and J. Xia, "Event detection and popularity prediction in microblogging," Neurocomputing, vol. 149, 2015, pp. 1469–1480.

[15] M. Avvenuti, S. Cresci, A. Marchetti, C. Meletti, and M. Tesconi, "Ears (earthquake alert and report system): A real time decision support system for earthquake crisis management," in Proceedings of the 20th ACM SIGKDD International Conference on Knowledge Discovery and Data Mining, ser. KDD '14. New York, NY, USA: ACM, 2014, pp. 1749–1758.

[16] R. Lee, S. Wakamiya, and K. Sumiya, "Discovery of unusual regional social activities using geo-tagged microblogs," World Wide Web, vol. 14, no. 4, Jul. 2011, pp. 321–349.

[17] M. Schinas, S. Papadopoulos, G. Petkos, Y. Kompatsiaris, and P. A. Mitkas, "Multimodal graph-based event detection and summarization in social media streams," in Proceedings of the 23rd ACM International Conference on Multimedia, ser. MM '15. New York, NY, USA: ACM, 2015, pp. 189–192.

[18] H. Samet, "The quadtree and related hierarchical data structures," ACM Computing Surveys (CSUR), vol. 16, no. 2, 1984, pp. 187–260.

[19] K. Gimpel et al., "Part-of-speech tagging for twitter: Annotation, features, and experiments," in Proceedings of the 49th Annual Meeting of the Association for Computational Linguistics: Human Language Technologies: Short Papers - Volume 2, ser. HLT '11. Stroudsburg, PA, USA: Association for Computational Linguistics, 2011, pp. 42–47.

Extended Named Entity Recognition Using Finite-State Transducers: An Application To Place Names

Mauro Gaio, Ludovic Moncla

Laboratoire d'Informatique, Université de Pau et des Pays de l'Adour (LIUPPA)
64000 Pau, France
Email: mauro.gaio@univ-pau.fr
ludovic.moncla@univ-pau.fr

***Abstract*—The textual geographical information is frequently organized around spatial named entities. Such entities have intrinsic ambiguities and Named Entity Recognition and Classification methods should be improved in order to handle this problem. This article describes a knowledge-based method implementing a full process with the aim of annotating in a more precise way the spatial information in the textual documents. This gain in accuracy guarantees a better analysis of the spatial information and a better disambiguation of places. The backbone of our proposal is a construction grammar and a cascaded finite-state transducers. The evaluation shows that the introduced concept of hierarchical overlapping, is very helpful to detect a local context associated with Named Entities.**

***Keywords*–Geo-information processing; Geo-spatial Web Services and processing; Geo-spatial data mining.**

I. INTRODUCTION

Different from other forms of geographical data, text-based spatial descriptions are subject to all sorts of ambiguities that prevent effective use [1]. 'Geocoding' textual documents refers to the function of creating unambiguous representation (i.e., footprint) of those text-based spatial descriptions. Significant efforts have been invested in geocoding, however, in order to achieve such a function it is clear that one must first correctly annotate spatial descriptions in the text. Such process is commonly known as 'geoparsing'.

The purpose of this article is to describe a method for implementing a full geoparsing process. A formal grammar describes the concept of extended spatial named entity and their relations with movement verbs. A cascaded finite-state transducers implements a parser with respect for the grammar rules. The parser annotates places and their spatial and verbal relations in order to produce an output including the more detailed description as possible.

We introduce the concept of 'Extended Named Entity' as an entity built with both categories of proper names [17] (i.e., pure and descriptive), and that can be composed of one or more other concepts. Whereas most NERC systems, such as OpenCalais [2], DBpedia Spotlight [2], OpenNER [3], CasEN [4] and Stanford NER [5], usually only consider pure proper names.

We argue that for a fine-grained task, such as marking, classifying and disambiguating spatial named entities, it is essential to consider more accurately the spatial information in relation with named entities [6].

The paper is structured as follows. In Section II, we present the theoretical background and some work useful to implement an automatic process on extracting valuable spatial information in texts. In Sections III-A and III-B, we describe the core principles for establishing our construction grammar. In Section III-C, we briefly describe the implemented solution and we assess the results of a series of evaluations, and Section IV concludes this paper.

II. BACKGROUND AND RELATED WORK

In computational linguistics, parsing is the process of analysing natural language data in accordance with the rules of a formal grammar. In order to automatically parse such data, it is initially necessary to agree on the grammar to be used. Syntactic parsing, then, is the task of recognizing a sentence and assigning a syntactic structure to it. Parsers can be viewed as searching through the space of possible parse trees to find the correct representation for a given input, using two basic search strategies: top-down search and bottom-up search. The top-down strategy tries to build the correct tree from the root node to the leaves, whereas in the bottom-up strategy the parser starts with the words of the input, and tries to build trees from the leaves to the root node, by applying, one by one the rules of the grammar.

Alongside the development of these parsers the notion of construction grammar emerged. This kind of grammar evolved out of work initiated by [7]–[9] and assigns a major role to the concept of construction as a theoretical entity. As specified by [10] the elements of the grammar are constructions: a construction is a pattern used to generate the elements of a language, or to extract these elements from an instance produced from a language. Construction grammars may specify a semantics that differs from the sum of the lexical meanings of its components. Construction grammars can reuse concepts already employed in other linguistic theoretical frameworks, such as Noun Phrase (NP) or Verb Phrase (VP), or Prepositional Phrase (PP). In this kind of construction, a feature structure is usually used to represent the elements of the language. A feature structure is a set of attribute-value pairs; the value can be atomic or another feature structure. A feature structure can be represented as a directed acyclic graph (DAG), with the nodes corresponding to the variable values and the paths to the variable names. Often however, feature structures are written as follows:

$$\begin{bmatrix} \text{role} & target \\ \text{named entity} & \begin{bmatrix} \text{component} & noun\,phrase \\ \text{category} & descriptive \\ \text{type} & location \end{bmatrix} \end{bmatrix}$$

Local and global ambiguities are perhaps the trickiest problem that parsers have to tackle. This problem is particularly important when the parser is based on a complex grammar. In the literature, many strategies have been proposed to remove as many ambiguous cases as possible. Currently, in tasks known as Named Entity Recognition and Classification (NERC) the problem of ambiguities remains unresolved for some contexts. The notion of 'Named Entity' (NE) was formally established at the Sixth Message Understanding Conference (MUC-6, 1995). From the beginning the notion included names of persons, locations and organisations, but also numerical expressions of time, date, money, etc.

A considerable amount of work in NERC research takes the language factor as a parameter and in this body of work a significant proportion is devoted to the study of English, but French is also considered [11] [12], as well as other languages. The impact of literary genre (narrative, memoir, journalism, etc.) and domain (supply of raw materials, market or economic intelligence, politics, etc.) is a problem that has been more recently addressed in the NERC literature. Globally approaches for named entity parsing cover a huge variety of strategies, methods and representations. These approaches are generally classified in two main categories, data-driven approaches and knowledge-based approaches. One of the earliest research papers in the field of NERC was written by [13]. Her approach was based on heuristics and handcrafted rules, in other words was knowledge-based, this is also the case of our proposal. This kind of approach do not require a complete parse for all the input. A shallow parse of input sentences may be sufficient; as it is usually the case in information extraction systems that focus on the segments in a text that are likely to contain valuable information. Many different methods can be used, but, it should be mentioned that a finite-state automaton is probably the most widely used mathematical device to implement shallow parsers. Some implementations make use of cascaded finite-state transducers to produce tree-like representations. Because regular languages and relations can be encoded as finite automata they can be more easily manipulated than more complex languages; cascaded finite-state transducer principle have therefore turned out to be very useful for linguistic applications, in particular for shallow parsing. Generally, there are different finite-state transducers at different stages. Each stage bundles a set of items in a package that will be considered as a single element in the next stage.

Parsing that is solely concerned with geographical data is known as geoparsing and aims at extracting keywords and keyphrases describing geographical references from unstructured text. There are currently several types of specific ambiguity involved in geoparsing and more specifically with the problem of toponym recognition.

Toponym disambiguation is defined as a subtask of toponym resolution and is complementary to the subtask of toponym recognition. It involves associating a non-ambiguous location with a place name [14]. According to [15], the approaches for disambiguating toponyms can be classified in three categories: supervised or data-driven approaches, map-based approaches and knowledge-based approaches. Data-driven approaches are based on machine learning algorithms and exploit non-geographical content and events to build probabilistic models using spatial relationships between entities (i.e., persons, organisations) and places. As pointed out by [16], a place is more likely to be located near other places mentioned around it. Knowledge-based approaches aim at considering semantic relations between named entities, concepts or key terms such as social, associative or lexical relatedness and not only co-occurrence statistics of terms. These methods use knowledge sources (gazetteers, ontologies, etc.) to determine whether other related toponyms in the knowledge source are also referred to the document, or exploit additional information from the toponyms, such as importance, size or population counts. Finally, map-based disambiguation approaches use other unambiguous and georeferenced toponyms found on the same document as context for disambiguation.

As previously mentioned, NERC approaches are classified in two main categories, data-driven approaches and knowledge-based approaches. The main drawback of data-driven approaches is the lack of classified collections and the need for large corpora of annotated ground truths. Knowledge-based methods are more suitable for approaches based on domain-specific corpus analysis and rules are described in a readable way and are easy to modify and maintain. This is the case in our proposal, where the goal is to design and implement a parser, based on a bottom-up stategy, for recognising and classifying places in a dynamic space context mentioned in French, Spanish or Italian texts.

III. ANNOTATING SPATIAL DESCRIPTIONS

A. Extended Named Entity (ENE) structure

According to [17] there are two categories of proper names: pure and descriptive. Pure proper names can be simple (i.e., composed of a single lexeme) or complex (i.e., composed of several lexemes) and are composed of proper names only. Descriptive proper names refer to a composition of proper names and common names (i.e., expansion). In other words, descriptive proper names overlap pure proper names. Descriptive proper names refer to a NE built with a pure proper name and a descriptive expansion. This expansion can change the implicit type (e.g., location, person, etc.) of the initial pure proper name.

We define several levels of overlapping (0, 1, 2, etc.) for the representation of ENE. Each level is encapsulated in the previous level.

Level 0: refers to pure proper names. It can be seen as the core component of an ENE. Thus, we consider NE as a special kind of ENE. Examples (1) illustrate level 0 entities:

[*Aragón*] → one entity (location)
[*Greenpeace*] → one entity (organisation) (1)
[*Charles de Gaulle*] → one entity (person)

Level 1: refers to descriptive proper names composed of a pure proper name (i.e., an entity of level 0) and a common noun (i.e., expansion). The following examples (2) show the representation of ENE. In these cases, and according to a same given ontology, descriptive expansions may not change the implicit or default nature of the object described by the proper name; they just specify the nature or the feature type.

comunidad autónoma de [*Aragón*]
'autonomous community of Aragón'
(2)
ufficio italianno di [*Greenpeace*]
'Greenpeace Italian office'

However, when the associated term has not the same type of the intrinsic or default type of the pure proper name, it defines a new entity that overlaps the pure proper name one. The following examples (3) show that an entity may contain the name of another entity, and that the new entity may have a different type, examples (3b. - 3c.).

a. *Delta del* [*Ebro*]
'Ebro Delta'
→ two entities, ***Ebro*** (location) and ***Delta del Ebro*** (location)

b. *siège social de l'* [*Unicef*]
'Unicef headquarters' (3)
→ two entities, ***Unicef***(organisation) and ***siège social de l'Unicef*** (location)

c. *sindaco di* [*Genova*]
'mayor of Genoa'
→ two entities, ***Genova*** (location) and ***sindaco di Genova*** (person)

Level >1 : refers to a descriptive proper name composed of another descriptive proper name. ENE of level >1 are built with ENE of level 1 and with one or more descriptive expansions, as shown on the examples (4a. - 4b.). The behavior is the same as for the previous level, i.e., the expansion can change the type of the object described by the ENE of level 1. In fact, there is not really a limit to the overlapping. However, it is quite uncommon to find an ENE of a level greater than 3. The example (4c.) show an ENE of Level 3.

a. *portavoce della* [*Villa Médicis a* [*Roma*]]
'spokesperson of the Villa Médicis in Rome'

b. *club de pelota vasca de la* [*ciudad de* [*San Sebastián*]]
'Basque pelota club of San Sebastian city' (4)

c. *dépression karstique dans le* [territoire aride au sud de la [*région* d' [Aragon]]]
'karstic depression in the arid land south of the Aragon Region'

We have considered the annotation of ENE as a shallow parsing and the grammar to be used as a specific construction. The core of the grammar is given in 5.

With this kind of grammar and with a parser based on a bottom-up strategy each level of the ENE can be marked, from the pure proper name to the whole ENE and it can distinguish between two types of ENE, 'absolute' refering to standard spatial ENE and 'relative' refering to spatial ENE associated with spatial relations (i.e., 'offset' and 'measure').

$$\begin{array}{rcl} S & \rightarrow & ENE \\ ENE & \rightarrow & ENEA \mid (Term)\ ENER \\ ENER & \rightarrow & Offset\ ENEA \mid Offset\ ENER \\ ENEA & \rightarrow & (Term)\ ProperNoun \mid Term\ ENEA \\ Term & \rightarrow & Nominal\ Det \\ Nominal & \rightarrow & Noun \quad \mid \quad Nominal\ Noun \end{array} \qquad (5)$$

$Offset$ can be seen as an adverbial clause. For instance, taking example (4c.), using the proposed NERC process it produces the results represented in feature structure form in Fig. 1.

```
ENER [ level  3
       type   place name
       comp.  NP,OFFSET,
       ENER [ level  2
              type   place name
              comp.  NP,IN,OFFSET,
              ENEA [ level  1
                     type   location
                     cat.   descriptive
                     comp.  NN,IN,
                     ENEA [ level 0
                            type location
                            cat.  pure
                            comp. NNP
                            lex.  Aragon ]
                     lex.   région d'Aragon ]
              lex.   territoire aride au sud
                     de la région d'Aragon ]
       lex.   dépression karstique dans le territoire
              aride au sud de la région d'Aragon ]
```

NP=Noun phrase, NN=Noun, IN=Preposition, NNP=Proper noun, singular

Figure 1. The annotation of an ENE.

With respect to the specific problem of the NERC category of place names, this makes it possible, in particular, to move beyond reducing a place to a name and then geocoded with a single set of coordinates, a model that is still predominant in Geographic Information Science [18].

Standard NER tools consider only the entity 'Aragon Region', and therefore lead to inaccuracies in classification and/or disambiguation. Of course this must be consistent with the discourse context.

B. Movement verbs and Extended Spatial Named Entity structures

In view of our aim of automatically producing the more detailed description to achieve a better disambiguation, we propose to use additional information in relation with NE. For a better understanding of the spatial context of a NE, the linguists have highlighted the importance of the use of motion verbs, especially in Romance languages [19]. That is why we opted for taking into account movement verbs in the parsing process.

The core of the 'VT' grammar proposed hereafter can be seen both as a specialisation and as an extension of the ENE construction grammar. The symbol V represents a set of movement verbs and the symbol T a set of n-tuples, i.e., a composition of elements belonging respectively to three sets: SO a set of spatial offsets, TG a set of geographical noun phrases and E a set of ENE.

Consider the following sentence 6:

descendre sur le territoire aride au sud de la région d'Aragon.
'go down onto the arid land south of the Aragon region.' (6)

Example (6) has the following VT structure = (v,t), with: v = *descendre*, t = *sur le territoire aride au sud de la région d'Aragon*. With t respectively composed of: $tg_3 = \emptyset$, so_3 = *sur*, ENE_2 = *territoire aride au sud de la région d'Aragon*, tg_2 = *territoire aride*, so_2 = *au sud de*, ENE_1 = *la région d'Aragon*, tg_1 = *région*, $so_1 = \emptyset$, ENE_0 = *Aragon*. The set SO of spatial offsets is composed of locative phrases in which, at least in verb-framed languages such as French, the role of prepositions is central. A large number of studies have shown that prepositions are involved in the operation of spatial tracking, or location. With respect to the location concept, following the conclusions of work conducted according to Talmy's [20] and Vandeloise's [21] proposals, prepositions contribute significantly to bringing together two entities: a locator and a localised entity (i.e., a landmark and a target in Vandeloise's terms). The phrase used as locator must have spatial properties that facilitate its identification and the explanation of the spatial relationship in which it is involved. Linguistically, there are three kinds of phrases that can serve as locators: noun phrases including a name with spatial properties, noun phrases indicating distance, e.g., *le refuge se trouve à trois kilomètres ou à une heure de marche* ('the refuge is three kilometers or an hour's walk away') or orientation, e.g., *prendre la bretelle de droite* ('take the exit on the right') and noun phrases evoking an activity that may be associated with a place, e.g., *je me rendais au cours de natation* ('I was on my way to my swimming lesson').

The first category of phrases used as locator is the most common one and it can be associated to the greatest number of prepositions. The proposed VT construction grammar relies only on this category. In this category, the included name can be of two types: place names and the names of concrete objects (objects that can be located in the same place at the same time), in other words the ENE elements contained in the set E. Frequently, a particular sub-group consisting of noun phrases referring to specific parts of a locator (the peak, the bottom, the slope, the interior) is considered separately. They are unique in that they are considered suggestive of spatial properties only if they are in relation with ENE via prepositions such as *de* (from) and *à* (to, at). In the VT structure, the set TG represents this sub-group of noun phrases.

What can be retained from the literature is that the same prepositional phrase can be used to describe a variety of spatial situations, and that the discriminating factors are at the level of modalities of action. As pointed out by various studies, location is a static principle unless a dynamic component related to the verb also operates. Moreover, languages are not fully part of one category or the other [22]. For instance, in English, which is mostly a satellite-framed language, there are many verbs, such as: 'enter, exit, ascend, descend', that refer both to Motion and Path. Conversely, in verb-framed languages there are also some satellite-framed expressions such as *partir de* ('to leave'), *partir à* ('to go') where the path is encoded in the French prepositions *de* and *à*.

[23] proposed to classify motion verbs according to the 'aspectual' properties of movement called hereafter 'polarity'. The three polarities are initial (e.g., to leave), median (e.g., to cross) and final (e.g., to arrive). Without changing the intrinsic polarity of the verb, the preposition can change what could be called the focus of the displacement. More specifically, the association of a motion verb with a spatial preposition can change the focus of the displacement and take on the polarity of the preposition instead of that of the verb. Undeniably, 'leaving from Paris' and 'leaving for Paris' are two expressions with radically opposite focus of the displacement. If we consider the role played by the name, in one case, the place name is the origin of the displacement, and in the other case the place name is the destination. The place name *Paris* is the target, so the polarity of the whole expression may be considered as final.

The VT construction grammar aims to be a computational synthesis of the work on the means used by the language to express displacement, the work on the functioning of movement verbs in a sentence, and the work on the combinatorial principles of these verbs with different prepositions. The core of the grammar is given in 7.

$$
\begin{array}{rcl}
S & \rightarrow & V\ T \\
V & \rightarrow & Verb \mid Verb\ SO \\
C & \rightarrow & Conjonction \mid , \\
LT & \rightarrow & ENE\ C\ T \\
T & \rightarrow & (SO)\ (det)\ ENE \mid \\
 & & (SO \mid ENE)\ T \mid (SO)\ LT
\end{array} \tag{7}
$$

SO can be seen as a spatial adverbial clause.

Of course, in order to take into account the combinations, which by their structure are inconsistent with French, the real grammar is more complex. The VT construction grammar reuse a sub-set of the concepts employed in a traditional parts-of-speech (POS) grammar.

The bottom-up parser, based on the real grammar and implemented with a cascade of transducers, can be viewed as searching through the space of possible parse trees to find the correct parse tree for a given 'VT' phrase. Then if a correct parse tree is found the ENE becomes a candidate to be an Extended Spatial Named Entity (ESNE).

Finally, consider the following sentences :

Emprunter successivement ***rue des Capucins*** *et* ***rue de Compostelle****.*
'Walk down **Capucins Street** and then **Compostelle Street**.'
Prendre à gauche après l'entrée de ***l'usine de Fontanille****.*
'Turn left after the entry to the **Fontanille factory**.' (8)
Suivre la route depuis le ***hameau Lic*** *jusqu'à la* ***Chapelle Saint-Roche****.*
'Follow the road from the **hamlet Lic** to the **Chapelle Saint-Roche**.'

These sentences are extracted from a French hiking description. For each of them the cascade of transducers found a correct parse tree. So each marked ENE becomes a potential ESNE but first all the ambiguities must be removed. In fact, most of the descriptive proper names used to build the ENE in these sentences are very common proper nouns and moreover refer to small localised objects. These are specific aspects that may cause ambiguity.

For our experiments we used the multilingual Perdido corpus [24], which is a TEI [25] compliant gold-standard corpus containing 90 hiking descriptions (French, Spanish and Italian) manually annotated. Hiking descriptions are a specific type of document describing displacements using geographical information, such as toponyms, spatial and motion relations, and natural features or landscapes. The corpus analysis shows that only 2% of ENE are not referring to spatial entities. Furthermore, 53% of the occurrences of ESNE are contained within a VT structure and 47% are associated with feature types (i.e., 53% of ESNE belong to the level 0) and a very few number of ESNE (3%) are built with more than one expansion (level >1). Additionally, about 59% of verbs are motion verbs. Median and final motion verbs are the most frequent ones and only 3% of verbs belonging to a VT structure refer to verbs of perception.

C. NERC Processing and Evaluation

As we saw above, we consider only two types of named entities: spatial and non-spatial, and ENE and ESNE are considered as described in the previous sections. With respect to the NERC task, we implemented the construction grammars previously described using an hybrid solution combining a pre-processing POS analysis, a cascaded finite-state transducers for annotating the segments in a text containing valuable information, and external resources for the named entity classification task. The pre-processing component of the Perdido processing chain (PPC) transforms and pre-annotates raw texts with different process: sentence splitting, tokenisation, lemmatisation, and POS tagging. These shallow linguistic tasks are language dependent and are done by standards POS taggers. We propose to integrate different POS taggers in order to solve language or performance issues. Thus, we developed an integration framework designed to handle the output provided by different POS taggers, which use various tag-sets to assign grammatical categories of words. The integration framework implements a generic transformation to standardise tag-sets in order to turn the POS taggers output into a compliant input format for the next component of the PPC. The main component of the PPC deals with the automatic annotation of ENE and geospatial information such as VT structures. The proposed cascaded finite-state transducers, which annotates spatial information and ENE was developed using the CasSys program available in the Unitex platform [26]. For the development of the PPC, we have followed the principles introduced for the development of the CasEN system [27], which implements a combination of two cascaded finite-state transducers. The first one called *analysis cascade* is the core of the annotation process, it executes a sequence of transducers which annotate elements in a specific order. The second cascade called *synthesis cascade* transforms the output of the first cascade (XML-CasSys) into the TEI-compliant XML markup language described in [28]. We have designed web services [29] for the POS and NERC components of the PPC. The Perdido POS web service returns the result of the POS processing using the Unitex compliant input format and the Perdido NERC web service returns the TEI-compliant XML results.

The NERC task was evaluated using both manual POS processed texts (POS 100% corrected) and a fully automatic process (automatic POS processed texts) in order to show the

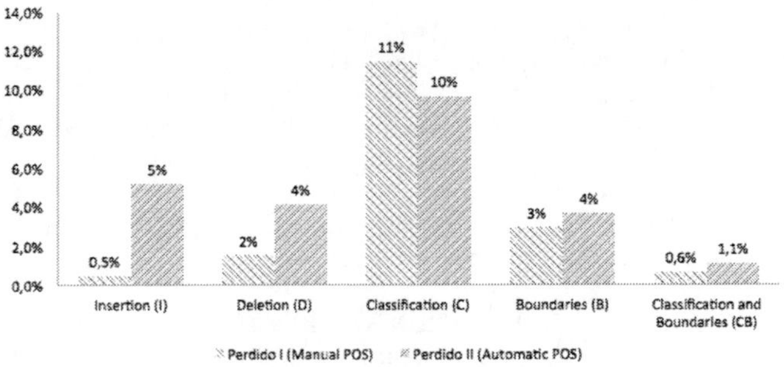

Figure 2. Comparison of the percentage of slot errors of Perdido I and Perdido II (French).

percentage of errors introduced during the pre-processing step of our method. The configuration for experiments done with manually corrected POS is called Perdido I hereafter and the configuration for experiments done with POS automatically processed Perdido II.

TABLE I. NUMBER OF CORRECTLY DETECTED ENE WITH PERDIDO I AND II (FRENCH).

	N	*Perdido I*		*Perdido II*	
level 0	304	235	77%	244	80%
level 1	332	302	91%	280	84%
level 2	20	16	80%	17	85%
level 3	4	0	0%	1	25%
total	660	553	84%	542	82%

Table I shows the number of ENE that were correctly detected by Perdido I and Perdido II without any errors and the column 'N' shows the reference number of ENE in the French Perdido gold-standard corpus. The evaluation of the automatic NERC task gives a number of correct recognition (i.e., true positives) of 553 ENE with Perdido I and 542 ENE with Perdido II over a total number of 660 ENE, which represents 84% and 82% respectively with Perdido I and Perdido II. For further details concerning the evaluation of the results, we used the SER metric [30] which represents the total slot error rate taking into account the different types of errors related with the NERC task (i.e., insertion, deletion, classification, boundary detection and both classification and boundary detection).

Fig. 2 shows the comparison of the percentage of the different slot errors used in the SER metric. Each bar on this chart refers to the percentage of errors, thus, the lower the percentages are, the better the results are. Concerning errors of insertion (i.e., false positives), it can be seen that Perdido II (5%) makes more errors than Perdido I (0.5%). This can be explained by the fact that as Perdido I is based on a manually corrected POS pre-processing, there is no ambiguity or mistake concerning which words are proper names or not. This can explain also errors of deletion, 4% with Perdido II and only 2% with Perdido I. Then the difference of 1% between Perdido I and Perdido II concerning classification errors is not significant. Indeed, the percentage of classification errors refers to the number of errors over the number of detected entities (i.e., deletion errors are not taken into account in the calculation). The evaluation process gives a total SER of 10% with Perdido I and 17% with Perdido II. As expected, the

Perdido I configuration, which is based on a manual POS analysis, obtains better results than the Perdido II configuration. Approximately seven percent of the errors are introduced by the POS pre-processing step of our method. However, considering the different levels of encapsulation (ENE) and all the different types of errors, 17% of SER and 82% of correct recognition of ENE is a good score.

IV. Conclusion and Future Work

With respect to the annotation of spatial information used to extract geographical data from text-based spatial descriptions, we have proposed a geoparser based on construction grammars implemented with two cascaded finite-state transducers. As a computational synthesis of the work on the expression of space and motion in natural languages, we described the construction grammar VT which aims to mark and formalise the relations between ENE, geographical terms, spatial relations and movement verbs. We have shown that the hierarchical overlapping introduced by the concept of ENE is very helpful to detect a local context associated with NE. For instance, the local context contained within ESNE, such as feature types, helps to produce a detailed description that can be used for a better analysis of the spatial information and a better disambiguation of places. The feasibility of our proposal has been evaluated using a corpus of hiking descriptions and obtains an overall SER score of 17%.

To our knowledge NERC is an important pre-processing step for most of these tasks and automatic NERC process for Indo-European languages might be more or less challenging (e.g., for German it is especially challenging). Our proposal relies on the TEI standard which is widely used in digital humanities and linguistics for Indo-European languages. Thus, the work in progress is to define several other specific finite-state transducers, each one adapted to the specific needs of a given Indo-European language but all based on the same generic core layer. The proposed generic core layer may be used to create and share pre-processed corpus.

Acknowledgment

This work has been partially supported by: the Communauté d'Agglomération Pau Pyrénées (CDAPP) and the Institut National de l'Information Géographique et Forestiére (IGN) through the PERDIDO project; the Spanish Government (project TIN2012-37826-C02-01); and the Aragon and Aquitaine Regional Governments cooperation programme through the YACA project.

References

[1] R. R. Larson, "Geographic Information Retrieval and Spatial Browsing," GIS and Libraries: Patrons, Maps and Spatial Information, Apr. 1996, pp. 81–124.

[2] OpenCalais, http://www.opencalais.com/, 2017, [accessed 2017-01-12].

[3] OpenNER, http://opennlp.apache.org/, [accessed 2017-01-12].

[4] CasEN, http://tln.li.univ-tours.fr/Tln_CasEN_eng.html, [accessed 2017-01-12].

[5] Stanford-NER, http://nlp.stanford.edu/ner/, [accessed 2017-01-12].

[6] L. Moncla, W. Renteria-Agualimpia, J. Nogueras-Iso, and M. Gaio, "Geocoding for texts with fine-grain toponyms: An experiment on a geoparsed hiking descriptions corpus," in Proceedings of the 22Nd ACM SIGSPATIAL. Dallas, TX, USA: ACM, 2014, pp. 183–192.

[7] C. J. Fillmore, "Syntactic Intrusions and The Notion of Grammatical Construction," Annual Meeting of the Berkeley Linguistics Society, vol. 11, no. 0, Jun. 1985, pp. 73–86.

[8] G. Lakoff, Women, fire, and dangerous thinks – What categories reveal about the mind. University of Chicago Press, 1987.

[9] R. W. Langacker, Foundations of Cognitive Grammar: Volume I: Theoretical Prerequisites. Stanford, CA: Stanford University Press, 1987.

[10] Y. Yannick-Mathieu, "La Grammaire de Construction," Approches syntaxiques contemporaines, no. 48, 2003, pp. 43–56.

[11] T. Poibeau, "Extraction automatique d'information: du texte brut au web sémantique," in Extraction automatique d'information: du texte brut au web sémantique. Hermès Lavoisier, 2003.

[12] N. Friburger and D. Maurel, "Finite-state transducer cascades to extract named entities in texts," Theoretical Computer Science, vol. 313, no. 1, Feb. 2004, pp. 93–104.

[13] L. F. Rau, "Extracting Company Names from Text," in Artificial Intelligence Applications. Miami Beach: IEEE, 1991, pp. 29–32.

[14] J. L. Leidner, Toponym Resolution in Text: Annotation, Evaluation and Applications of Spatial Grounding of Place Names. Universal-Publishers, Jan. 2007.

[15] D. Buscaldi and P. Rosso, "A conceptual density-based approach for the disambiguation of toponyms," Int. J. Geogr. Inf. Sci., vol. 22, no. 3, Jan. 2008, pp. 301–313.

[16] D. A. Smith and G. Crane, "Disambiguating Geographic Names in a Historical Digital Library," in Proceedings of the 5th European Conference on Research and Advanced Technology for Digital Libraries, ser. ECDL '01. London, UK: Springer-Verlag, 2001, pp. 127–136.

[17] K. Jonasson, Le nom propre. Duculot, Louvain-la-Neuve, Belgium, 1994.

[18] R. S. Purves and C. Derungs, "From Space to Place: Place-Based Explorations of Text," International Journal of Humanities and Arts Computing, vol. 9, no. 1, Mar. 2015, pp. 74–94.

[19] M. Aurnague, "How motion verbs are spatial: The spatial foundations of intransitive motion verbs in French," Lingvisticae Investigationes, vol. 34, no. 1, 2011, pp. 1–34.

[20] L. Talmy, How language structures space, ser. Berkeley cognitive science report. Berkeley, CA, Etats-Unis: Cognitive Science Program, Institute of Cognitive Studies, University of California at Berkeley, 1983, no. 4.

[21] C. Vandeloise, L'Espace en français. Sémantique des prépositions spatiales. Editions du Seuil, 1986.

[22] S. Pourcel and A. Kopecka, "Motion expression in French: typological diversity," Durham & Newcastle working papers in linguistics, vol. 11, 2005, pp. 139–153.

[23] J.-P. Boons, "La notion sémantique de déplacement dans une classification syntaxique des verbes locatifs," Langue Française, no. 76, 1987, pp. 5–40.

[24] L. Moncla, M. Gaio, J. Nogueras-Iso, and S. Mustière, "Reconstruction of itineraries from annotated text with an informed spanning tree algorithm," International Journal of Geographical Information Science, vol. 30, no. 6, 2016, pp. 1137–1160.

[25] TEI, "Text encoding initiative," http://www.tei-c.org/, 2017, [accessed 2017-01-12].

[26] Unitex, "Unitex/gramlab: an open source, cross-platform, multilingual, lexicon- and grammar-based corpus processing suite," http://www-igm.univ-mlv.fr/~unitex/, 2017, [accessed 2017-01-12].

[27] D. Maurel, N. Friburger, J.-Y. Antoine, I. Eshkol-Taravella, and D. Nouvel, "Cascades de transducteurs autour de la reconnaissance des entités nommées," TAL, vol. 52, no. 1, 2011, pp. 69–96.

[28] L. Moncla and M. Gaio, "A Multi-layer Markup Language for Geospatial Semantic Annotations," in Proceedings of the 9th Workshop on Geographic Information Retrieval, ser. GIR '15. Paris, France: ACM, 2015, pp. 5:1–5:10.

[29] PERDIDO, "Expanded named entity annotation service," http://erig.univ-pau.fr/PERDIDO/api.jsp, 2017, [accessed 2017-01-12].

[30] J. Makhoul, F. Kubala, R. Schwartz, and R. Weischedel, "Performance measures for information extraction," in In Proceedings of DARPA Broadcast News Workshop, 1999, pp. 249–252.

Cascading Geospatial Content Services

CASE: European Location Framework

Lassi Lehto
Department of Geoinformatics and Cartography
Finnish Geospatial Research Institute, NLS Finland
Masala, Finland
e-mail: lassi.lehto@nls.fi

Abstract— **The concept of service cascade can be seen as a solution for the data aggregation needs set forth for instance by the basic INSPIRE principle, according to which European level Spatial Data Infrastructures (ESDIs) can be built on top of national level SDIs. The research described in this paper has been conducted in the context of a major EU project, called European Location Framework (ELF). The main goal of the work discussed in this paper has been to facilitate European level access to national master datasets using direct access download services that conform to Web Feature Service (WFS) specification. Content aggregation is based on the Cascading WFS approach and carried out as on-the-fly process. Service cascade is not formally specified in the WFS standard, thus the ELF Cascading WFS has to be taken as an experimental implementation with some significant limitations. Altogether 83 national download services have been successfully included into the ELF Cascading WFS, providing access to over 120 different feature types from 11 INSPIRE themes in 13 European countries.**

Keywords-service cascade; content aggregation; Web Feature Service; European SDI.

I. INTRODUCTION

Providing aggregated European-wide access to geospatial data resources maintained on national level is the ambitious goal of the INSPIRE process (Infrastructure for Spatial Information in the European Community) [1] and other similar integration initiatives. Service cascade is presented in this paper as a solution for facilitating access to national content to support Pan-European applications. The paper presents the process of providing a centralized access point to geospatial data, requested from several national INSPIRE-compliant Download Services [2].

The research described in this paper has been carried out in the context of a major EU project, called European Location Framework (ELF), initiated by EuroGeographics (EG), the European level representative of the European National Mapping and Cadastral Agencies (NMCAs) [3]. The ELF project aims at developing European-wide INSPIRE-compliant services based on geodata resources maintained by the EG's membership. The ELF project started in March 2013 and ended in October 2016 [4]. The project has 30 participant organizations, 13 of them representing EU/EFTA member states as official NMCAs. Thus the data resources accessible by the project have quite extensive spatial coverage across Europe, see Fig. 1.

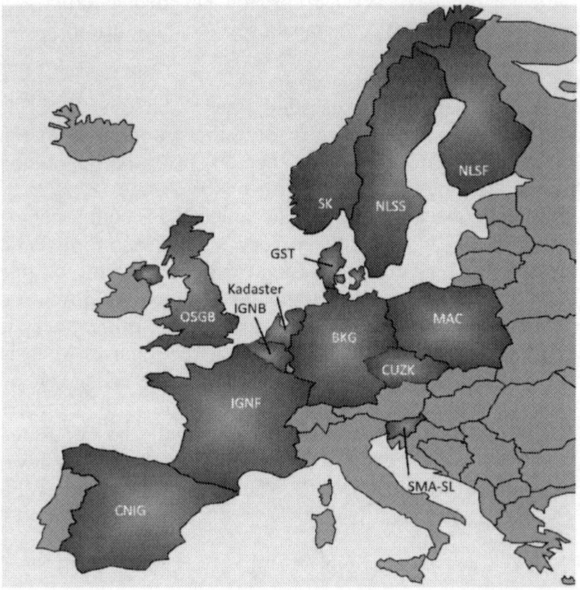

Figure 1. The countries participating in the European Location Framework project. The label indicates the National Mapping and Cadastral Agency (NMCA) of each country.

The ELF project includes a work package specifically focusing on data provision and service development. In this work package there is a subtask that focuses on the issues related to service cascade [5]. The author of the paper has been responsible for this subtask in the ELF project. The approach presented in this paper covers this development and discusses specifically the provision of European level download services based on data services delivering content on national level. The approach is based on the principle of a Cascading Web Feature Service (WFS) [6].

Section II introduces the concept of service cascade and its implementation in the download services of the ELF platform. Section III provides a more detailed description of the ELF Cascading WFS module and Section IV discusses its most significant limitations. The paper ends with concluding remarks in Section V.

II. SERVICE CASCADE

A. *Principle*

The concept of service cascade is discussed in this paper, as a solution for data aggregation needs. According to the service architecture model of the Open Geospatial Consortium (OGC), the basic idea in service cascade is that a service access point can be configured as a content source for another service, actually making this latter service a client of the source service [7]. Service cascade can be regarded as an implementation of the basic INSPIRE principle, according to which European level Spatial Data Infrastructures (ESDIs) can be built on top of the national level SDIs. This can be seen as the most cost-effective way for building services on multiple levels of local administration inside a single country as well. In the past, service cascade has been studied for instance in the context of metadata service integration [8].

B. *Query Distribution*

When implementing cascaded integration over a set of national services, one has to resolve the problem of spatial query distribution on one hand, and the cross-border fusion of geospatial content on the other.

The main tasks of the ELF Cascading WFS component is to determine, to which national services the incoming WFS GetFeature –query must be forwarded, depending on the location of the query's bounding box (query window) and the requested feature types. The bounding box of the query is overlaid with the polygonal national boundaries dataset stored in the ELF Cascading WFS's local PostgreSQL/PostGIS database. As a result, all countries involved in the query are identified. Then the requested feature types are checked to determine, which country level services have to be queried. The ELF Cascading WFS approach is depicted in the Fig. 2.

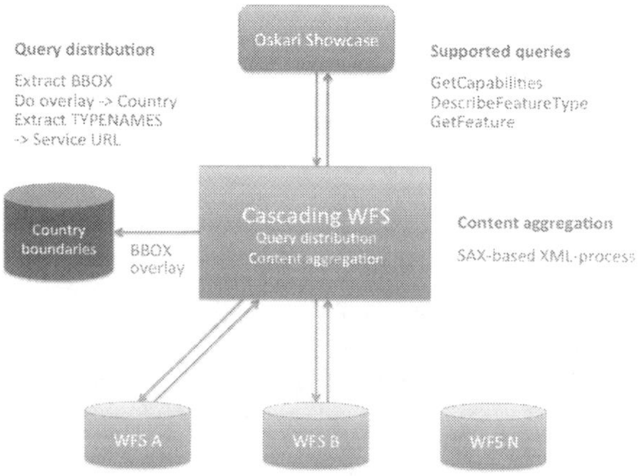

Figure 2. Cascading WFS service architecture of the ELF platform.

C. *Content Aggregation*

The goal of the ELF platform is to support the end user in accessing geospatial data content aggregated on the European level, and directly from national services, too. Thus, the cascading approach aims at supporting real-time aggregation of content from a set of distributed national data sources. One of the new challenges encountered, when accessing national services from European-level applications, is the need to introduce spatial integration capabilities to the traditional service cascade approach. At the moment only thematic integration is supported in the existing cascade mechanisms of the OGC service implementations (Web Map Service, WMS) [9]. In that setup, every single map layer is served by one and only one back-end service.

If only one backend service is involved in the Cascading WFS query, the process is straightforward. The single service is accessed, and the resulting dataset is returned to the calling application without further processing. However, if two or more services are involved in the case of a cross-border query, the Cascading WFS dispatches several parallel query threads to access the national services. The returning data streams are processed in the order they become ready. The datasets are merged into a single response message stream using a SAX-based XML-processing model [10], as depicted in Fig. 2.

The Cascading WFS has to create the root element (FeatureCollection) of the resulting dataset and include all required XML namespace declarations. In addition, the Cascading WFS fills in the boundedBy-element using the bounding box of the query, as a rough indication of the spatial extent of the resulting dataset. Then the content streams of the individual background responses are written out in the order they become ready, taking away the FeatureCollection and boundedBy-elements from the individual streams. Finally, the FeatureCollection element is closed by the Cascading WFS.

As the source data sets conform to the data models defined in the INSPIRE schemas and the extensions developed in the ELF project, data content is semantically harmonised already on the state level. Content aggregation done on the cascading level thus does not need to be concerned about the semantic harmonisation of the data sets to be aggregated. Issues related to edge matching of content on the border were not treated in this subtask of the ELF project.

D. *Client Applications*

The ELF Cascading WFS functionality has been tested with a wide set of test queries using a standard Web browser. The POST-queries have been tested from browser using a service-side POST-module that forwards the queries to the service interface. In addition, the Cascading WFS has been successfully tested with the QGIS client application with the WFS 2.0 plugin installed [11]. Integration with a showcase application based on the Finnish Open Layers-derived map client library, Oskari, has also been tested [12]; see Fig. 2.

III. IMPLEMENTATION

The Cascading WFS implementation is currently running on the governmental cloud platform of the Norwegian NMCA, as a Java Servlet on top of a Tomcat Web application server. Backend national services are queried by simultaneously dispatching a set of threaded query processes. The responses are returned to the client application in the order they become ready.

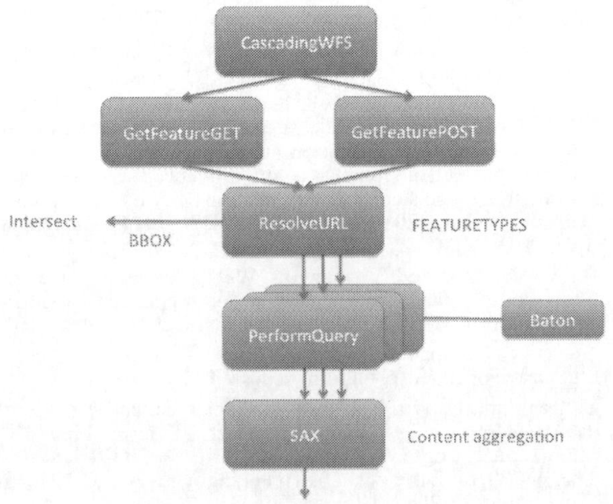

Figure 3. Internal structure of the ELF Cascading WFS implementation.

A baton-based approach is used to prevent parallel threads from writing to the response stream simultaneously. The fact that backend queries are run in a parallel fashion introduces a potential performance benefit to the system, when compared with the traditional way, in which the individual country level services are queried in a sequential manner. Exact values for the performance gain have not yet been determined. The internal modules of the ELF Cascading WFS implementation are depicted in Fig. 3.

IV. Limitations

The ELF Cascading WFS access interface has certain significant restrictions. Most importantly, it requires that the query must always have a bounding box defined. This can be presented as a BBOX –parameter of a GET query, or as a <fes:BBOX> -element inside either the FILTER –parameter of a GET query or inside the <Filter> -element of a POST query. If there are several <Query> -elements in a single POST type GetFeature request, they have to contain the same <fes:BBOX> value.

The Coordinate Reference Systems (CRSs) that are supported by the Cascading WFS include Web Mercator (EPSG:3857 or EPSG:900913), WGS84 (EPSG:4326), ETRS89 (EPSG:4258) and Lambert Equal Area (EPSG:3035). Whether a given CRS is supported by the backend national level service, varies from country to country.

The GetCapabilities response message of the ELF Cascading WFS is based on dynamic GetCapabilities – queries run on the backend national services. This way the GetCapabilities response of the Cascading WFS will better reflect the real status of the backend services. However, there are certain limitations. The GetCapabilities response defines the spatial extent of each feature type only by one single rectangle. As the spatial extents of the backend services are typically distinct, the extent definitions in the GetCapabilities response of the Cascading WFS soon become misleading. Because the other parameters, like the list of supported CRSs, must be defined as the greatest common denominator, some capabilities of the backend services remain hidden from the client application.

The COUNT –parameter affects each background service individually. For instance, if COUNT has a value of 1000 and the request is cross-border involving two countries, the maximum number of resulting features is 2000. If a sorting operation is requested, the result of each background service is sorted individually. The order of the response datasets inside the combined result is arbitrary (the responses are returned in the order they become ready).

ELF Cascading WFS supports only the following WFS 2.0.0 requests: GetCapabilities, DescribeFeatureType and GetFeature. In the case of the GetFeature request, ELF Cascading WFS does not support the FEATUREID –type query.

Feature identifiers must be globally unique for the Cascading WFS to work. In the case of the INSPIRE feature identifiers, this is handled properly by using a well-defined namespace mechanism. Some of the ELF national services already use feature identifiers with URI-based namespace prefixes, which automatically ascertains global uniqueness. However, this becomes crucial in the case of the XML ID-typed attributes used in geometry elements. These values must also be kept unique in the content aggregation phase, for instance by prepending them with the namespace prefix, or by some other mechanisms.

V. Conclusion

Real-time content aggregation that is tested in the ELF project is based on the principle of Cascading WFS. ELF Cascading WFS does not support the full-fledged WFS service interface specification. It has certain significant restrictions, like the fact that the query must always contain a bounding box.

A content request coming from a client application is first analyzed by the Cascading WFS to determine, which national level services must be included into the process. Then the request is forwarded to the involved national services, the resulting datasets are merged together, and finally returned back to the calling application. The analysis on the service inclusion is based on the bounding box of the query and on the requested feature types. The bounding box is overlaid on top of the dataset of national borders to determine, which countries the query overlap. The actual service on the country level is then selected, depending on the requested feature type.

Altogether 83 national download services from 13 different countries have been connected to the ELF Cascading WFS. These services provide access to over 120 feature types from 11 INSPIRE themes.

It can be said that the discussed research goals of the project have been reached, as the ELF Cascading WFS can be said to be being functionally ready. However, a lot of work remains to be done to extend the spatial coverage of the served data sets and further improve their compatibility, for instance in the area of edge matching.

The ELF project has ended in Oct 2016. The service infrastructure is being maintained and even extended over the two years' transition period by the ELF participant organisations. More countries and services will be added and the quality of the data content be improved. After the transition period, the service infrastructure is going to be handed over to an operator that will maintain the ELF service platform on behalf of the EuroGeographics and the involved NMCAs.

The development of the ELF Cascading WFS service will also continue. New joining services must be configured into the service and tested. More rigorous testing of the ELF Cascading WFS itself, as it concerns both functionality and performance, will also continue.

ACKNOWLEDGMENT

The ELF project has been funded by the European Commission, Grant Agreement No 325140.

REFERENCES

[1] European Commission, INSPIRE Directive. http://eur-lex.europa.eu /LexUriServ/LexUriServ.do?uri=OJ:L:2007:108:0001:0014:EN:PDF Accessed 17 Nov 2016

[2] European Commission, COMMISSION REGULATION (EC) No 976/2009 of 19 October 2009 implementing Directive 2007/2/EC of the European Parliament and of the Council as regards the Network Services. http://eur-lex.europa.eu/legal-content/EN/TXT/PDF/?uri=CELEX:02009R0976-20101228&from=EN. Accessed 17 Nov 2016

[3] EuroGeographics, Home Page. http://www.eurogeographics.org Accessed 17 Nov 2016

[4] European Location Framework, Project Home Page. http://www.elfproject.eu Accessed 17 Nov 2016

[5] L. Lehto, P. Latvala and J. Kähkönen, Service Cascade as a Means for Pan-European Access to National Geodata Content CASE: European Location Framework. The Sixth International Conference on Advanced Geographic Information Systems, Applications and Services, "GEOProcessing 2014", Mar 23 – 27, 2014, Barcelona, Spain, CD-ROM.

[6] P. A. Vretanos [ed.], OpenGIS Web Feature Service 2.0 Interface Standard. http://portal.opengeospatial.org /files/?artifact_id=39967 Accessed 17 Nov 2016

[7] Open Geospatial Consortium, Home page. http//www.opengeospatial.org Accessed 17 Nov 2016

[8] Y. Deng and Q. Wu, Research on the harvest and cascade of catalogue service in GeoGlobe Service Platform. Proc. 18th International Conference on Geoinformatics: GIScience in Change (Geoinformatics 2010) Peking University, Beijing, China, June, 18-20, 2010

[9] J. de la Beaujardiere [ed.], OpenGIS Web Map Server Implementation Specification. http://portal.opengeospatial.org/files/?artifact_id=14416 Accessed 17 Nov 2016

[10] Simple API for XML, Home Page. http://www.saxproject.org Accessed 17 Nov 2016

[11] QGIS, Home Page. http://www.qgis.org/en/site/ Accessed 17 Nov 2016

[12] Oskari Platform, Home Page. http://oskari.org Accessed 17 Nov 2016

A Cost-Efficient Method for Big Geospatial Data on Public Cloud Providers

Joao Bachiega Junior, Marco Antonio Sousa Reis *
Aletéia Patrícia Favacho de Araújo, Maristela Holanda **
Department of Computer Science
University of Brasilia
Brasília/DF, Brazil
* e-mail: {joao.bachiega.jr, marco.antonio.sousa.reis}@gmail.com
** e-mail: {aleteia, mholanda}@unb.br

Abstract—**The rise of big geospatial data creates the need for an environment with powerful computational resources to process this large amount of geographical information. Spatial Cloud Computing is a solution to this problem as it offers facilities to overcome the challenges of a big data environment, providing significant computer power and vast storage. However, the software to process this data requires great performance capacity. These requirements are met by SpatialHadoop, a fully-fledged MapReduce framework with native support for spatial data. This paper presents a cost-efficient method for processing geospatial data on public cloud providers, optimizing the number of data nodes in a Hadoop cluster according to dataset size. Tests have proven that it can optimize the use of computational resources for available SpatialHadoop datasets.**

Keywords - Big geospatial data; Hadoop; SpatialHadoop; Spatial Cloud Computing

I. INTRODUCTION

Big geospatial data is the emerging paradigm for the infinite amount of information that has become available to users with the development and widespread use of Geographical Information System (GIS) softwares, delivering hundreds of TiB up to several PiB per hour [1][7]. Big data is defined by some authors [2][3] according to three essential aspects: i) *Variety* – referring to the different types of data, with more than 80% of them in an unstructured form; ii) *Volume* – the tremendous amounts of data generated each second; iii) *Velocity* – the speed at which new data is being produced. Recently, new aspects were included in the big data definition [7]: *Veracity* – how trustworthy the data is; *Value* – referring to the importance that the data has to the business; *Variability* - referring to data whose meaning is constantly changing and *Visualization* – how the data is presented, readable and accessible to users.

The rise of cloud computing and cloud data stores has been a precursor to, and a facilitator of the emergence of big data [9]. Consequently, to support the computational demand big data has caused, mainly for geospatial data, Yang and Huang [4] have proposed Spatial Cloud Computing, an infrastructure that helps conduct relevant computing and data processing, which is characterized by its sufficient computing capability, low energy cost, fast response to spike computing needs, and a wide accessibility to the public when needed.

An important property of clouds is their capability to increase and decrease computational resources without impact on applications. NIST [4] identified elasticity as an essential characteristic of cloud computing: “capabilities can be elastically provisioned and released, in some cases automatically, to scale rapidly outward and inward commensurate with demand. To the consumer, the capabilities available for provisioning often appear to be unlimited and can be appropriated in any quantity at any time”.

Moreover, Kramer and Senner [1] assert that the cloud offers virtually unlimited resources in terms of processing power and memory, and that the faster geospatial data is processed, the higher its practical value will be. However, public cloud providers, such as Amazon AWS [24], Microsoft Azure [25], Google Cloud [26] among others, charge computational resources by the minute or by byte transferred, which is extremely costly. Therefore, using the computational resources in the most efficient way is essential to minimize costs.

Big Geospatial data demands a large number of resources to store and process information. The amount of computational resources required by this vast volume of information grows in an asymptotic way and each wasted resource represents a significant financial loss, which could have been avoided. Faced with this dilemma, some methods have been developed to process big data [2]. Among them, Apache Hadoop, a programming framework for distributed computing using the divide and conquer (or Map and Reduce) method to break down complex big data problems into small units of work and process them in parallel. Specifically for big geospatial data, some applications have been developed using Hadoop concepts [9], such as the following: i) “GIS Tools on Hadoop”, that work with the ArcGIS product; ii) Parallel-Secondo as a parallel spatial Data Base Management System (DBMS) that uses Hadoop as a distributed task scheduler; iii) MD-HBase extends HBase, a non-relational database for Hadoop, to support multidimensional indexes; iv) Hadoop-GIS extends Hive, a data warehouse infrastructure built on top of Hadoop with a uniform grid index for range queries and self-join. Finally, Eldawy and Mokbel [9] presented SpatialHadoop, a fully-fledged MapReduce framework with native support for spatial data with better performance when compared to all the other applications listed.

This article presents a cost-efficient method for determine the cluster size for processing big geospatial data using SpatialHadoop on public cloud providers. The goal is to optimize the use of computational resources to reduce costs. Section II covers concepts of SpatialHadoop. Section III presents concepts about Spatial Cloud Computing. Section IV presents the system architecture. The methodology used to develop this method is explained in Section V and the previous work done in this area is discussed in Section VI. The tests carried out and results obtained are shown in Section VII and Section VIII contains the conclusion and some suggestions for future work.

II. SPATIALHADOOP

Hadoop is the most popular technique for working with big data. It uses a MapReduce paradigm that break big problems in small ones and process these jobs in a distributed computation [9]. SpatialHadoop was developed as a fully-fledged MapReduce framework with native support for spatial data. It was built on Hadoop base code, adding spatial constructs and the awareness of spatial data inside the core functionality of traditional Hadoop.

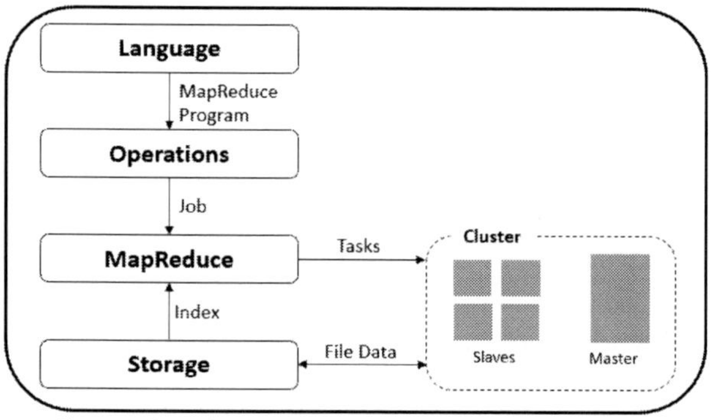

Figure 1. SpatialHadoop high-level architecture. Adapted by [9]

SpatialHadoop is composed of four main layers, namely language, operations, MapReduce and storage. All of them execute in a cluster environment with one master node that breaks a MapReduce job into smaller tasks, carried out by slave nodes [9]. The high-level architecture of SpatialHadoop is shown in Fig. 1.

A. Language Layer

The language used by SpatialHadoop is Pigeon, a simple high-level SQL-like language, derived from Pig Latin. It is compliant with the Open Geospatial Consortium's (OGC) simple feature access standard, which is supported in both open source and commercial spatial DBMS. Pigeon supports OGC standard *data types* including point, linestring and polygon, as well as OGC standard *functions* for spatial data import/export, querying and manipulation. Spatial *operations* are also included.

The spatial functionality is implemented as user-defined functions (UDFs), which are seamless to integrate with existing non-spatial operations in Pig Latin and also makes it compatible with all recent versions of Pig that support UDFs [11].

B. Operations Layer

This layer encapsulates the implementation of various spatial operations that use the spatial indexes and the new components in the MapReduce layer. According to [10], the operations layer is composed of:

- *Basic Operations*: among the available spatial operations, three of them were chosen as basic operations in SpatialHadoop due to their popular use. These basic operations are range query, k-nearest neighbor (knn) and spatial join [9].
- *CG_Hadoop*: a suite of scalable and efficient MapReduce algorithms for various fundamental computational geometry problems, namely, *polygon union, skyline, convex hull, farthest pair, and closest pair* [12]. These operations take advantage of spatial indexes available in SpatialHadoop to achieve better performance than traditional Hadoop environments.
- *Spatial Data Mining*: operations developed using spatial data mining techniques.

C. MapReduce Layer

Similar to Hadoop, the MapReduce layer in SpatialHadoop is the query processing layer that runs MapReduce programs [9]. However, contrary to Hadoop where the input files are non-indexed heap files, SpatialHadoop supports spatially-indexed input files. In Hadoop, the input file goes through a FileSplitter that divides it into n splits, where n is set by the MapReduce program, based on the number of available slave nodes. Then, each split goes through a RecordReader that extracts records as key-value pairs that are passed to the map function.

SpatialHadoop enriches traditional Hadoop systems with two main components: i) *SpatialFileSplitter* - an extended splitter that exploits the global index in input files to perform early pruning of file blocks not contributing to the answer, and ii) *SpatialRecordReader* - which reads a split originating from spatially indexed input files and exploits the local indexes to process it efficiently.

D. Storage Layer

There are two challenges when using traditional spatial indexes in Hadoop. First, traditional indexes are designed for the procedural programming paradigm, while SpatialHadoop uses the MapReduce programming paradigm. Secondly, traditional indexes are designed for local file systems, while SpatialHadoop uses the Hadoop Distributed File System (HDFS), which is inherently limited as files can be written in an append-only manner, and once written, they cannot be modified [10].

To solve this limitation, SpatialHadoop creates two index layers - global and local. The global index is applicable on a cluster's master node, while local indexes organize data in each slave node. It is therefore possible for SpatialHadoop to support the following spatial index structures [9]:

- *Grid file:* a simple flat index that partitions the data according to a grid such that records overlapping each grid cell are stored in one file block as a single partition. To simplify, we use a uniform grid assuming that data is uniformly distributed;

- *R-tree:* in this indexing technique records are not replicated, which causes partitions to overlap. This makes it more efficient for range queries where partitions that are completely contained in query range can be copied to output and no reduplication step is required;
- *R+-tree:* a variation of the R-tree where nodes at each level are kept disjoint, while records overlapping multiple nodes are replicated to each node to ensure efficient query answering. In this indexing technique, SpatialHadoop adjusts the size of each partition based on data distribution such that the contents of each partition ensure load balancing. Records in each partition are stored together as one HDFS block in one machine.

Eldawy et al. [13] developed four more indexing techniques for SpatialHadoop, namely, Z-curve, Hilbert curve, Quad tree, and K-d tree, but these techniques are not as widely used as the others are.

Before executing queries and operations, the dataset needs to be indexed and this task occurs in the partitioning phase. The indexing algorithm runs in three steps, where the first step is fixed and the last two steps are customized for each partitioning technique. The first step computes the number of desired partitions, *n*, based on file size and *HDFS block capacity*, both of which are fixed for all partitioning techniques. The second step reads a random sample, with a sampling ratio, from the input file and uses this sample to partition the space into n cells such that the number of sample points in each cell is at most $\lfloor k/n \rfloor$, where k is the sample size. The third step actually partitions the file by assigning each record to one or more cells. Boundary objects are handled using either the distribution or replication methods. The distribution method assigns an object to exactly one overlapping cell and the cell has to be expanded to enclose all contained records. The replication method avoids expanding cells by replicating each record to all overlapping cells but the query processor has to employ a duplicate avoidance technique to account for replicated records.

III. Spatial Cloud Computing

Although computing hardware technologies, including a central processing unit (CPU), network, storage, RAM, and graphics processing unit (GPU), have been advanced greatly in past decades, many computing requirements for addressing scientific and application challenges, such as applications for big geospatial data processing, go beyond existing computing capabilities [4].

These challenges require the readiness of a computing infrastructure that can [20]: i) better support discovery, access and utilization of data and data processing so as to relieve scientists and engineers of IT tasks, allowing them to focus on scientific discoveries; ii) provide real-time IT resources to enable real-time applications, such as emergency response; iii) deal with access spikes; and iv) provide more reliable and scalable service for massive numbers of concurrent users to further public knowledge.

Cloud computing offers facilities to overcome the challenges of a big data environment, providing heightened computer power and vast storage. In the most used definition for cloud computing, NIST [4] indicates five essential characteristics, namely: on demand self-service, broad network access, resource pooling, rapid elasticity, and measured service.

However, other characteristics are relevant when providing a spatial cloud computing environment. Akdogan et al. [20] proposed a cost-efficient partitioning of spatial data in clouds. This partitioning method considers location-based services and optimizes the storage of spatial-temporal data by making it possible to turn-off idle servers, thereby reducing costs.

Yang et al. [20] defines Spatial Cloud Computing as the cloud computing paradigm that is driven by geospatial sciences, and optimized by spatiotemporal principles for enabling geospatial science discoveries and cloud computing within a distributed computing environment. The intention is to supply the computational needs for geospatial data intensity, computing intensity, concurrent access intensity and spatiotemporal intensity.

A. Public Cloud Providers

According to NIST [4], there are four deployment models for clouds, namely private, community, public and hybrid. Specifically to public clouds, [4] defines how the cloud infrastructure is provisioned for open use by the general public. In this model of cloud deployment, services are charged in a pay-per-use method at some level of abstraction appropriate to the type of service (e.g., storage, processing or bandwidth). When working with big geospatial data, the volume of data and the power of processing are always high and, consequently, expensive.

Amazon AWS is, according to the "Gartner Magic Quadrant for Cloud Infrastructure as a Service", the leading Public Cloud Provider [27]. It offers "Elastic Map Reduce" (EMR) that uses Hadoop fundamentals and is integrated with other services available from providers, such as storage, data mining, log file analysis, machine learning, scientific simulation, and data warehousing. Our tests were conducted in an Amazon AWS environment.

IV. System Architecture

To support the method proposed in this paper, an architecture composed of three layers, namely Web Interface, Storage and SpatialHadoop (Fig. 2), was put together.

The main characteristics of each layer are described below:

- *Web Interface Layer*: a user-friendly interface to receive inputs and show results. In this layer, the user selects an available dataset (or uploads one if it is new) and defines the following parameters for the application: queries and operations, indexing (Grid, R-Tree, R+-Tree) and stickiness.

- *Storage Layer*: this layer stores all datasets available to the application and saves the results after application execution.
- *SpatialHadoop Layer*: this is the core layer. It is responsible for provisioning the SpatialHadoop cluster with one master node and *n* data nodes. The quantity of data nodes is defined based on dataset size, as shown in Section V. After provisioning the cluster, this layer indexes the dataset (based on user choice in the Web Interface layer), processes queries and operations and saves the results file back in the Storage Layer.

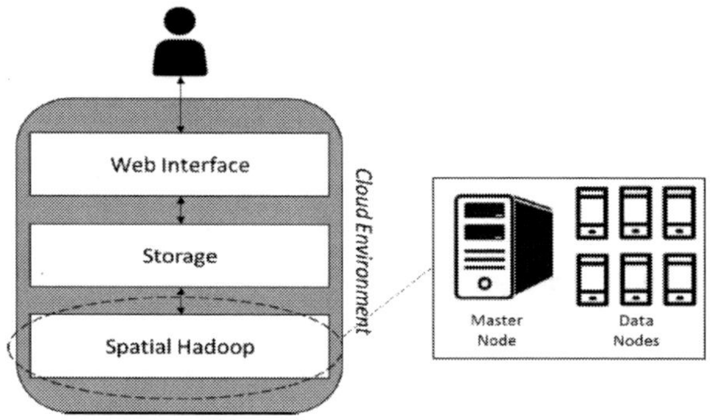

Figure 2. System Architecture Overview.

In the proposed method, all three layers were designed to use a public cloud environment. It is also possible to allocate the Web Interface Layer and the Storage Layer to different environments. However, it is important to consider that public cloud providers usually charge users for each gigabyte stored and transferred, and this can affect the total cost.

V. METHODOLOGY

A common uncertainty for Hadoop environment administrators is how to define the cluster size infrastructure. In a static environment, like a private cloud, most of the time the computational resources are limited and big geospatial data grows faster, requiring ever more resources. On the other hand, in public cloud providers the computational resources are unlimited, but users are charged for them, so it is very important to define a cost-effective environment.

A twenty-node cluster can be necessary to process SpatialHadoop queries and operations on a 100Gb dataset, but it is overprovisioned to work on a dataset of only 5Gb. To solve this problem, a formula to calculate the quantity of data nodes based on dataset size is fundamental. Adapting the proposal by [6] and [23], the following formula can be used to determine the ideal number of data nodes in a SpatialHadoop environment on public cloud providers:

$$DN = \left\lceil \frac{T}{d} \right\rceil \quad (1)$$

DN represents the total data nodes needed; *T* is the total amount of data and *d* is the disk size in each node.

It is necessary to calculate *T* because the total amount of data used in a SpatialHadoop application is not only the volume of the dataset. To calculate *T*, the following formula can be used:

$$T = \frac{C \; x \; R \; x \; S}{(1 - i) * (1 + w)} \quad (2)$$

C represents the compression rate of the dataset, required because SpatialHadoop can work with compressed files. When no compression is used, the value must be 1. *R* is the number of replicas of data in HDFS and *S* represents the size of the dataset. The notation *i* refers to the intermediate working space dedicated to temporarily storing results of Map Tasks. Finally, *w* represents the percentage of space left (wasted) to HDFS.

To demonstrate the use of these formulas, let us consider a real Open Street Map (OSM) dataset of 96Gb of total size (2.7 billion records) [28]. Without compression ($C = 1$), without replication ($R = 1$), considering $i = 25\%$ and $w = 20\%$, the value obtained for *T* is 106.67. Considering that each data node has a disk with 32Gb ($d = 32$) it is possible to conclude that the ideal number of data nodes (*DN*) is 4.

Changing any other parameter value can affect the number of data nodes in cluster. For example, using the same values for parameters *C, R, S* and *w* ($C = 1$, $R = 1$, $S = 96$, $w = 20\%$), and changing the value for *i* to 40% the number of data nodes (*DN*) grows to 5. This result will affect application performance and, also the total cost of environment.

VI. TESTS AND RESULTS

A SpatialHadoop environment was built using Amazon AWS Elastic MapReduce to test the proposed method. Although all three layers of the system architecture – Web Interface, Storage and SpatialHadoop – were allocated on a cloud provider, the focus of performance and costs used in this test scenario were specifically on the SpatialHadoop layer.

Table I presents the instances configurations used to run the tests on Amazon AWS.

TABLE I. INSTANCES CONFIGURATIONS ON AMAZON AWS.

Function	vCPUs	Memory	Disk (SSD)	Price (US$)
Master	8	15	160 Gb	0.42 / hour
Data	4	7.5	80 Gb	0.21 / hour

The datasets used were extracted from Open Street Map and Tiger and are available to download on the SpatialHadoop site [28]. The clusters created for the tests were composed of one master node and the quantity of data nodes based on the formula shown in Section V, considering the following values to the others parameters: $C = 1$, $R = 3$, $i = 25\%$ and $w = 20\%$. Details about datasets and number of data nodes are described in Table II.

TABLE II. DATASETS AND DATANODES.

Dataset	Size	Records	Data nodes
LinearWater	9.0 Gb	8.4 million	1
Roads	7.7 Gb	20 million	1
Buildings	26.0 Gb	115 million	2
Lakes	9.0 Gb	8.4 million	1

Once parameters were defined in the Web Interface Layer and the dataset was stored in the Storage Layer, the SpatialHadoop Layer was configured to execute the following steps:

- *Provisioning Cluster:* a defined request is sent to a cloud provider, with the number and type of master node, and data nodes.
- *Transfer Dataset:* copy an existing dataset from Storage Layer to data nodes.
- *Index Dataset:* apply the user-defined index type to dataset.
- *Queries and Operations:* executes the user-defined queries and operations.
- *Save Results:* saves the result file – usually a text file – on Storage Layer to be accessed by the user.
- *Turn-off Cluster:* to avoid wasting of computational resources and increasing financial costs, all the clusters (master node and data nodes) are turned off, unless some stickiness parameter was defined by the user.

Table III presents the runtime of each task in a test environment. The values present an average of 3 execution for the smallest (Roads) and the biggest (Buildngs) datasets. The queries – KNN and Range Query – and the indexing type *Grid* were chosen randomly, and could be changed by any query or operation and indexing type.

TABLE III. TIME MEASURED IN EACH TASK.

Task	Smallest Dataset (seconds)	Biggest Dataset (seconds)
Provisioning Cluster	300	420
Transfer Dataset	60	120
Index Dataset	600	3540
KNN	10	8
Range Query	8	6
Save Results	2	2
Turn-off Cluster	100	164
TOTAL Time	1080	4260

The indexing task is very important to ensure SpatialHadoop is high performing. Note that the majority of time is spent on the index process, but once it is finished, the queries are done very quickly. A comparassion of the runtime of the indexing task for the Buildings Dataset, using a cluster with 2 datanodes, is presented in Fig. 3.

Since the cluster to support the Smallest Dataset (1 master node and 1 data node) costs US$ 0.63/hour, the total cost to process these two queries was US$ 0.19. The cost of the cluster to support the large dataset (composed of 1 master node and 2 data nodes) is US$ 0.84/hr, so the cost of processing these queries was US$ 0,99.

If this cluster had been created without considering the dataset´s size – and other parameters defined in the formula – it would had been necessary to consider the largest dataset available to ensure that any query or operation could be executed in this cluster. Considering all datasets available to download on the SpatialHadoop webpage [28], the largest dataset – an OSM file with 137Gb of size and 717M records about road networks represented as individual road segments – would require a cluster composed of 1 master node and 6 data nodes. The total cost of this cluster would be US$ 1.68 per hour and running the small dataset (18 minutes) would cost US$ 0.50, costing 263% more than was really needed

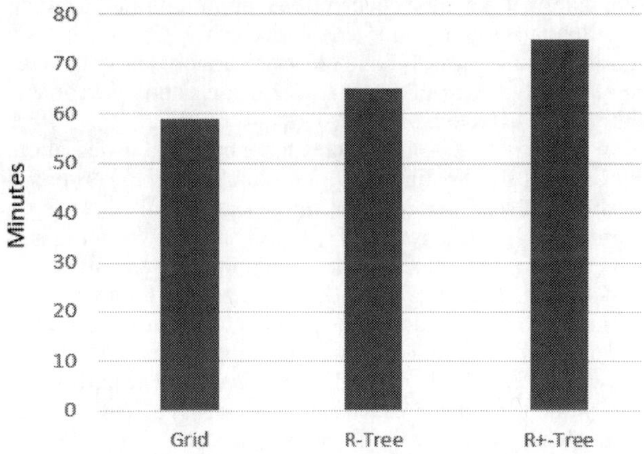

Figure 3. Index task runtime for Buildings Dataset.

Analyzing all datasets availabe on the SpatialHadoop webpage [28], and considering the scenario and parameters defined in our test environment ($C = 1$, $R = 3$, $i = 25\%$ and $w = 20\%$), only 7 from a total of 33 datasets needed more than 1 data node to be executed. On the other extreme, only 1 dataset needed a 6-node cluster. Processing any other datasets wastes computational resources if the proposed formula is not applied.

TABLE IV. TOTAL COST OF CLUSTER.

Number of Data Nodes	Total cluster lifecycle time	Total Cost
1 (defined by formula)	20 minutes	US$ 0.21
2	19 minutes	US$ 0.27
4	17 minutes	US$ 0.36

Table IV presents the total cluster lifecycle time and cost to process the queries KNN, Spatial Join and Range Query using the Lakes dataset using the number of instances proposed by the formula (1), and also using 2 and 4 instances. However, even though the total time of execution is higher, the cost is lower. This occurs because there is a low reduction in the indexing task runtime (only 1 minute per core added).

VII. Related Work

SpatialHadoop was presented in 2013 by Eldawy and Mokbel [14] as the first fully-fledged MapReduce framework with native support for spatial data. In this article, the authors used a demonstration scenario created on an Amazon AWS, with a 20 node cluster to compare SpatialHadoop and traditional Hadoop in three operations, namely, range query, knn and spatial join.

Also in 2013, Eldawy et al. [12] presented CG_Hadoop, which is a suite of scalable and efficient MapReduce algorithms for various fundamental computational geometry problems - polygon union, skyline, convex hull, farthest pair, and closest pair – comparing the performance of these computational geometry operations on traditional Hadoop and SpatialHadoop and concluded that SpatialHadoop algorithms significantly outperform Hadoop algorithms as they take advantage of the spatial indexing and components within SpatialHadoop.

In recent years, some articles have been published about improvements to SpatialHadoop. Mokbel et al. [15] proposed a web-based road-network, traffic generator, called, MNTG. Alarabi et al. [16] created TAREEG, a MapReduce-based web service that uses SpatialHadoop fundamentals for extracting spatial data from OpenStreetMap. Eldawy et al. [17] used SpatialHadoop to query and visualize spatio-temporal satellite data in an application called SHAHED. Eldawy et al. [18] created HadoopViz, a MapReduce framework for extensible visualization of Big Spatial Data. All of these studies were developed in static and dedicated clusters.

A modular software architecture for processing big geospatial data in the cloud was presented by [1]. Since the proposed framework is not affected by whether the cloud environment is private or public, a third-party tool – Ansible – was used to execute provisioning scripts.

Finally, in 2016, Das et al. [19] proposed a geospatial query resolution framework using an orchestration engine for clouds. However, the cloud environment used was private and no dynamic allocation of computational resources was performed.

None of these works present a method to optimize the use of computational resources and reduce financial costs on public cloud providers when using SpatialHadoop to process big geospatial data.

This paper presents a cost-efficient method to process geospatial data on public cloud providers, optimizing the number of data nodes in a SpatialHadoop cluster according to dataset size.

VIII. Conclusion and Future Works

SpatialHadoop is a MapReduce framework for big geospatial data that has high performance but requires a computational infrastructure that can be expensive. When working on public cloud providers, in which each computational resource is charged for, it is necessary to look for a cost-effective solution.

The method proposed in this paper achieves the goal of supporting a SpatialHadoop environment on public cloud providers, while avoiding the waste of computational resources. The formula to define the number of data nodes was validated in a test scenario, resulting in a cost savings of approximately 263%.

As future works we suggest optimizations on performance that can be obtained using task nodes – for job processing only - and data nodes together. In this way, it is possible to apply scalability in SpatialHadoop applications based on user-defined threads. Formulas to calculate other computational resources – CPU and memory – based on datasets and queries or operations can also be defined.

References

[1] M. Krämer and I. Senner, "A modular software architecture for processing of big geospatial data in the cloud." In Computers & Graphics, pp. 69-81, 2015.

[2] S. Seref and S. Duygu, "Big data: A review." In International Conference on Collaboration Technologies and Systems (CTS), pp. 42-47, 2013.

[3] J. S. Ward and A. Barker, "Undefined by data: a survey of big data definitions." arXiv:1309.5821, 2013.

[4] P. Mell and T. Grance, "Draft NIST working definition of cloud computing," [Online]. Available from: http://csrc.nist.gov/groups/SNS/cloud-computing/index.html [acessed: 2016-11-01]

[5] N. R. Herbst, S. Kounev, and R. Reussner, "Elasticity in cloud computing: What it is, and what it is not." Proceedings of the 10th International Conference on Autonomic Computing (ICAC 13), pp. 23-27, 2013.

[6] Hadoop Online Tutorial. Formula to calculate NDFS nodes storage. [Online]. Avilable from: http://hadooptutorial.info/ formula-to-calculate-hdfs-nodes-storage/ [acessed: 2016-11-03]

[7] J. Pramila, "Cloud Architecture for Big Data." International Journal of Engineering and Computer Science, pp. 12757 – 12765, June, 2015.

[8] E. S. A. Ahmed, and A. S. Rashid, "A Survey of Big Data Cloud Computing Security." International Journal of Computer Science and Software Engineering (IJCSSE), pp. 78-85, 2014.

[9] A. Eldawy and M. F. Mokbel, "Spatialhadoop: A mapreduce framework for spatial data." In 2015 IEEE 31st International Conference on Data Engineering, pp. 1352-1363, 2015.

[10] A. Eldawy, "SpatialHadoop: towards flexible and scalable spatial processing using mapreduce." Proceedings of the 2014 SIGMOD PhD symposium, pp. 46-50, 2014.

[11] A. Eldawy and M. F. Mokbel, "Pigeon: A spatial mapreduce language". In 2014 IEEE 30th International Conference on Data Engineering, pp. 1242-1245, 2014.

[12] A. Eldawy, Y. Li, M. F. Mokbel, and R. Janardan, "CG_Hadoop: computational geometry in MapReduce." The 21st ACM SIGSPATIAL International Conference on Advances in Geographic Information Systems, pp. 294-303, June, 2014.

[13] A. Eldawy, A. Alarabi, and M. F. Mokbel, "Spatial partitioning techniques in SpatialHadoop." Proceedings of the VLDB Endowment, pp. 1602-1605, 2015.

[14] A. Eldawy and M. F. Mokbel, "A demonstration of SpatialHadoop: an efficient mapreduce framework for spatial data." Proceedings of the VLDB Endowment, pp. 1230-1233, 2013.

[15] M. F. Mokbel et al., "A demonstration of MNTG-A web-based road network traffic generator," In 2014 IEEE 30th International Conference on Data Engineering, pp. 1246-1249, March, 2014.

[16] L. Alarabi, A. Eldawy, R. Alghamdi, and M. F. Mokbel, "TAREEG: a MapReduce-based web service for extracting spatial data from OpenStreetMap". In 2014 ACM SIGMOD International Conference on Management of data, pp. 897-900, 2014.

[17] A. Eldawy et al., "Shahed: A mapreduce-based system for querying and visualizing spatio-temporal satellite data". In 2015 IEEE 31st International Conference on Data Engineering, pp. 1585-1596, April, 2015.

[18] A. Eldawy, M. Mokbel, and C. Jonathan, "HadoopViz: A MapReduce framework for extensible visualization of big spatial data." In 2016 IEEE International. Conference on Data Engineering (ICDE), pp. 601-612, 2016.

[19] J. D. Das, A. Ghosh, and R. A. Buyya, "Geospatial Orchestration Framework on Cloud for Processing User Queries". In 2016 IEEE International Conference on Cloud Computing for Emerging Markets, pp. 19-21, 2016.

[20] A. Akdogan, "Cost-efficient partitioning of spatial data on cloud". In 2015 IEEE International Conference on Big Data, pp. 501-506, 2015

[21] C. Yang et al., "Spatial cloud computing: how can the geospatial sciences use and help shape cloud computing?" International Journal of Digital Earth, pp. 305-329, 2011.

[22] C. Qu, R. N. Calheiros, and R. Buyya, "Auto-scaling Web Applications in Clouds: A Taxonomy and Survey." arXiv:1609.09224. 2016.

[23] Distributed System Archicteture. Hadoop cluster size. [Online]. Available from: https://0x0fff.com/hadoop-cluster-sizing/ [acessed: 2016-10-26]

[24] Amazon AWS. [Online]. Available from: https://aws.amazon.com [acessed: 2016-11-04]

[25] Microsoft Azure. [Online] Available from: https://azure.microsoft.com [acessed: 2016-11-04]

[26] The Google Cloud Provider. [Online] Available from: https://cloud.google.com [acessed: 2016-11-04]

[27] Magic Quadrant for Cloud Infrastructure as a Service, Worldwide. [Online]. Available from: https://www.gartner.com/doc/ reprints?id=1-2G2O5FC&ct=150519. [acessed: 2016-11-02]

[28] SpatialHadoop Datasets. [Online]. Available from: http://spatialhadoop.cs.umn.edu/datasets.html [acessed : 2016-11-03]

Combining Ground Penetrating Radar Scans of Differing Frequencies Through Signal Processing

Roger Tilley, Hamid Sadjadpour
Department of Electrical Engineering
University of California, Santa Cruz
Santa Cruz, CA. 95064
Email: rtvax@soe.ucsc.edu, Email: hamid@soe.ucsc.edu

Farid Dowla
Lawrence Livermore National Laboratory
Livermore, CA. 94550
Email: dowla1@llnl.gov

Abstract— **Interference reduction is vital in delivering a clear usable signal, whether in the form of beamforming in a noisy environment of radar target responses, or effective communication in the presence of noise for mobile phone users, as examples. The methods used to render a cleaner signal can also be used to combine signals of various frequencies. In this paper we explore using an optimization problem solver, the Expectation-Maximization Algorithm, to define the weights to be used to combine multiple Ground Penetrating Radar frequency scans over the same target area. This approach exploits the Gaussian Mixture Model feature to combine the scans to produce a cleaner image at depth. Our method demonstrates a measured improvement toward producing a cleaner image.**

***Keywords-** Ground Penetrating Radar; Expectation-Maximization; Gaussian Mixture Model; Maximum Likelihood Parameter Estimation; Finite Difference Time Domain Method; GprMax*.

I. INTRODUCTION

Ground Penetrating Radar (GPR) signal scans are used to illuminate terrain and buried objects at various depths. The frequency scan that generates the best illumination is different for each depth. In general, higher frequencies image objects and terrain closer to the surface in great detail while lower frequencies image objects deeper with less fidelity. Developing a way to combine high and low frequencies suggests that the resolution of the combined signal is increased to a lower depth. Determining how to weight each frequency signal to be combined for an optimal result, poses as an optimization problem to solve. In the literature a few methods have been proposed to solve this problem with varying success, all with a very similar approach. Methods by Dougherty[1], Booth[2] and Bancroft[3] all discussed ways to weight each signal used in the sum of each system of frequency traces.

Dougherty's effort to enhance the original GPR data involved direct wave removal, bandwidth enhancement, and cross-correlation analysis. Dougherty aligned each trace by the direct arrival pulse. Scaled each trace by the L2 norm of the direct arrival pulse then simply summed the frequency traces after removing the direct arrival pulse and equally weighting each trace.

Booth used weights derived from the maximum value of the frequency spectra of each trace. The value used to equalize the spectra provided the signal trace weighting prior to summation. Booth's weights were derived from a time-variant least squares analysis of the amplitude spectra of each frequency data set, referred to as optical spectral whitening.

Bancroft uses a ramped summation method where the higher frequency data is suppressed by the same amount the lower frequency data is enhanced over a portion of the two way transit time of a GPR trace, determined by Bancroft and referred to as amplitude envelope equalization.

Absent from these works are optimization problem solvers. We have chosen to investigate the use of an optimization problem solver referred to as the Expectation-Maximization (EM) Algorithm; using the data mixture feature of the EM Algorithm to develop optimal weights.

In this paper, we illustrate the EM Algorithm data mixture feature as it relates to GPR scans of different frequencies. The paper is organized as follows. In SECTION II, we describe the EM Algorithm data mixture process. In SECTION III, we present an EM algorithm test case. In SECTION IV, GPR scans over the same area are processed using EM Algorithm tools developed to combine the frequencies. SECTION V draws some conclusions from using this approach.

II. EXPECTATION-MAXIMIZATION ALGORITHM

The EM Algorithm, is often used to group like items contained in complex mixtures. Another use is to solve incomplete data problems by performing Maximum Likelihood (ML) Parameter estimation. An offshoot use for the EM algorithm is determining the membership weights of points in a cluster within a finite Gaussian mixture model [4][9]. This feature will be exploited to combine several frequency scans into a composite wave. The entire data set can be represented by other mathematical distributions but we used Gaussian because it is often used when the distribution for the real-valued random variables is unknown.

We can define a finite mixture model $f(x;\theta)$ of K components as mixtures of Gaussian functions:

$$f(\underline{x};\theta) = \sum_{k=1}^{K} \alpha_k p_k(\underline{x}|\,\theta_k) \qquad (1)$$

Where:

- $p_k(\underline{x}|\theta_k)$ are K mixture components with a distribution defined over $p(\underline{x}|\theta_k)$ with parameters $\theta_k = \{\underline{\mu}_k, C_k\}$ (mean, covariance)
- $p_k(\underline{x}|\theta_k) =$

$$\frac{1}{(2\pi)^{d/2}\,|C_k|^{1/2}} e^{-\frac{1}{2}(\underline{x}-\underline{\mu}_k)^T C_k^{-1}(\underline{x}-\underline{\mu}_k)} \quad (2)$$

- α_k are the mixture weights, where $\sum_{k=1}^{K} \alpha_k = 1$.
- $\{\underline{x}_i, \dots\dots\dots, \underline{x}_n\}$ Data set for a mixture component in d dimensional space.

In each iteration of the EM Algorithm, there are 2 steps, the Expectation step (E-step) and the Maximization step (M-step). In this case the E-Step computes the conditional expectation of the group membership weights (w_{ik}'s) for $\underline{x}_i$'s , adding unobservable data given θ_k. The M-Step computes new parameter values $(\alpha_k, \underline{\mu}_k, C_k)$ to maximize the finite mixture model using the membership weights. The E-Step and M-Step are repeated until stopping criteria is reached (convergence). Convergence is signaled by the log-likelihood of $f(\underline{x};\theta)$ not appearing to change substantially from one iteration to the next.

E-Step –

$$w_{ik} = \frac{p_k(\underline{x}_i|\theta_k) * \alpha_k}{\sum_{m=1}^{K} p_m(\underline{x}_i|\theta_m) * \alpha_m} \quad (3)$$

for $1 \le k \le K,\ 1 \le i \le N;$

with constraint $\sum_{k=1}^{K} w_{ik} = 1$

M-Step –

$$N_k = \sum_{i=1}^{N} w_{ik} \quad (4)$$

$$\alpha_k^{new} = \frac{N_k}{N}, \text{ for } 1 \le k \le K \quad (5)$$

$$\underline{\mu}_k^{new} = \left(\frac{1}{N_k}\right) \sum_{i=1}^{N} w_{ik} * \underline{x}_i \quad (6)$$

for $1 \le k \le K$

$$C_k^{new} =$$

$$\left(\frac{1}{N_k}\right) \sum_{i=1}^{N} w_{ik} * \left(\underline{x}_i - \underline{\mu}_k^{new}\right)\left(\underline{x}_i - \underline{\mu}_k^{new}\right)^T \quad (7)$$

Convergence (log likelihood of $f(\underline{x};\theta)$) –

$$\text{Log}\, l(\vartheta) =$$

$$\sum_{i=1}^{N} \log f(\underline{x}_i;\theta) =$$

$$\sum_{i=1}^{N}\left(\log \sum_{k=1}^{K} \alpha_k p_k(\underline{x}_i|\theta_k)\right) \quad (8)$$

III. Expectation-Maximization Algorithm Test Case

As a test case, we constructed a series of six sine waves (50, 150, 250, 350, 450 and 550 Hz) noted in Fig. 1, Fig. 2 and Fig. 3, which when weighted properly sum to the square wave of Fig. 4. As noted in Fig. 5, the result is not quite a square wave but well on the way. The apparent error can be attributed to the constraints associated with this implementation; specifically group membership weights, w_{ik} and/or mixture weights, α_k each constrained to sum to one. The weights normally sum to greater than 1 dependent on the number of signals added together. The constructed sine waves are harmonics of the square wave used

.

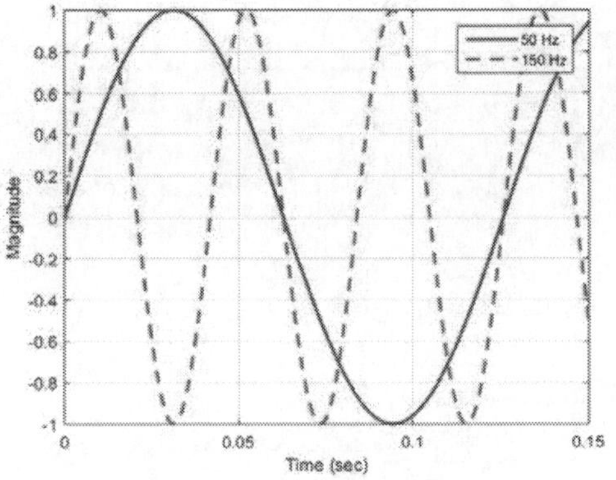

Fig. 1 – Sine wave frequencies 50-150 Hz

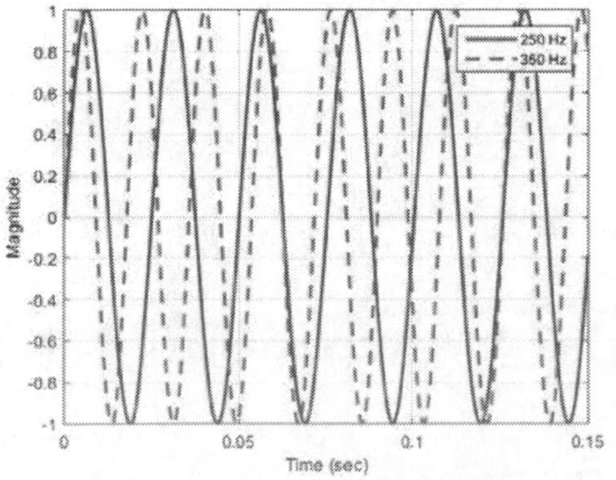

Fig. 2 –Sine wave frequencies 250, 350Hz

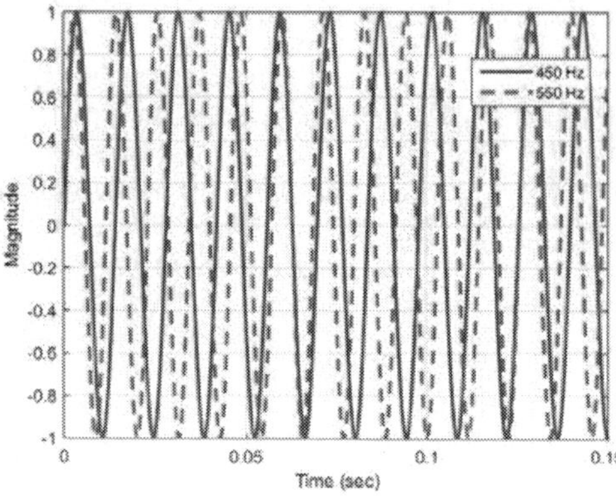

Fig. 3 – Sine wave frequencies, 450-550 Hz

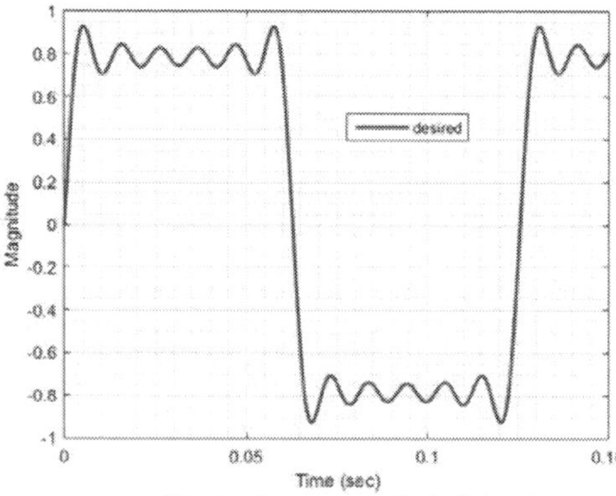

Fig. 4 – Square wave desired signal

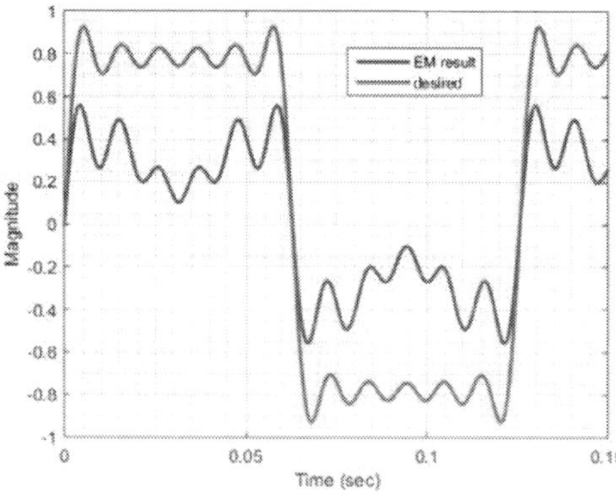

Fig. 5 – EM algorithm result with desired signal

IV. PROCESSING GPR SCANS AT VARIOUS FREQUENCIES

A fictional area was defined using a Finite Difference Time Domain (FDTD) [5][6][7] modeling software package. A Proprietary package in development similar in operation to the popular GprMax software program by A. Giannopoulos [8] was used to model a defined space. The space consisted of a Transmitter (Tx) and Receiver (Rx) suspended 5 meters above the ground in air with a target (perfect electrical conductor) buried 10 meters below ground in a moist-sand medium with a relative permittivity (ε_r) of 9.0 and an electrical conductivity of 0.001 mS/m. The transmitter and receiver were moved along the length of the defined space as shown in Fig. 6 for a total of 36 scans at 0.25 meters per step. The Tx starts at 0.5 meters ending at 9.5 meters, and the Rx starts at 0.75 meters ending at 9.75 meters well within the defined space of 10 meters in length by 25 meters in depth.

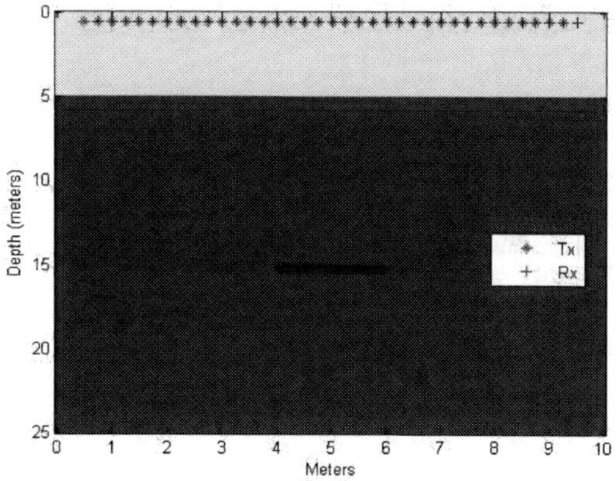

Fig. 6 Defined Space with buried target at 15 meters depth and Tx's & Rx's 5 meters above ground.

GPR scans over the same defined space were run at 20, 30, 50, 100, 500 and 900MHz. The resultant 2-D display for each frequency is shown in Figs. 7-14. Note that in each case the object is correctly identified at approximately 10 meters below ground, approximately 15 meters below Tx's and Rx's or approximately 240 ns from the direct arrival signal (black line on plot). In Fig. 12 and Fig. 14, a display of each trace is shown to better depict the target return signal. The direct arrival signal and ground bounce (radar return from the ground) are shown (see arrow 1 in Fig. 7). Arrow 2 in Fig. 7 denotes the target reflection at depth. In the 30MHz trace result (Fig. 8), the target is indicated by arrow 3. The remaining unlabeled arrows indicate the target reflection at depth for the indicated scan frequency. Of note, is the length of the line indicating the target in frequency scans 100MHz and below, representing limited if not non-existent edge detection. For this analysis the test area length is less than half the depth (25 meters depth by 10 meters length), more like a bore hole, contributing to the limited target edge detection. Arrow 4 (Fig. 14) exhibits better edge detection.

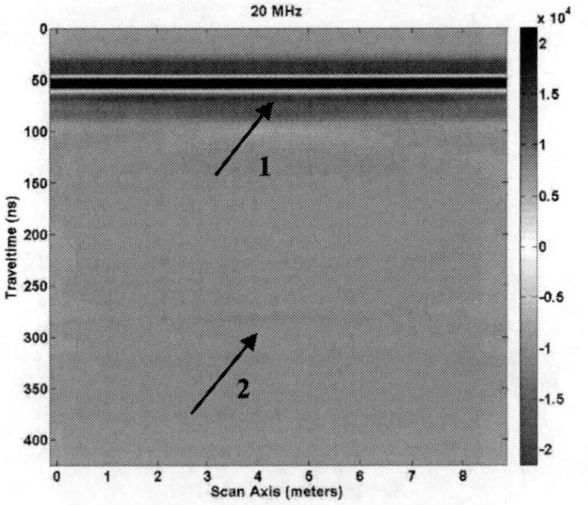

Fig. 7 2-D GPR scans 20MHz

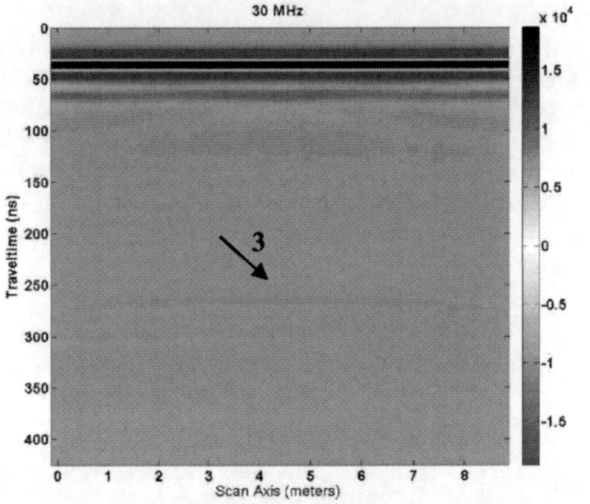

Fig. 8 2-D GPR scan 30 MHz

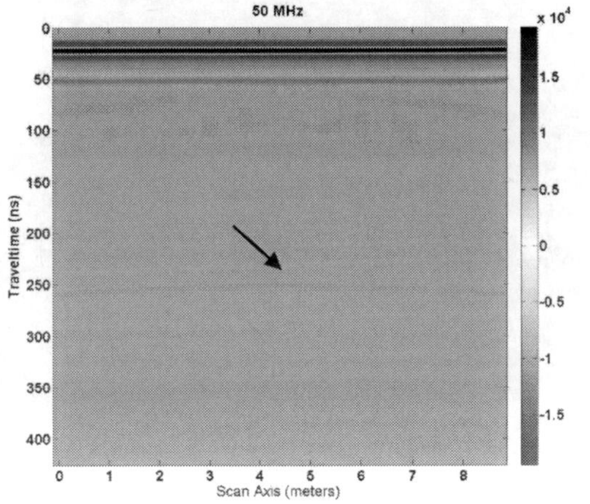

Fig. 9 2-D GPR scan 50 MHz

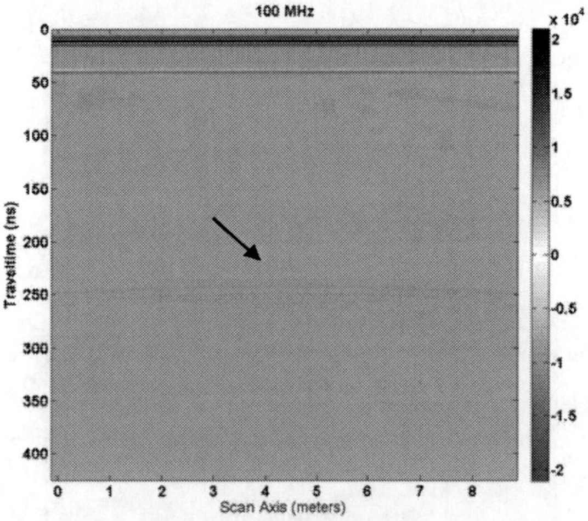

Fig. 10 2-D GPR scan 100MHz,)..

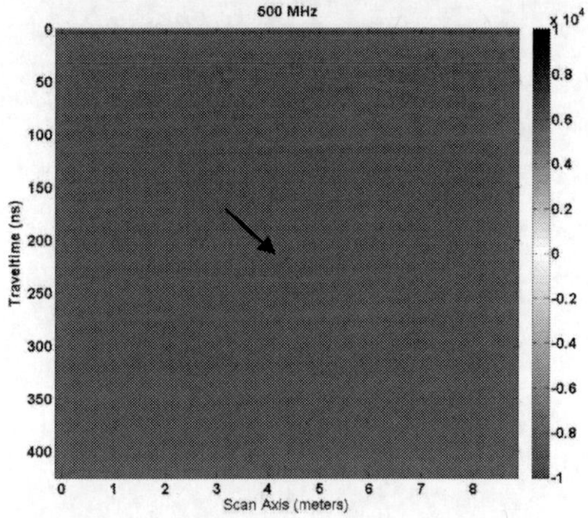

Fig. 11 GPR scan 500MHz

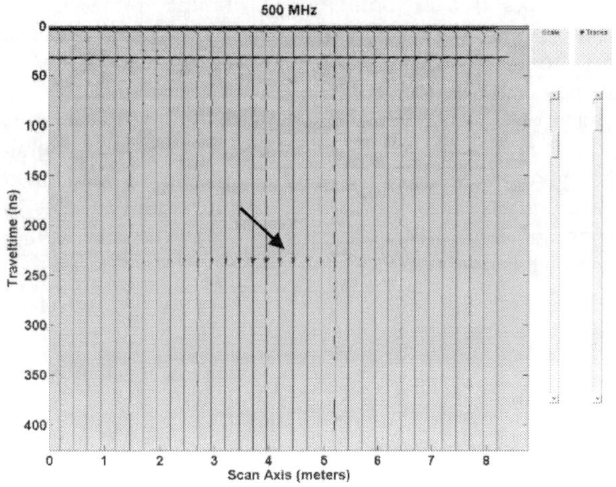

Fig. 12 GPR scan 500MHz (individual traces)

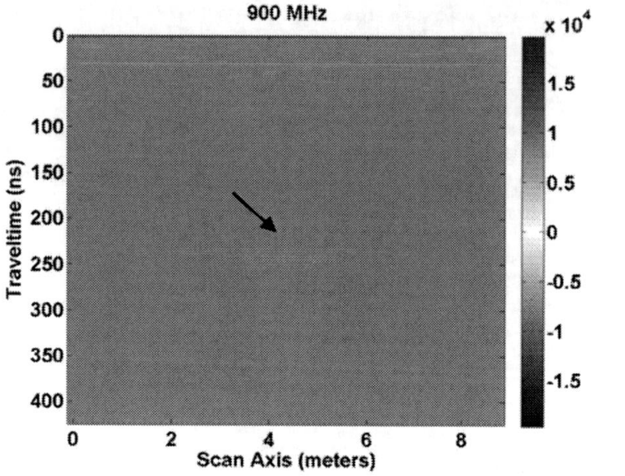

Fig. 13 GPR scan 900MHz (normal 2 D image display)

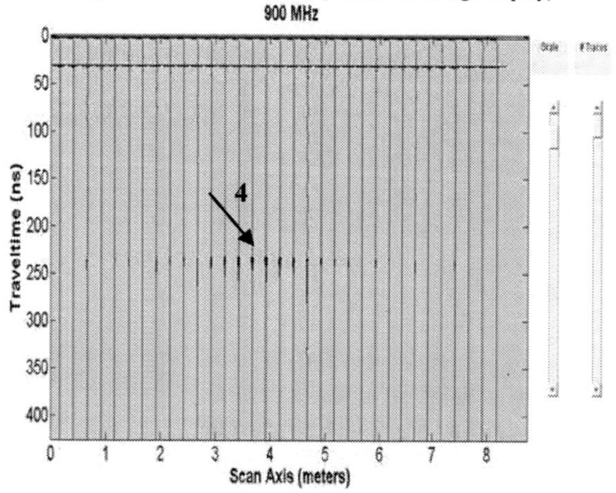

Fig.. 14 GPR scan 900MHz (individual traces)

In all of the GPR scan results, of note is that as the frequency is increased, the area where the target exists is more pronounced. The opposite occurs as the scan frequency is lowered.

Fig. 15 shows the result of adding each of the frequencies together having removed the direct arrival signal and scaling each signal max value to the same magnitude. A broad area of target reflection is shown from approximately 240 ns to 320 ns in depth (two-way travel time); a very rough indication of target depth.

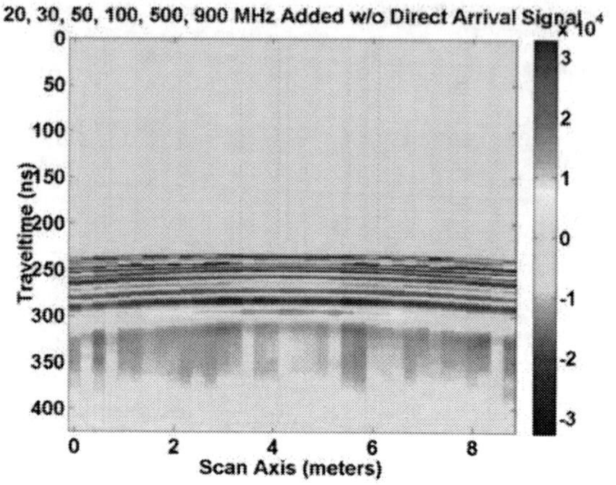

Fig. 15. Sum of frequency signals with direct arrival and ground bounce signals removed.

Fig. 16 and Fig. 17, show the same signals combined using the EM algorithm to determine the weight of each signal. Fig. 17 shows the EM processed individual signal traces. The area that is being scanned is more like a bore hole, twice as deep as it is wide. This accounts for the broad reverse "u-shaped" area that begins at target depth. The existence of lower frequencies in the sum broadens the output result.

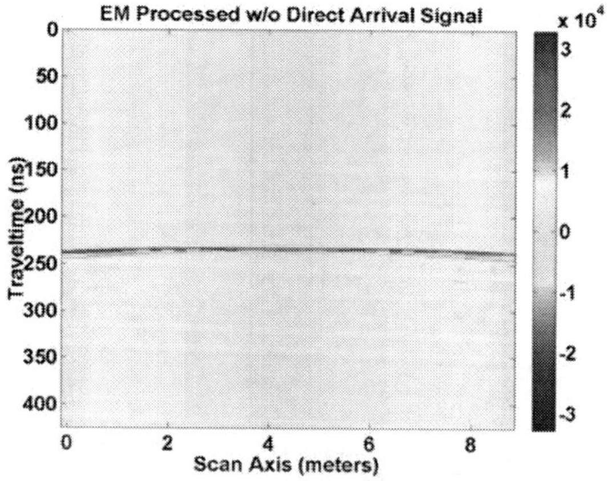

Fig. 16 EM sum of frequency signals with Direct Arrival and ground bounce signals removed.

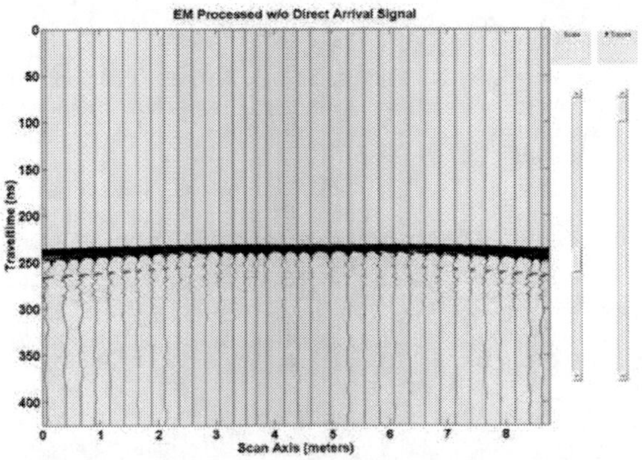

Fig. 17 EM processed signal traces with Direct Arrival and ground bounce signals removed.

As a test, a more complex structure was developed. This structure, Fig. 18, consists of an area 30 meters in length and 25 meters in depth with little or no space above ground, (0.15 meters), for the Tx and Rx used. The Tx and Rx are swept along the scan axis length starting at 0.5 meters (Tx) and ending at 24.85 meters with spacing between the Tx and Rx the same as before (0.25 meters). The number of GPR scans is 145. The electrical conductivity of the ground is the same as before but the relative permittivity (ε_r) is 3.0 for dry sand. Buried in the ground at 8 different levels (4.565m, 6.065m, 8.565m, 10.065m, 12.815m, 14.065m, 16.565m and 18.065m) are sheets of corrugated aluminum, modelled as perfect electrical conductors for ease of computation. Each sheet is approximately 2 meters in length and 0.1 meters thick. The GPR scanning frequencies are the same as before. The result for the EM method, shown in Fig. 19, identifies 8 targets at very close to the correct depth (approximately 50ns, 70ns, 100ns, 116ns, 148ns, 160ns, 190ns and 208ns for two-way travel time at a velocity in the medium of 0.1732 m/ns for the defined relative permittivity) with edges depicted reliably but with less fidelity as one descends in depth. Fig. 20 displays the individual GPR traces instead of the image response.

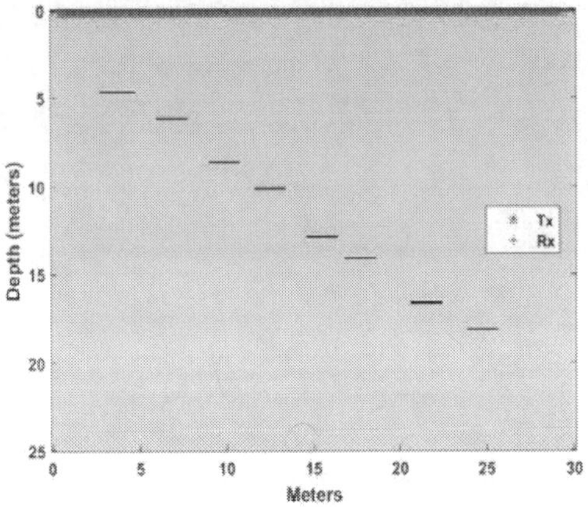

Fig. 18 EM algorithm Test Case, (8) 2m long plates, 0.1m thick

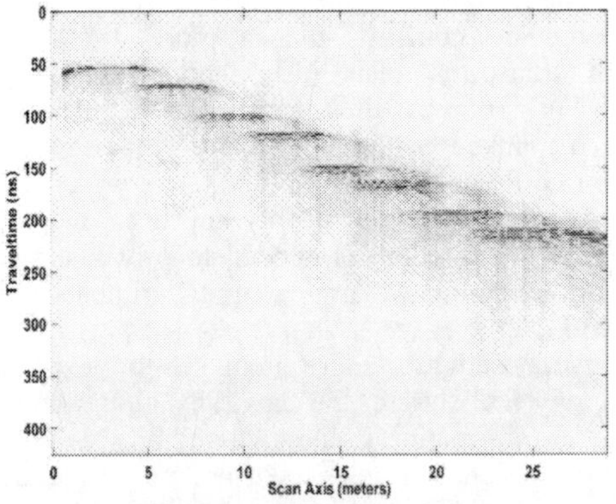

Fig. 19 GPR scan result for complex structure

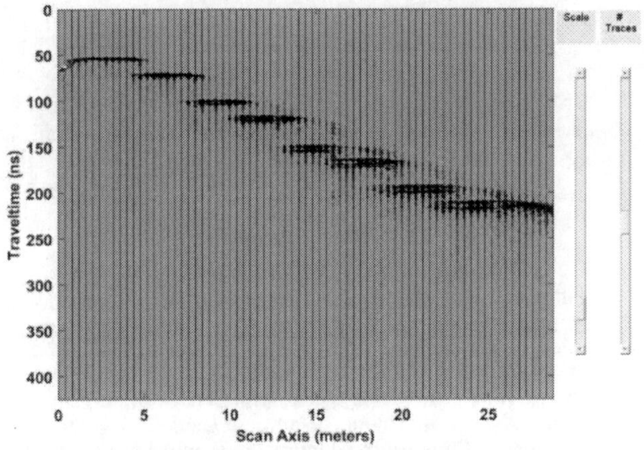

Fig. 20 EM processed signal traces for complex structure

V. CONCLUSIONS AND FUTURE WORK

We have shown that the Expectation and Maximization Gaussian Mixture Model approach to summing sine waves of a particular set of frequencies (harmonics of a square wave), works reasonably well. It is not, however, without problems associated with the magnitude of the calculated weights. As discussed earlier, the mixture weights are constrained to sum to 1; this is not what occurs in actuality. The result of summing sine waves was encouraging enough to continue this approach to GPR scans. Since actual equipment and a suitable target area were not available, computer codes were used to generate the scan area, the target, the type of material for the medium, and the resultant scans at several frequencies. The number of frequencies to use for this analysis was not defined at any time. We have illustrated that the computer code results is very similar to actual scans reported in an earlier paper [10]. We have further shown that just removing the direct arrival signal, the ground bounce, equalizing the magnitude of each frequency and adding the signals together is not sufficient. The result, though it points out the area of interest, the depth where the target appears is not well defined, Fig. 15. The depth indicator line is spread over 10s of nanoseconds. However, the EM method confirms that a more definitive depth indication transpires than just adding the frequencies together, Fig. 16. A final test using a more complex structure demonstrates the viability of the EM algorithm method for GPR analysis, Figs. 19-20.

Our results illustrate that this approach is promising, however, further research is needed to prove its capability using more complicated simulated experiments and field experiments.

This work suggests more items to be explored like removing any DC shift in the data, any global background (mean trace) information in the data and any "wow" (signal interference, which manifests itself as low frequency signal added to the signal trace). Lining up each signal trace by the peak direct arrival pulse and reprocessing the data or looking at how the spectral bandwidth has been changed, are a few methods to investigate.

ACKNOWLEDGMENT

This work was performed under the auspices of the U.S. Department of Energy by Lawrence Livermore National Laboratory under Contract DE-AC52-07NA27344.

REFERENCES

[1] M. E. Dougherty, P. Michaels, J. R. Pelton, L. M. Liberty, "Enhancement of Ground Penetrating Radar Data Through Signal Processing", Symposium on the Application of Geophysics to Engineering and Environmental Problems 1994, pp. 1021-1028, Jan 1994, DOI 10.4133/1.2922053

[2] A. D. Booth, A. L. Endres, T. Murray, "Spectral Bandwidth Enhancement of GPR Profiling Data Using Multiple-Frequency Compositing", Journal of Applied Geophysics, vol 67, pp. 88-97, Jan 2009, DOI 10.1016/j.jappgeo.2008.09.015.

[3] S. W. Bancroft, "Optimizing the Imaging of Multiple Frequency GPR Datasets using composite Radargrams: An Example from Santa Rosa island, Florida", PhD dissertation, University of South Florida, 2010.

[4] Padhraic Smyth, "The EM Algorithm for Gaussian Mixtures, Probabilistic Learning: Theory and Algorithms, CS274A", University of California, Irvine, Department of Computer Science, Lecture Note 4.

[5] A. P. Annan, "Electromagnetic Principles of Ground Penetrating Radar," in Ground Penetrating Radar Theory and Applications, M. J. Harry, Ed., ed Amsterdam: Elsevier, pp. 1-40, 2009, ISBN: 978-0-444-53348-7.

[6] A. Tavlove, "Review of the formulation and Applications of the Finite-Difference Time-Domain Method for Numerical Modeling of Electromagnetic-Wave Interactions with Arbitrary Structures," Wave Motion, vol. 10, pp. 547-582, Dec 1988, DOI 10.1016/0165-2125(88)90012-1.

[7] N. Blindow, D. Eisenburger, B. Illich, H. Petzold, and T. Richter, "Ground Penetrating Radar," in Environmental Geology, Ed. Springer Berlin Heidelberg, pp. 283-235, 2008, DOI 10.1007/978-3-540-74671-3_10.

[8] A. Giannopoulos, "Modelling Ground Penetrating Radar by GprMax", Construction and Building Materials, vol. 19, pp. 755-762, Dec 2005, DOI 10.1016/j.conbuildmat.2005.06.007.

Article in Conference proceedings:

[9] J. J. Verbeek, N. Vlassis, and B. Kröse, "Efficient Greedy Learning of Gaussian Mixtures",The 13th Belgian-Dutch Conference on Artificial Intelligence (BNAIC'01),pp. 251-258, 2001, INRIA-00321510.

[10] R. Tilley, F. Dowla, F. Nekoogar, and H. Sadjadpour, "GPR Imaging for Deeply Buried Objects: A comparative Study based on FDTD models and Field Experiments, Selected Papers Presented at MODSIM World 2011 Conference and Expo; pp. 45-51, Mar. 2012; (NASA/CP-2012-217326); (SEE 20130008625) .

A Comparative Study of the Characteristics of Collisions Involving Bicycles on Frequently and Infrequently Used Bicycle Routes

Joshua James Coniglio, Jianhong (Cecilia) Xia and Mark Ryan
Department of Spatial Sciences
Curtin University
Perth, Western Australia
email:joshua.coniglio@hotmail.com, c.xia@curtin.edu.au and mark_ryan.au@outlook.com

***Abstract*— Cycling is a popular and sustainable transport mode. However, cyclists make up three percent of all road fatalities and fifteen percent of all road hospitalisations in Australia. Limited studies have been conducted to investigate the characteristics of Bicycle Motor Vehicle Crashes (BMVC) from a spatial perspective. This paper aims to compare the characteristics of BMVC on frequently and infrequently used bicycle routes within the Perth metropolitan region. It is broken down into two parts. The first part was to identify the frequently and infrequently used recreational bicycle paths based on Strava heat maps. The second task uses market segmentation with the Expectation-Maximisation (EM) algorithm to identify the major characteristics involved in BMVC on frequently and infrequently used routes. Through the findings presented in this study, the overall safety of these frequently used bicycle routes was determined.**

Keywords- freqently used bicycle route; bicycle crash characteristics; bicycle motor vehicle crashes; spatial distribution.

I. INTRODUCTION

Over the last decade, cycling has become increasingly popular not only as an environmentally friendly form of transportation, but as a healthy recreational activity undertaken individually or as part of a group. Cycling also poses more risk to severe injury in the event of a crash because the human body is unprotected against any hazardous road environments [1]. Various studies conducted by researchers into the risk factors involved in cycling related incidents along with the road and crash characteristics that contributed to the bicycle crashes. However, there is limited research comparing the characteristics of motorists, cyclists and vehicles on frequently used and unfrequently used routes.

The main objective of this study is to identify the most frequently used bicycle routes within the Perth Metropolitan area and relate these routes to BMVC to evaluate the safety of these cycling routes. The purpose behind this study is to reduce the number of incidents involving cyclists in Perth by analyzing Perth's current cycling infrastructure and major crash characteristics involved in order to provide recommendations for improvement. The rest of this paper is organized as follows. Section II describes the related studies according to the crash locations. Section III explains the methods used. Section IV addresses the results. The discussion and conclusions close the paper in Section V.

II. LITERATURE REVIEW

This review primarily focuses on identifying hazardous environments for cyclists by examining the crash locations with the highest percentage of crashes and the road and driver characteristics, which may influence these crashes. The four main crash sites include crashes in traffic, on shared paths, off-road crashes and in cycle lanes.

A. *In Traffic Crash Locations*

According to Meuleners, Lee, and Haworth [2], 92.5 percent of recorded cyclist crashes occurred within the Perth Metropolitan area, whilst the remaining 7.5 percent were located in rural areas [2]. This suggests that urban areas have more hazardous road environments that can threaten the safety of cyclists and increase their likelihood of suffering a severe injury. Severe injuries refer to cases where the victim is hospitalized or killed following a crash. One of the most severe crash sites are in traffic crashes, where a cyclist is travelling on the road but not within a bicycle lane. A study in the Australian Capital Territory by Rome et al. [4] in 2014 identified that 31.9 percent of cycling crashes occurred in traffic and of those, 35.4 percent involved a motor vehicle [4]. Crashes between cyclists and motor vehicles, particularly cars, pose the greatest threat to the safety of cyclists. This is supported by Stevenson et al. [5] whose research into the safety of cyclists within an Australian urban road environment identifies that a cyclist has a 3.6 greater chance of being severely injured in a crash involving a motor vehicle than any other crash type [5].

B. *Crashes on Shared Paths*

The next type of crash site that contributes to high crash statistics are shared paths, which account for 36.1 percent of crashes according to the results from the analysis conducted by Rome et al. [4]. Shared paths are off-road routes that are accessible by both cyclists and pedestrians. These paths however are often mistaken as bicycle only paths by cyclists thus justifying why cyclists were travelling at high speeds when they crash. Of the crashes that occurred on a shared path, 16.4 percent involved pedestrians, whilst 23.3 percent involved other cyclists. The cyclist either crashed into another road user or crashed trying to avoid a collision [4].

Consequently, shared paths are associated with crashes that result in serious injuries suffered by cyclists. An important safety measure that could be implemented to reduce the percentage of shared path crashes could be to recognize shared paths by installing signs near the paths. This measure would be a cost effective attempt to communicate this information to cyclists and may encourage them to slow down.

C. *Off-Road Crashes*

Off-road paths is a broad term used to describe several locations that contribute to over half of the cycle related crashes that occur within Western Australia. Such locations include "sidewalks, driveways, yards, cycle paths, bike trails and parking areas" [2, p 1223]. Despite 58 percent of the crashes being located off-road, cyclists injured off-road were less likely to go to hospital to receive care than those injured on the road. As a result, many bicycle related crashes are not reported to police if the injuries sustained are only minor and do not require medical treatment [2]. From these off-road crashes, 82 percent and therefore the majority occurred on footpaths, which ran parallel to a road. Footpaths can be classified as off-road paths that accounted for 16.8 percent of all bicycle crashes within the Australian Capital Territory [4]. This is a relatively low percentage though compared to the Western Australia study, reinforcing the idea that many off-road crashes are not reported and therefore cannot be included in crash statistics. A study by Wegman, Zhang, and Dijkstra [6] suggests that a vital issue in relation to cycling crash data is the underreporting of such crashes to the appropriate authorities [6].

D. *On-Road Cycle Lane Crashes*

The final type of crash site is on-road cycle lanes these are small lanes located on and run parallel to the road, and are dedicated to cycle traffic. They also assist in separating cyclists from motor vehicles in an attempt to improve road safety for cyclists [3]. Only 7.9 percent of crashes occur within on-road cycle lanes, which is the lowest percentage of crashes compared to any other crash site [4]. As a result, it can be debated that on-road cycle lanes are the safest way for a cyclist to travel. To back up this theory, multiple arguments can be made; firstly, on-road cycle lanes have the lowest number of crashes, secondly, it is illegal for a motor vehicle to cross over a solid line into the bicycle lane unless the line is broken. Lastly, there is a greater chance of an incident being reported to the police because the lane is located on a public road and the majority of these incidents often involve a motor vehicle [1].

III. METHODS

This section presents data collection methods, the study areas and data analysis methods.

A. *The Study Area and Bicycle and Motor Vehicle Crash Data*

The area of focus for this study is the Perth metropolitan area located in Western Australia (WA). The Western Australian road network was acquired from the Department of Transport (DoT) and was clipped to the study area. DoT also provided the shared paths data that consisted of shared paths, recreational shared paths and the principle shared paths. Lastly, the WA boundary was provided by Main Roads (See Figure 1).

For this study, Main Roads provided their BMVC data from 2005 to 2014. This data contained 12057 records, of which 5755 were bicycle crashes. This total of bicycle crashes was lower than expected considering the ten-year time period, suggesting that many more crashes occurred but were not reported and therefore not included in the data. This needs to be taken into consideration when using the data throughout the study. The other records were all the motorized vehicles involved in bicycle crashes. These records are therefore referred to as vehicular crashes. It is possible for multiple vehicles and one bicycle to be involved in a crash, thus the reason why there are more vehicle records than bicycles.

B. *Frequently Used Bicycle Routes*

Multiple acquisition approaches were considered in order to obtain data in regards to the frequently used bicycle routes. As the main focus of this study, it was crucial that this data was accurate and current to ensure that the results and any recommendations based on the results were reliable. The first approach considered was using a GPS device attached to the bicycles of multiple frequent cyclists so that different routes could be acquired. The disadvantage of this approach however was that the data could be biased based towards the route preferences of those cyclists and therefore was not a good representation of all cyclists in Perth.

The second approach was the use of existing data collected by Run and Cycling Tracking on the Social Network for Athletes (Strava). Strava is a mobile application that utilises mobile Global Positioning System (GPS) to record the routes of runners and cyclists worldwide. Using this data, Strava developed a global heat-map that displays the most highly used paths by runners and cyclists. An inquiry was sent to Strava requesting their cycling data for the Perth metropolitan area to be used for this study but no response was ever received. As a result, a third approach was ultimately taken.

The frequently used bicycle routes data was obtained by digitising the data from a road network and the shared paths data based on Strava's global heat-map. Care, time and precision was required to ensure the data was accurate in accordance with this heat-map. The shared paths data was used to obtain any paths that were not located along roads such recreational paths around the Swan River. The resulting digitized routes are therefore the most frequently used recreational cycling routes

For simplicity, these frequently used paths are referred as the popular routes, which are highlighted in the Strava heat-map and all other paths are known as the unpopular routes.

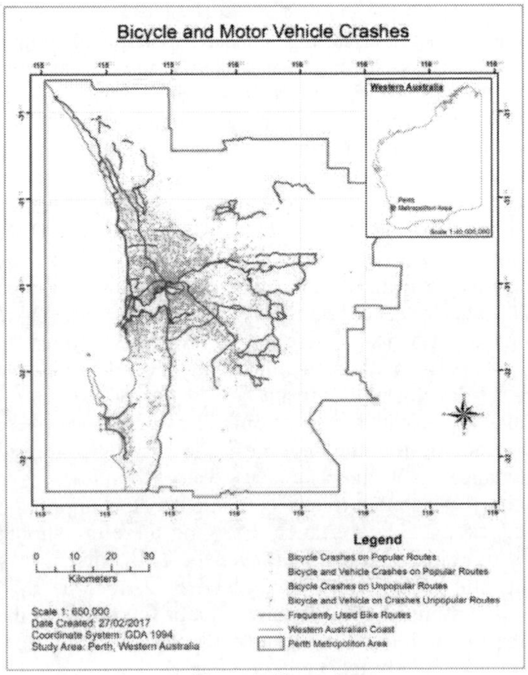

Figure 1. The study area

C. *Identification of Major Characteristics of Drivers and Vehicles of BMVC.*

A data mining approach was taken for the second part of the analysis to identify the dominant characteristics of each variable involved in BMVC on the identified popular and unpopular routes. These characteristics will in turn identify vulnerable populations that are more prone to severe crashes. Data mining uses existing information to generate new information for a particular purpose. The method chosen to implement this approach is known as market segmentation with the use of the EM algorithm. Market segmentation is the process of separating a market into smaller groups known as market segments based on the similar characteristics from the market [7]. The EM algorithm is a clustering based algorithm that identifies the dominant characteristics of objects by implementing maximum likelihood principles. For model-based clustering, this algorithm is also known as mixture modelling and can be used for both categorical and numerical data.

The crash data was broken down into four subsets so that cyclist crash characteristics on frequently used routes could be easily compared against those on infrequently used routes. Vehicle crashes were also of interest because each case that involved at least one vehicle in the crash data also involved a cyclist. As a result, characteristics of vehicles could have been contributing factors that caused the crashes to occur. For example, a drunk driver could hit a cyclist so the driver's alcohol level would be an important factor that caused the crash. The original crash data was first broken down into bicycle only crashes and vehicle crashes. Using the frequently used bicycle routes (line geometry) and the crash sites (point geometry) within a Geographic Information System (GIS), the second task was to determine an appropriate distance (in metres) to classify if a bicycle crash had occurred on a frequently used route. Three distances were tested and the most appropriate was chosen.

Firstly, a distance of 0 metres was used meaning the bicycle crashes had to intersect with the line geometry of the popular route. However, only 2 crash sites out of 5755 records actually intersected with the popular routes line because the majority of crashes were slightly offset from the line. A distance of 10 metres was then implemented but crashes that occurred on roads parallel to the popular routes (i.e., in the other lane) were also selected. Ultimately, a distance of 5 metres was chosen because it selected all crashes on popular routes without selecting crashes in the opposing lanes near the popular routes. In other words, crashes within a 5 metre proximity of the popular routes were selected and classified as having occurred on the popular route. Crashes that occurred on unpopular routes are therefore the inverse of the popular routes selection. The same process was carried out for the vehicular crashes. Table I summarises the number of records for the four subsets. The last task was to clean the data by converting numerical data to categorical data because the data provided by Main Roads used numbers to represent categories.

TABLE I. NUMBER OF RECORDS PER CRASH SUBSET

	Bicycle Crashes	Vehicular Crashes	Total
Popular Routes	591	597	1188
Unpopular Routes	5164	5705	10869
Total	5755	6302	12057

According to Xia et al. [7], there are three main steps involved to carry out this analysis. The first is to identify the spatial patterns involved. For this study there are only two patterns of interest, which are the crashes on popular routes compared against the crashes on the unpopular routes. The second step was to apply market segmentation with the EM algorithm to the variables for each crash subset using software called Weka. This generates between one to seven market segments in a table based on the characteristics inputted. In total, 10 tables were created so each crash subset had a table for each variable. Tables for the vehicle variable were not required for the bicycle crash subsets because the vehicle is a bike, thus there are no data in regards to the bike itself. The last step was to distinguish the major characteristics by interpreting the results from step two.

IV. RESULTS

Using driver and vehicle variables, two tables were created from the results of the ten crash subset tables to identify the most statistically significant characteristics involved in bicycle and vehicular crashes. In each table, the dominant market segment is bolded for both cyclist and motorized categories for each movement pattern. The value in brackets indicates the percentage of the market that belongs to that cluster. The dominant value under each characteristic in each market segment (i.e., each row) is also shaded. Characteristics with empty cells were not involved in the analysis of that crash subset because the characteristic was not deemed as relevant. Tables II to III show the results for each variable.

For crashes on the popular routes, in the first row of Table II for example, 68% of bicycle crashes on popular routes involved a male between the ages of 40 to 49 who were wearing protective gear and only minor property damage was sustained as a result of the crash. This is therefore the largest and most significant market segment for that crash subset. The other two segments were dominated by young male cyclists aged between 20-29, the majority of which were hospitalized or required medical attention. While for crashes on the unpopular routes, middle-aged male cyclists aged between 30-39 in segment 6 dominated and only minor property damage was sustained as a result of the crash. Young male cyclists aged between 10-19 in segment 5 dominated and the majority of them did not wear protection. We did not find any noteworthy characteristics for motorists, except minor injuries were dominant for all segments of the motorists.

In Table III, 73% of the vehicular crashes on popular routes involved a car with a four-cylinder engine manufactured between 2000 and 2009 while the remaining 27% of the market had a six-cylinder engine. Segment 2 contains 73% of the vehicular crashes on popular routes and therefore is the dominant group. For vehicular crashes on unpopular routes, segment 1 is the most dominant with 60% of the market falling within this segment. The results from this segment are the same to that of segment two from the popular routes movement pattern. However, segments 4 and 5 are worth noting because the dominant vehicle in segment 4 is a station wagon rather than a car and segment 5 is the same as segment one for the popular routes. Together, segments four and five equal to just over a quarter of the market.

V. DISCUSSION AND CONCLUSIONS

The major characteristics of cyclists, drivers and motor vehicles were discovered. One vulnerable population were teenagers involved in severe bicycle crashes on the unpopular routes without wearing helmets. The age group of male drivers varied from young adults to middle aged who wore protective equipment such as seatbelts and were usually involved in incidences resulting in minor property damage. In incidences involving such drivers however, inattention and fatigue were the defining characteristics that would have caused the crash. Fatigue not only affects a drivers' reaction time but leads to inattention. This threatens the safety of cyclists regardless if they are within an on-road cycle lane because cyclists on the road rely on other road users to overtake them safely. Surprisingly, the injuries sustained by crashes involving fatigue and inattention are minor but could have been much worse, especially in the case of a vehicle colliding with a cyclist.

Of the major vehicle characteristics, modern cars with four cylinder engines were mostly involved in crashes and could be related to the high number of crashes caused by young adults not paying attention while driving. Consequently, there is strong causation that the young drivers were using their phones whilst driving and therefore not paying attention to the road as it is easier to use a mobile device while driving a small automatic vehicle.

In conclusion, the most frequently used recreational bicycle routes were identified using Strava's global heat-map. The major characteristics involved in bicycle-related crashes on and off the popular routes were also identified. The market segmentation method with the use of the Expectation-Maximisation algorithm successfully divided the crash data for each variable into groups that share common characteristics. These groups were examined in depth in comparison to each other and several justifiable theories were developed as a result.

Overall, the popular recreational bicycle routes were found to be safe despite the high traffic flow and urgent need of maintenance. Not many crashes were found to have occurred on the popular routes compared to the unpopular routes, suggesting they are much safer and therefore should be utilised by regular recreational cyclists. This in turn, may reduce the number of cyclists involved in dangerous road incidents by diminishing the risk. The major limitation of the study is the methodology in defining popular and unpopular routes. Strava is mainly for recreation purpose. Many bicycle trips, with other purposes, such as work, haven't been considered. In the future, other social media tool, such as Bikemap, can be used for understanding bike travel behavior in Perth in a more holistic way.

TABLE II. DRIVERS' CHARACTERISTICS

Market Segments of Significant Crash Patterns for Driver Characteristics

Movement Patterns	Cyclist vs Motorist	Market Segments	Sex		Age								
			M	F	1 to 9	10 to 19	20 to 29	30 to 39	40 to 49	50 to 59	60 to 69	70 to 79	80 to 89
Popular Routes	Cyclist	1 (0.68)	365.1	40.2	30.3	4.6	29.3	63.5	216.0	48.5	15.4	2.9	1.8
		2 (0.08)	38.6	12.8	2.1	17.4	19.3	2.4	9.0	2.0	2.2	2.8	1.1
		3 (0.23)	88.3	52.0	21.6	5.0	29.5	28.1	21.9	23.4	10.4	6.3	1.1
	Motorist	1 (1)	389.0	210.0	40.0	34.0	282.0	61.0	58.0	57.0	46.0	23.0	7.0
Unpopular Routes	Cyclist	1 (0.11)	483.4	80.6	84.0	46.7	76.9	120.0	128.2	69.2	31.8	13.0	1.3
		2 (0.25)	1238.2	64.2	140.7	119.8	274.9	96.6	389.6	199.3	64.0	21.3	3.2
		3 (0.09)	71.9	416.8	44.3	48.2	144.4	116.0	72.9	46.9	18.7	3.1	1.1
		4 (0.07)	535.2	19.3	36.1	83.4	35.5	272.9	36.5	60.8	19.5	8.0	8.8
		5 (0.07)	331.4	42.9	52.2	151.3	87.8	34.6	33.9	11.3	5.3	2.0	2.9
		6 (0.37)	1684.8	207.2	48.7	111.6	70.5	1595.9	32.0	24.5	9.7	4.6	1.7
	Motorist	1 (0.99)	3427.9	2230.0	545.0	309.0	799.0	678.0	2319.9	526.0	303.0	138.0	44.0
		2 (0.01)	50.1	1.0	1.0	1.0	1.0	1.0	50.1	1.0	1.0	1.0	1.0

Movement Patterns	Cyclist vs Motorist	Market Segments	Protection		Severity					Alcohol	Inattention		Fatigue		Purpose of Travel	
			Worn	Not Worn	Fatal	Hospitolised	Medical	PDO Major	PDO Minor	Level	Yes	No	Yes	No	Private	Business
Popular Routes	Cyclist	1 (0.68)	387.7	17.6	1.2	77.6	113.0	41.8	174.6							
		2 (0.08)	28.8	22.6	1.5	26.9	8.3	2.2	15.5							
		3 (0.23)	129.5	10.8	1.4	26.5	97.7	5.0	12.8							
	Motorist	1 (1)	587.0	12.0	2.0	111.0	214.0	54.0	221.0	0.0	583.0	16.0	597.0	2.0	564.0	35.0
Unpopular Routes	Cyclist	1 (0.11)	545.9	18.1	3.1	408.5	70.2	19.4	65.8							
		2 (0.25)	1294.1	8.4	2.2	80.1	583.4	89.6	550.2							
		3 (0.09)	466.5	22.3	2.6	82.6	252.8	8.3	145.4							
		4 (0.07)	471.6	82.9	6.8	45.7	438.9	28.2	37.9							
		5 (0.07)	32.9	341.4	14.1	172.5	122.1	11.6	57.0							
		6 (0.37)	1611.0	281.0	2.2	80.7	131.5	285.9	1394.7							
	Motorist	1 (0.99)	5593.9	64.0	22.0	866.0	1695.0	505.0	2573.0	0.0	5519.9	138.0	5650.9	7.0	5280.9	376.0
		2 (0.01)	50.1	1.0	4.0	11.0	18.0	3.0	18.0	0.9	48.1	3.0	50.1	1.0	38.1	1.0

TABLE III. VEHICLES' CHARACTERISTICS

Market Segments of Significant Crash Patterns for Vehicle Characteristics

Movement Patterns	Bicycle vs Vehicle	Market Segments	Year Manufacture						Number Cylinder			U Type			
			1960 to 1969	1970 to 1979	1980 to 1989	1990 to 1999	2000 to 2009	2010 to 2014	4	6	8	Car	Utility	4WD	Station Wagon
Popular Routes	Vehicle	1 (0.27)	3.0	2.0	9.0	38.0	107.0	9.0	1.0	128.0	21.0	98.0	8.0	15.0	22.0
		2 (0.73)	1.0	2.0	8.0	60.0	307.0	63.0	436.0	1.0	1.0	300.0	41.0	11.0	53.0
Unpopular Routes	Vehicle	**1 (0.6)**	1.8	3.0	120.4	543.3	2734.5	44.0	3380.4	29.8	12.3	2766.6	233.0	81.3	41.4
		2 (0.07)	1.7	3.9	28.4	306.7	18.6	28.7	8.0	345.3	23.7	275.2	20.6	41.8	14.7
		3 (0)	1.0	1.1	2.9	1.0	17.1	11.1	2.0	1.3	1.2	1.5	1.3	1.5	1.1
		4 (0.12)	2.1	1.2	7.9	77.1	519.6	100.7	418.9	254.7	14.4	25.7	18.0	24.8	597.0
		5 (0.14)	2.4	6.7	13.7	33.7	708.4	26.1	24.9	665.9	78.3	559.4	99.0	56.6	26.2
		6 (0)	1.0	1.0	1.0	1.0	1.0	1.0	1.0	1.0	1.0	1.0	1.0	1.0	1.0
		7 (0.06)	2.0	2.2	15.7	16.2	18.8	317.3	330.8	15.0	7.0	277.6	30.2	13.0	35.6

REFERENCES

[1] S. Boufous, L. D. Rome, T. Senerrick, and S. Ivers, "Risk factors for severe injury in cyclists involved in traffic crashes in Victoria, Australia," Accident Analysis and Prevention vol. 49, pp. 404-409, 2012, doi: 10.1016/j.aap.2012.03.011.

[2] L. B. Meuleners, A. H. Lee, and C. Haworth, "Road environment, crash type and hospitalisation of bicyclists and motorcyclists presented to emergency departments in Western Australia," Accident Analysis and Prevention vol. 39, pp.1222-1225, 2007, doi: 10.1016/j.aap.2007.03.006

[3] J. Parkin, and C. Meyers, "The effect of cycle lanes on the proximity between motor traffic and cycle traffic," Accident Analysis and Prevention, vol. 42, pp. 159-165, 2010, doi: 10.1016/j.aap.2009.07.018.

[4] L. D. Rome, S. Boufous, T. Georgeson, T. Senserrick, D. Richardson, and R. Ivers, "Bicycle Crashes in Different Riding Environments in the Australian Capital Territory," Traffic Injury Prevention, vol. 15, pp. 81-88, 2014, doi:10.1080/15389588.2013.781591.

[5] M. Stevenson, M. Johnson, J. Oxley, L. Meuleners, B. Gabbe, and G. Rose, "Safer cycling in the urban road environment: study approach and protocols guiding an Australian study," Journal of the International Society for Child and Adolescent Injury Prevention, vol. 21, pp. 1-5, 2014, doi:10.1136/injuryprev-2014- 041287.

[6] F. Wegman, F. Zhang, and A. Dijkstra, "How to make more cycling good for road safety?" Accident Analysis and Prevention, vol. 44, pp. 19-29, 2012, doi:10.1016/j.aap.2010.11.010.

[7] J. Xia, F. H. Evans, K. Spilsbury, V. Ciesielski, C. Arrowsmith, and G. Wright, "Market segments based on the dominant movement patterns of tourists," Tourism Management, vol.31, pp. 464-469, 2010, doi:10.1016/j.tourman.2009.04.013

Spatio-temporal Analysis and Visualisation of Incident Induced Traffic Congestion Using Real Time Online Routing Information

A Case Study of Fremantle South, Perth, Western Australia

Arfanara Najnin, Jianhong (Cecilia) Xia, Graeme Wright and Ting (Grace) Lin
Department of Spatial Sciences,
Curtin University,
Kent Street, Bentley, Perth, Western Australia
e-mail: 18126208@postgrad.curtin.edu.au
e-mail: C.Xia@curtin.edu.au
e-mail: graemewright2408@gmail.com
e-mail: zju.grace@gmail.com

Abstract— **Traffic congestion triggered by incidents is extremely challenging because of its random occurrence. Incident Induced Traffic Congestion (IITC) usually refers to a form of non-recurrent congestion, which can be measured based on travel time variation after an incident has occurred. This study aims to analyze the spatio-temporal pattern of travel time variation induced by incidents using a case study of Fremantle South, Western Australia. The travel time data and information were collected from the TOMTOM® online routing system through TOMTOM® API. Around ninety-nine origin-destination (O-D) pairs were generated and geocoded to collect travel time information in three different periods, i.e., morning peak (7:00 am to 9:00 am), evening peak (4:00 pm to 6:00 pm) and off peak (1:00 am to 3:00 am) for six months from March 15, 2016 until September 15, 2016. Simultaneously, around 1047 records of incident location information have been collected in the vicinity of the study area. To understand the road network performance, travel time variation and delay were estimated using the Travel Time Index (TTI) measure. The spatial and temporal pattern of travel time variations were analyzed and visualized using specialized geo-spatial tools and techniques. The paper displays the spatial and temporal pattern of IITC in different circumstances that can be used for better traffic management and planning. An attempt will be made to generate various IITC scenarios using Geographic Information System (GIS) tools and techniques. These scenarios may be used for further research to understand the behaviour of road networks due to the occurrence of incidents for the development of congestion mitigation strategies.**

Keywords- Incident Induced Traffic Congestion (IITC); Online Routing, Travel Time delay; Spatio-temporal Data Analysis; Data visualization; GIS.

I. INTRODUCTION

At present, ensuring proper planning and management of the transport sector is a universal issue. Besides, an emerging challenge for transport planning is to mitigate traffic congestion in a sustainable way. There is no concrete definition of congestion. Congestion can be defined as the travel time delay from the origin to destination during peak hours [1]. Factors, such as, high travel demand, low supply of road network and incidents on roads may lead to traffic congestion or travel delay. Different agencies and researchers tend to define incidents in a different way. According to the Traffic Incident Management Handbook, the term "incident" can be defined as occurrence of any non-recurring event that reduces the roadway capacity or abnormally increases highway demand [2]. Congestion caused by incidents is usually defined as non-recurrent congestion, which can be measured based on travel time variation in a certain location. Hence, location and time of incident, and travel time variation are two significant factors to measure the spatio-temporal distribution of IITC. Four general aspects to measure congestion are duration, extent, intensity and reliability [3].

To measure congestion a real-time travel information system is becoming a significant objective. Global Navigation Satellite System (GNSS) technologies such as Global Positioning System (GPS) floating car data, GPS probe vehicle (moving vehicle equipped with vehicle tracker) or cell phone tracking are worthy methods for collection of non-stationary spatial data such as real time traffic flow and travel time information along the road network. Google API and TOMTOM API are two widely known Web-data-portal techniques that have been developed with the integration of GPS equipped floating car data. GPS floating car data is a potential source to collect data without using any vehicle detection technique [4]. A very few studies have been carried out to understand traffic congestion features using empirical data on traffic states from Web portal information [5].

Previous studies suggest that Travel Rate Index (TRI) [6], Congestion Index (CI) [7]-[11], Travel Time Index (TTI) [12] [13] and Speed Performance Index (SPI) [14] are the most widely used indices to quantify congestion and IITC. Among them, TTI has the benefit of assessing traffic congestion from a spatio-temporal perspective and it contains both recurring and incident circumstances encountered by urban travelers. Space and travel time variation are two significant features to measure congestion caused by incidents, which are indispensable elements for effective congestion and incident management [15]. On the other hand, incident information helps to generate different congestion scenarios based on random events that help identify route choice behaviour during incidents induced congestion [16]. Beforehand, most studies were focused to identify the major areas of concern due to incidents or crashes; thus, additional study is required to identify areas of concern through emphasis on non-recurrent traffic congestion.

Appropriate tools and techniques need to be identified to analyze and visualize IITC by considering the domains of space and time. Previously, several methods have been used to visualize and analyze spatio-temporal data on traffic congestion and incidents through human computer interaction. For instance, different graphical, cartographic and GIS tools such as, spider plots or radar graphs, line plots, scatter plots, box plot, QQ plot, Theme River, Comap, Self-organizing Map (SOM), contour map, pencil icons, spatial autocorrelation, spatio-temporal interpolation, cluster analysis etc. (), are widely used techniques to analyze, illustrate and visualize spatio-temporal information effectively [10] [17]-[22].

This study aims to analyze the spatio-temporal patterns of travel time fluctuation due to incident induced traffic congestion (IITC) in Fremantle South, Perth, Western Australia from real time traffic information to generate different IITC scenarios. Later, the generated scenarios (based on travel time variation) will be used to develop congestion mitigation strategies. The core hypothesis of this study is that, random events are the cause of non-recurrent congestion. The specific objectives of the study are as follows:

- Identify appropriate measures for IITC;
- Identify proper techniques to visualize and illustrate the spatio-temporal pattern of IITC;
- Evaluate and implement the techniques using a case study area.

Two major research questions were developed to fulfil the objectives:

- What is the appropriate measure to identify IITC pattern?
- Which visualization tools and techniques can be used to illustrate the information?

This paper consists of four main sections with a list of references. Section one (I) reflects the study background and target of this study. Section two (II) contains the materials and method including the study area delineation, data collection and pre-processing and detail about the approaches for data analysis and visualization of the outcomes. The study outcomes are highlighted in the results and discussion section. The study outcomes are highlighted in the results and discussion section (III). Finally, conclusions are drawn in section four (IV) based on study findings to address the research questions and to provide further research direction.

II. Materials and Method

The study outcomes will be generated by following a sequential approach. The spatio-temporal pattern of traffic delay has been estimated using TTI and demonstrated in a GIS environment using ArcGIS 10.4 e to generate various incidents induced congestion scenarios. To analyze the study data and visualize the outcomes ArcGIS 10.4 and MS Excel Analysis ToolPak-VBA have been used. Figure 1 demonstrates the conceptual framework for linking IITC data from a spatio-temporal perspective.

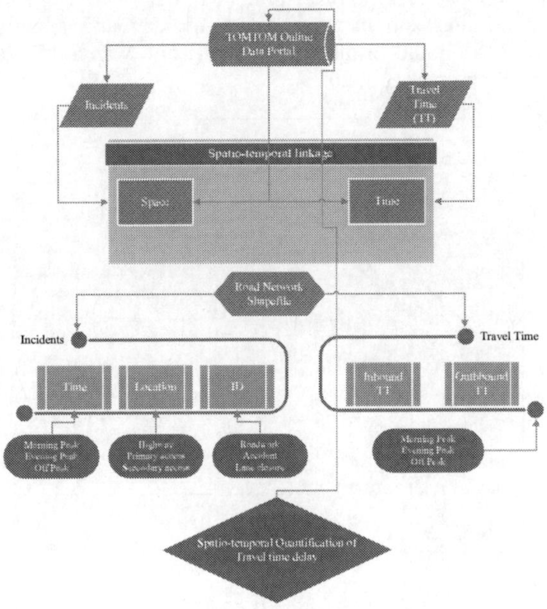

Figure 1. Conceptual framework of spatio-temporal analysis of IITC data

A. *Study Area Deliniation*

The Fremantle City Centre is a historical and touristic place in Western Australia. The market place or city centre (destination point) includes but is not limited to East Street, Queen Victoria Street/Adelaide Street, Market Street/South Terrace, Parry Street, Ord Street and the connecting roads. Queen Victoria Street and Adelaide Street are two major corridors inside the study area. This corridor is a busy link connecting Fremantle to Perth CBD and the surrounding suburbs. Canning Highway and South Street form the northern and southern study boundaries and eastern and western boundaries are Carrington Street, Mews Road and Cliff Street. The study area boundary and the location of Origin-Destination (O-D) points are shown in Figure 2.

B. *Data Collection and Pre-processing*

All the data and information were collected based on two major parameters of this study, i.e., travel time and records of incidents in the study area. The travel time information was collected from TOMTOM online routing system (TOMTOM® API) generated from GPS floating car data [23]. Around ninety-nine (99) O-D pairs were generated and geocoded to collect location specific data in two periods, i.e., morning (7:00 am-9:00 am) and evening (4:00 pm-6:00 pm) peak in each 15-minute interval. However, to get accurate real time information during free flow condition another time span at midnight from 01:00 am to 3:00 am travel time information was also collected.

The information was cross-checked with data collected from Google API. Travel time (TT) data were segregated as morning and evening peak, mid-day and late night hours from the original data set (from March 15, 2016 until September 15, 2016).

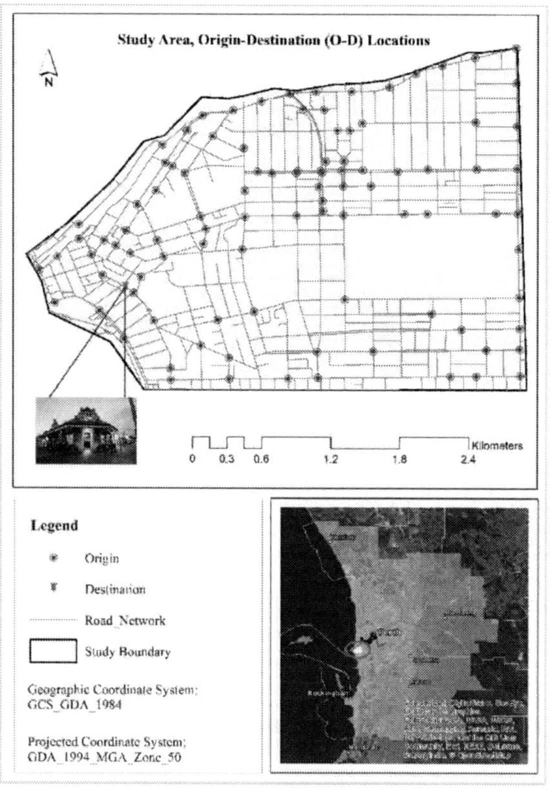

Figure 2. Study area boundary with Origin-Destination loaction, Fremantle, Perth

For the case of incidents, a bounding box was created within the vicinity of the study area and around 1047 records of incidents data were collected from the TOMTOM Traffic™ (the Online Traffic Incidents API). Finally, 747 records were identified after normalizing and overlaying the data with the study boundary. All the record were aggregated based on time and location during the analysis stage such as mean travel time during morning and evening peak, segment wise incident count per month etc. The road network data set was collected from Main Roads, Western Australia.

C. *Data Analysis and Visualization*

This section describes the spatio-temporal data analysis process, in addition to the illustration of study outcomes explained in the following sections.

1) Explore the General Pattern of Congestion

Exploratory analysis of spatial data, including statistical analysis and data visualization, were considered to generate the outcomes as the two major spatio-temporal data analysis techniques [24]. The average travel time (ATT) was calculated using an excel query and pivot table for each O-D (origin to destination) location during morning and evening peaks. The peak hour delay was measured using TTI based on average travel time during peak hour and free flow travel time. TTI was computed from Equation (1) [12]:

$$TTI = PTT/FFTT \qquad (1)$$

Where, TTI is the Travel Time Index, PTT is the actual travel time during peak hours and FFTT is the free flow travel time for the same O-D location.

Average TTI for each O-D pair was calculated based on morning and evening peak hours and free flow conditions. In addition, the average TTI for the total peak hour was estimated. This outcome reveals the general pattern of congestion through a line diagram.

Next, the road network was segmented according to location of O-D points using *network analyst* tool in ArcGIS. Then the segment wise travel time was calculated by subtracting the TT value of each O-D pair (location A) from O-D pair (location B) followed by a sequential location of travel time for each origin towards the destination. A model was developed in GIS to iterate the process 40 times to get TT value of all road segments. This outcome will be used to calculate segment wise delay that will demonstrate the spatio-temporal pattern of congestion in general (work in progress).

2) Mapping the Location of Incident

To define a unique ID for each incident, the find *identical tool* in ArcGIS was used to identify duplicate record of incidents. Then summary statistics were calculated to determine the maximum count of each incident and joined with the main data file. To define the projection of all the data sets, geographic coordinate system GDA 1994 was used and MGA Zone 50 was used as the projected coordinate system. The incident point data set was plotted and mapped in ArcGIS to visualize the location of incidents using the spatial analysis toolkit. Temporal patterns of incidents were analyzed using spider graphs and doughnut charts in MS Excel.

As the work is currently in progress, another subsequent initiative will be taken to identify incident hotspots using spatial analysis tools such as *Kernel Density Estimation* and *Ordinary Kriging* methods.

3) *Calculate Incident Frequency*

Around 683 incidents were identified through overlay analysis in ArcGIS by considering spatial joins between the two attributes, i.e., incidents and road segments. The incident rate in each segment was calculated using the frequency method for six months records, shown in Equation (2):

$$Loc_i = N_i/(L_i * T) \qquad (2)$$

Where, Loc_i is the incident rate at location i. N_i is the number of incidents identified at a certain location i over the period of T (total duration of recorded incidents) and L_i is the length of segment in metres.

A total of 131 days from the survey were identified (excluding public holidays and weekends). Total hours were then calculated by multiplying total days with the total recorded hours per day. In this study, six hours per day of data were recorded (2-hour morning peak, 2-hour evening peak and 2-hour off peak) with a total of around 786 hours.

4) *Identify the IITC Affected Road Segment, Is Congestion Associated with an Incident or Not?*

This section analyses and identifies major congested areas based on average TTI and incident rate per hour along the road network segments. Here, the association between TTI and the average incident rate from the previous calculation was explored. Both attributes from two different datasets were linked using the *spatial join* tool in ArcGIS. Then, the rate of incidents per segment were evaluated using the value of TTI. Later, a correlation analysis will be conducted between the number of incidents per segment or incident frequency and the average TTI per segment as further research.

5) *Spatial-temporal Pattern of IITC*

The spatio-temporal pattern of IITC for a major roadway was illustrated based on TTI of a specific day (with incident). The outcome was visualized through map and tables as shown in results and discussion section.

III. RESULTS AND DISCUSSION

A. *General Pattern of Congestion*

To understand the behaviour of road networks from a spatio-temporal perspective, the general pattern of congestion was analyzed without incidents. Here the travel time data was separated from the days with incidents. Then average TTI was calculated to estimate delay for each O-D pair. That provides a notion of re-current delay along the road network. Figure 3 illustrates the average travel time variations in morning peak (Avg_TT_Mor), evening peak (Avg_TT_Eve,), free flow average (AVG_FF) and average for whole peak hour travel time (AVG_Peak) in each O-D pair.

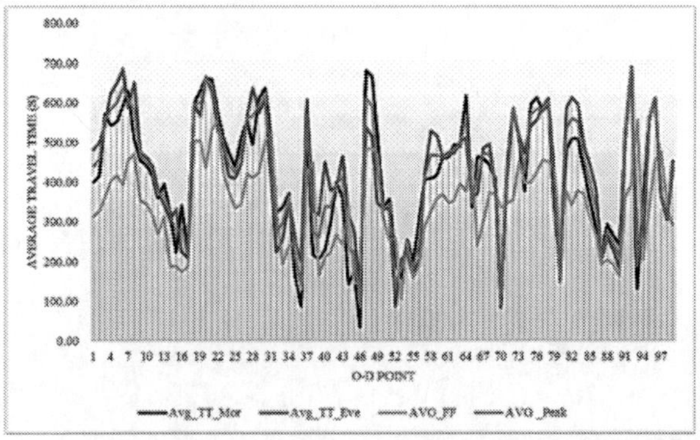

Figure 3. Average travel time variation (morning peak, evening peak and Free flow) per O-D pair;

According to the O-D point analysis, morning peak-hour travel times for pairs 1, 2, 5, 27, 83 and 85 are much higher than evening peak-hour travel times. Alternatively, pairs 37, 46, 52, 70 and 94 have minimum travel times both for the morning and evening peak hours that are lower than the free flow condition. This may happen due to a high rate of speeding by drivers.

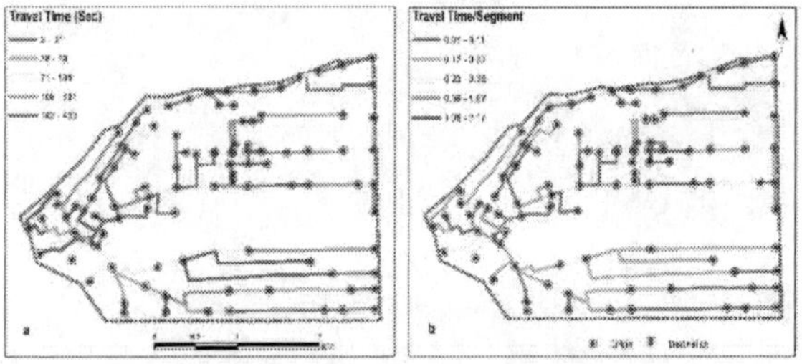

Figure 4. Travel time pattern in morning peak, 7:00 am along the road netwrok generated from *netwrok analyst* (a), normalized travel time for each road segmnet (b).

Morning peak-hour travel time was estimated for each road segment to explore the spatial pattern of congestion without incidents. Figure 4 (a) in the left side shows the distribution of travel time based on segment length (if the length is maximum then the value of TT was also maximum). Then the values were normalized with the lengths of road segments to get logical values of TT as shown in figure 4 (b). The north-west part of the study area near Canning highway was identified as mostly congested during peak periods.

B. *Incident Distribution*

The spatio-temporal distribution of incidents was analyzed using ArcGIS 10.4 and MS Excel Power Pivot. Figure 5 represents the locations of incidents based on category along the road network.

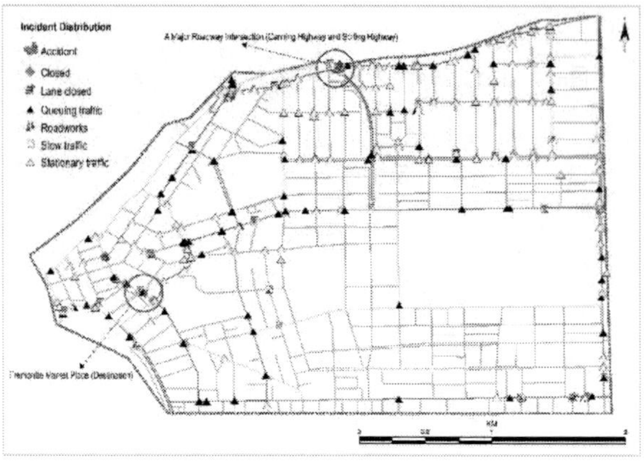

Figure 5. Spatial distribution of incidents based on categories

From the spatial distribution of incidents, only one record of an accident was found close to the Canning Highway and Stirling Highway intersection, which is a major intersection (Figure 5).

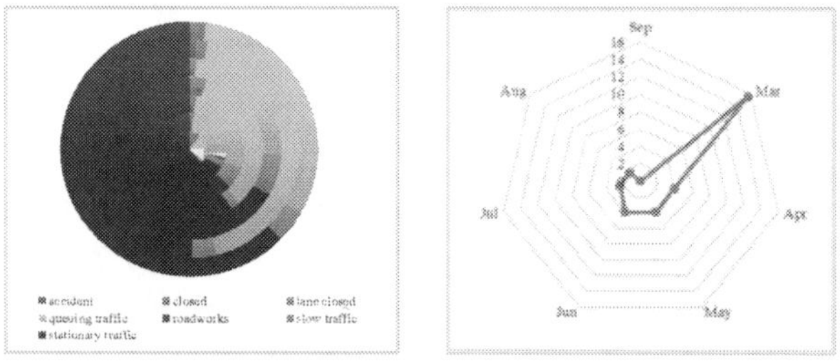

Figure 6. (a) Temporal distrbution of incident per month (March to September, 2016), (b) Amount of incidents overlay with road segments per month

Figure 6 illustrates the temporal pattern of incidents before and after overlay with the road segments. Most of the incidents generated stationary and queuing traffic. A very few number of (only two) accidents were reported in August 2016 over the whole study period, while a high number of incidents (how many) were found in March 2016

C. Incident Frequency

The hourly rate of incident per segment was calculated to measure the magnitude of incidents per segment along the whole road networks.

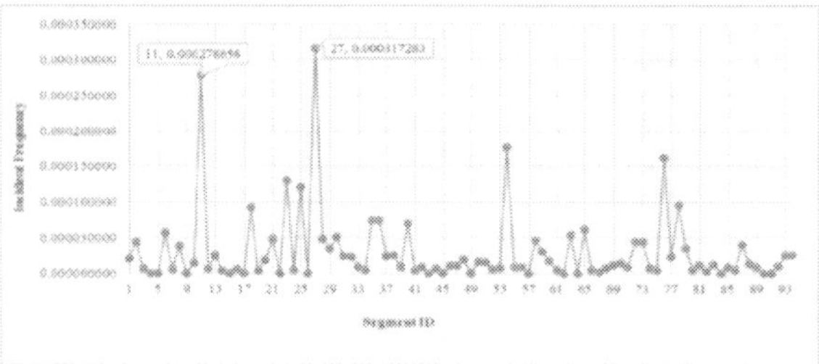

Figure 7. Incident rate per hour in each segment

Figure 7 describes the rate of incidents for each road segment. The maximum incident frequency rate were 0.0003 and 0.0002 near Staton Road to Stirling Highway and Queen Victoria Street to High Street (segments 11 and 27) respectively. This outcome will be used to select the date and location of incident for the next step of analysis.

D. Major Incident Induced Congested Road Segment

To identify a major congested road segment, travel time for a typical day was tested. Among the seven categories of incidents, an accident time of occurrence and location were selected to examine the impact on travel time for selected segments near the accident location. Hence, the evening peak hour TTI on Wednesday 17 August 2016 was analyzed to explore the spatio-temporal pattern of congestion, where the time of accident was recorded as 4:30 pm. From the result, segments 94 and 27 were identified as the most affected road section due to incident (accident).

E. Spatio-temporal Pattern of IITC

To explore the spatio-temporal pattern of congestion for road segments, the delay has been measured using the estimated average value of TTI during peak hours (morning peak, evening peak and total peak periods) as shown in Figure 8.

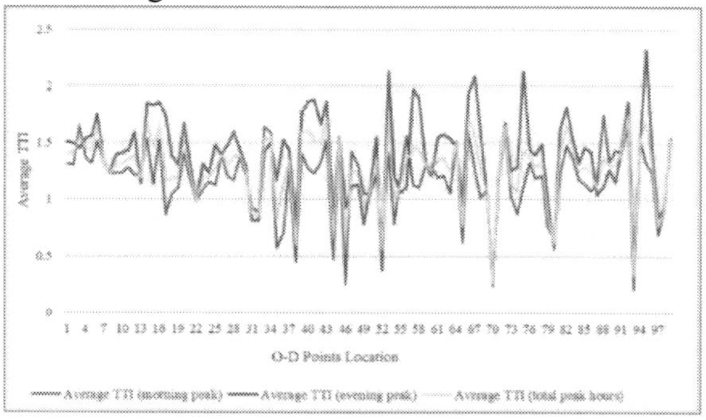

Figure 8. Estimated TTI value during Morning, evening and total peak periods

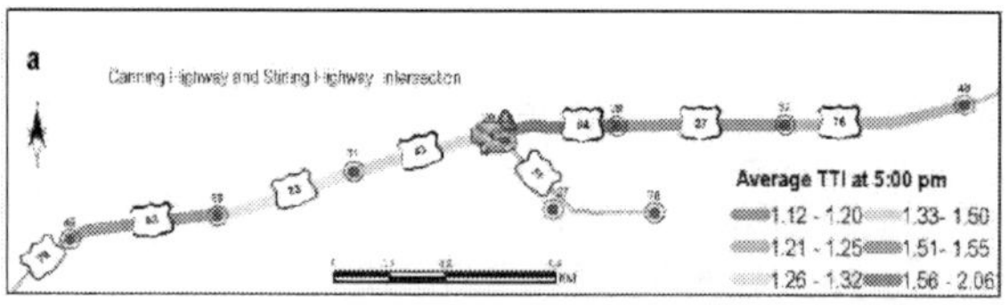

Figure 9. Spatial pattern of IITC during incindent at segment 43, 23, 63 at u/s and at 94, 27, 76 d/s

Figure 9 displays the pattern of congestion based on a single incident on 17 August near the Canning highway and Stirling highway intersection (segments 43, 23, and 63 in u/s and segment 94, 27 and 76 in d/s) during evening peak hour (5:00 pm) on 17 August 2016. Logically, upstream (u/s) segments close to the accident should be more impacted than u/s locations further away. Also, the nearest downstream (d/s) segments should have more impact due to incidents than those further away.

TABLE I. TTI VALUE OF U/S O-D POINTS TO AN ACCIDENT

Date (17/08/2016)	Average TTI Values (u/s segments)		
Time	O-D 69	O-D 71	O-D 26
16:00	1.13	1.32	1.50
16:15	1.13	1.32	1.50
16:30	1.12	1.31	1.49
16:45	1.12	1.31	1.49
17:00	1.12	1.30	1.48
17:15	1.11	1.29	1.46
17:30	1.10	1.28	1.45
17:45	1.09	1.27	1.43
18:00	1.07	1.25	1.41

TABLE II. TTI VALUE OF D/S O-D POINTS FROM AN ACCIDENT

Date (17/08/2016)	TTI Values (d/s segments)		
Time	O-D 28	O-D 37	O-D 48
16:00	1.71	1.52	1.22
16:15	1.70	1.52	1.22
16:30	1.71	1.52	1.23
16:45	1.69	1.51	1.21
17:00	2.06	1.51	1.20
17:15	1.67	1.50	1.19
17:30	1.66	1.49	1.18
17:45	1.65	1.48	1.17
18:00	1.63	1.47	1.16

Tables I illustrates the temporal pattern of IITC, where the closest u/s segment 43 (O-D point 71in u/s and O-D point 26 in d/s) was affected more than more distant u/s segments. Similarly, Table II illustrates how closer d/s segments 94 (O-D point 26 to O-D point 28) was affected more than more distant d/s segments. Next affected road segment in the d/s was 27.

IV. CONCLUSION AND FUTURE WORK

This study is part of an ongoing research program. The method will be used to further develop the research work. The aim of this paper was to explore and illustrate the spatio-temporal pattern of incident induced traffic congestion (IITC) on the road network using online traffic data. The study was designed to answer two research questions:

- What is the appropriate measure to identify IITC pattern?
- Which visualization tools and techniques can be used to illustrate the information?

This study attempts to explore appropriate tools and techniques to visualize and illustrate IITC that will be helpful for policy makers and the non-scientific community to understand congestion patterns along the road network. Travel time variation caused by incidents (vehicle crashes) were identified as the primary feature to define IITC. TTI has been identified as a useful index to measure the duration and extent of IITC. ArcGIS Network Analyst and Excel Analysis ToolPak-VBA are very useful tools to analysis and illustration of spatio-temporal data and outcomes.

From the preliminary analysis of incident and travel time data, segments 43 and 94 were found to be two major congested road sections due to an incident (accident). The preliminary assumption of this study was that random incidents are the cause of non-recurrent delay, and the results in Figure 9 and Tables I and II support the conclusion. This study attempts to explore suitable tools and techniques to visualize and illustrate IITC that will be helpful for the policy makers and non-scientific community to understand the congestion pattern along the road network.

The relationships between different spatial data attributes will be explored as further research work. To identify and evaluate the outcome of major congested road segment a correlation analysis will be carried out between two data parameter, i.e., travel time index and incident frequency rate based on space and time. In addition, the major area of concern or significant incident induced congested road segment will be identified using ArcGIS Network Analyst tool.

A major limitation of this study is the lack of data, especially information of travel demand and volume. To get robust results on incidents at least one-year of data should be used. Further research needs to develop more refined approaches to measure the spatial temporal dynamics of incident induced congestion.

ACKNOWLEDGMENT

This research work funded by the Australian Government under the Australian Post Graduate Award (APA) Scholarship. We express our thanks and gratitude to TOMTOM Developer and Main Roads, Western Australia for giving us the data access to conduct this research work.

REFERENCES

[1] WAAG, 2015, *Main Roads Projects to Address Traffic Congestion (2)*, Retrieved from Western Australian Auditor General, Main Roads, Western Australia.

[2] P. Farradyne, *Traffic Incident Management Handbook.* 2000, Federal Highway Administration Office of Travel Management.

[3] T. Lomax, S. Turner, and G. Shunk, *Quantifying Congestion.* 1997.

[4] C. Nanthawichit, T. Nakatsuji, and H. Suzuki, *"Application of Probe-Vehicle Data for Real-Time Traffic-State Estimation and Short-Term Travel-Time Prediction on a Freeway,"* Transportation Research Record, 2003. no. 1855, pp. 49-59.

[5] H. Rehborn, S. L. Klenov, and J. Palmer, *"An Empirical Study of Common Traffic Congestion Features Based on Traffic Data Measured in the USA, the UK, and Germany,"* Physica A: Statistical Mechanics and its Applications, 2011. vol. 390, no. 23-24, pp. 4466-4485.

[6] E. Hahn, A. Chatterjee, and M. S. Younger, *"Macro-Level Analysis of Factors Related to Areawide Highway Traffic Congestion,"* Transportation Research Record: Journal of the Transportation Research Board, 2002. vol. 1817, pp. 11-16.

[7] E. Necula, *"Analyzing Traffic Patterns on Street Segments Based on GPS Data Using R,"*

Transportation Research Procedia 2015. vol. 10, pp. 276-285.

[8] E. L. D. Oliveira, L. d. S. Portugal, and W. P. Junior, "*Determining Critical Links in a Road Network: Vulnerability and Congestion Indicators,*" Procedia - Social and Behavioral Sciences, 2014. vol. 162, pp. 158-167.

[9] C. Wang, M. A. Quddus, and S. G. Ison, "*Impact of Traffic Congestion on Road Accidents: A Spatial Analysis of the M25 Motorway in England,*" Accident Analysis and Prevention, 2009. vol. 41, no.4, pp. 798-808.

[10] B. H. Sibolla, T. V. Zyl, and S. Coetzee, "*Towards the Development of a Taxonomy for Visualisation of Streamed Geospatial Data,*" ISPRS Annals of Photogrammetry, Remote Sensing and Spatial Information Sciences, 2016. vol. III, no. 2, pp. 129-136.

[11] M. A. P. Taylor, J. E. Woolley, and R. Zito, "*Integration of the Global Positioning System and Geographical Information Systems for Traffic Congestion Studies,*" Transportation Research Part C, 2000. vol. 8, pp. 257-285.

[12] W. Eisele, Y. Zhang, E. Park, Y. Zhang and R. Stensrud, "*Developing and Applying Models for Estimating Arterial Corridor Travel Time Index for Transportation Planning in Small to Medium-Sized Communities,*" Transportation Research Record: Journal of the Transportation Research Board, 2011. vol. 2244, pp. 81-90.

[13] D. Schrank, B. Eisele, and T. Lomax, *2015 Urban Mobolity Scorecard.* 2015, Texas A&M Transportation Institute: Texas.

[14] F. He, X. Yan, Y. Liu, and L. Ma, "*A Traffic Congestion Assessment Method for Urban Road Networks Based on Speed Performance Index,*" Procedia Engineering, 2016. vol. 137, pp. 425 – 433.

[15] H. Zhang, and A. Khattak, "*Spatiotemporal Patterns of Primary and Secondary Incidents on Urban Freeways,*" Transportation Research Record: Journal of the Transportation Research Board, 2011. vol. 2229, pp. 19-27.

[16] J. Wahle, A. L. C. Bazzan, F. Klugl, and M. Schreckenberg, "*The Impact of Real-time Information in a Two-route Scenario Using Agent-based Simulation,*" Transportation Research Part C, 2002. vol.10, pp. 399–417.

[17] A. Asgary, A. Ghaffari, and J. Levy, "*Spatial and Temporal Analyses of Structural Fire Incidents and Their Causes: A Case of Toronto, Canada,*" Fire Safety Journal, 2010. vol. 45, no.1, pp. 44-57.

[18] Y. S. Park, H. Al-Qublan, E. Lee, and G. Egilmez, "*Interactive Spatiotemporal Analysis of Oil Spills Using Comap in North Dakota,*" Informatics, 2016. vol. 3, no. 2, p. 4.

[19] H. Roberto, B. Fernando, and L. Victor, "*Exploratory Geospatial Data Analysis Using the GeoSOM Suite,*" Computers, Environment and Urban Systems, 2012. vol. 36, no. 2, pp. 218-232.

[20] C. Plug, J. C. Xia, and C. Caulfield, "*Spatial and Temporal Visualisation Techniques for Crash Analysis,*" Accident Analysis and Prevention, 2011. vol. 43, no. 6, pp. 1937-1946.

[21] M. Grant, M. Day, R. Winick, A. Chavis, S. Trainor, and J. Bauer, *Showcasing Visualization Tools in Congestion Management*, in *Congestion Management Process: A Guidebook.* 2011. p.35.

[22] W. Aigner, H. Schumann, S. Miksch, and C. Tominski, *Visualization of Time-Oriented Data.* 2011. Springer.

[23] TOMTOM, *Measuring Real-time Traffic Data Quality based on Floating Car Data.* 2014.

[24] R. Haining, *Spatial Data Analysis: Theory and Practice.* 2003, Cambridge, United Kingdom: Cambridge University Press.

Proposal of a Decision Support System for Planning Bicycle Path Networks – An Approach Based on Graph Theory

Lucas José Machado[1], Diogo Bortolini[2], and Fabiano Baldo[3]

Departament of Computer Science
Santa Catarina State University – UDESC
Joinville, Santa Catarina, Brazil
E-mail: [1]lucasmachado.jose@gmail.com, [2]diogo.bortolini@udesc.br, and [3]fabiano.baldo@udesc.br

***Abstract*—Bicycle paths are increasingly becoming part of road infrastructure of cities. However, the expansion of bicycle paths network demands planning to prioritize investment in order to attend the population needs properly. The connectivity between bicycle paths is considered the most important issue pointed out by cyclists. In this work, it is assumed that the problem of planning bicycle path networks can be solved by using graph theory. Therefore, this work proposes a decision support to help planning bicycle path network, prioritizing the connectivity between the existing bicycle paths by using concepts of clustering, centrality and shortest path. In experiments performed in Joinville - Brazil, it could be seen that the proposed method can help specialists by promoting discussions about the bicycle path network connectivity. Also, it was observed that the usage of graph database increased considerably the solution performance.**

***Index Terms*—Graphs Theory; Centrality; Connectivity; Bicycle Paths; Decision Support System.**

I. INTRODUCTION

A proper bicycle path infrastructure allows cyclists to move safely due to the limitation of a specific space for this mean of transportation. However, such as road networks, the expansion of bicycle paths network also demands planning to prioritize investment in order to attend the population needs properly.

The bicycle path infrastructure needs to fulfill at least the following features: provide feeling of safe, present network connectivity and be pleasant and well kept [1]. Each one of the aforementioned characteristics causes direct impact on the bicycle path network quality and costs. Therefore, planning is mandatory in order to harmonise population needs and public budget.

According to Cardoso and Campos [2], the intersection between bicycle paths inside the network is considered the most important issue pointed out by cyclists in the interviews. Therefore, the planning of new bicycle paths should maintain or, preferably, increase the connectivity between the already existing bicycle paths on the network.

In this work, it is assumed that the problem of planning bicycle path networks can be fitted as a graph problem. Therefore, the objective of this work is to propose a decision support system to help planning the expansion of bicycle path network coverage, prioritizing the connectivity between existing bicycle paths by using concepts of clustering, centrality and shortest path from graph theory. The proposed solution was assessed on the bicycle path network from city of Joinville, Brazil.

The next sections are organized as follows. Section II presents a literature review of bicycle path planning, graphs and graph datadases. Section III makes an comprehensible review of related works. Section IV details the proposed solution. Section V presents the system developed. Section VI shows the results assessment. Section VII presents the conclusion and future works.

II. LITERATURE REVIEW

The present work addresses the following concepts: bicycle paths planning, graph theory and graph databases.

A. Bicycle Path Planning

Urban transportation comprises the set of means and services used to allow movements inside the cities. Within the existing means of transportation, bicycle has a special attention due to some features that it has compared to others [3]. It is cheaper and less pollutant, as well as it uses more rationally the road infrastructure when compared to other means. For these reasons, more investments are being made in bicycle transportation means in order to decrease the streets overcrowding caused by the massive use of cars.

Even being considered a safe transportation mean, many people are afraid to use bicycle, especially in crowded areas. However, studies show that many people accept to use bicycle when bicycle paths are available [4]. However, the existence of bicycle paths are not enough, they must be well kept and connected to each other as a integrated network. Isolated bicycle paths force the cyclist to share the space with motorised vehicles, which decreases considerably the safety and hence demotivates the usage of bicycles.

B. Graphs

A graph can be defined as a set of entities related to each other via relationships. Its visual representation describes entities as circles and the relationships as lines that connect the related entities. Nevertheless, formally a graph is defined as $G = (V, E)$, where V represents the set of vertex and E the set of edges [5]. In the scope of transportation networks, one of the possible approaches is to represent the intersections between the streets as entities (vertices) and the streets themselves as relationships (edges) between the intersections.

A graph presents a vast range of features and properties. The most important ones for this work are presented below.

1) *Vertex Degree*: the amount of edges incident to a vertex is called the vertex degree. To be considered incident on a vertex x the edge needs to connect x to a vertex y, where x and $y \in V$ [6].
2) *Shortest Path*: The shortest path in a graph is formed by the minimal set of non repeated vertices and a set of edges that connect these vertices in sequence. The size of this path is defined by the amount of edges that form it [7].
3) *Graph with Properties*: The properties are key-value pairs that may belong to vertices or edges, where each vertex and/or edge can have zero or more properties [5]. In a graph that represents a road network, the properties may identify the type of paving, unevenness and other street features.
4) *Graph Connectivity*: A graph is considered connected only if for every pair of vertices there is a path connecting both vertex, otherwise it is not connected. Although a graph may not be connected as a whole, it is possible to find pairs of connected vertices. This happens when there is at least one path that connects the pair [7].
5) *Centrality*: The centrality metrics are used to evaluate the importance of vertices and/or edges of a graph [8]. Some of them are: a) The degree centrality refers to the vertex degree; b) The proximity centrality refers to the distance of a vertex to all other vertices; c) The betweenness centrality classifies the vertices by the amount of times that each vertex participates on the shortest paths [8].
6) *Cluster*: Cluster means a set of elements that are grouped by an common feature [9]. The process used to identify clusters is called clustering [10]. The elements belonged to the same cluster are very similar, while the elements in different clusters have lower similarity [11]. The similarity can be verified by checking distances or comparing centrality metrics [11].
7) *Prediction of connections*: The prediction of connections aims to estimate the probability to have relationship between two elements on a network that are not directly connected yet [12]. This prediction is calculated analysing properties such as centralities, distances and so forth.

C. Databases

During the last decades the most used model for data persistence is the relational. However, it has not been conceived to storage graph. So, it performance considerably decreases as the graph stored increases [5]. This problem is faced especially in queries that perform recursive self-joins in order to find data indirectly related inside the graph.

An alternative to tackle the problems presented by the relational model is to use the graph model. The databases that implement this data model tend to remain the performance constant, even when the dataset grows, because the queries are localized to a portion of the graph. So, the execution time for each query is proportional to the size of the part of the graph traversed, rather than the size of the overall graph [5]. Another benefit is the flexibility of the graph model. It allows adding new types of vertices and new types of edges without compromising the existing network.

To select the graph database used in this work, it has been performed a evaluation of the three most popular graph databases from DBEngines [13]. The databases evaluated are Neo4J, OrientDB and Titan.

Having into account the analysis presented in [14] - [16], it has been selected the Neo4J. It presents the best performance in queries, as well as in shortest path and betweenness centrality computations. This can be explained because it was designed to optimize the execution of graph exploring algorithms, rather than insert and delete operations.

III. Related Works

This section presents a brief overview about each related work found in the literature.

Sevtsuk and Mekonnen [8] presented an approach to include builds, as schools, hospitals, houses and building, in the analysis of transportation networks modeled as a graph. These builds are represented as vertices connected to the streets through specific edges. This approach uses centrality metrics adapted specifically for analysing trasnportation networks with buildings.

Jun and Yikui [17] proposed a framework for constructing decision support systems for planning transportation networks. This framework had as objective to contribute for solving the limitations of traditional methods to fulfill the requirements of modern transportation systems. This framework describes the components and decision indicators needed to plan and assess any kind of transportation network.

Mishra, Welch and Jha [18] proposed the adaptation of graph connectivity metrics used in social networks to the scope of transportation networks. Most of this metrics are specializations of classical centrality metrics presented in graph theory.

Porta, Crucitti and Latora [19] presented a study demonstrating that the primal modeling is more appropriate to represent the streets in a transportation network for applying algorithms of vertex-centered analysis. Moreover, they emphasize the diversity of existing centrality metrics and explain how each one of them can be applied in the primal model.

Based on the review presented above, it can be noted that works like [8], [18] and [19] highlight that to represent a transportation network as a graph is considered a suitable approach. Besides that, all reviewed works state that centrality metrics can be applied in the connectivity analysis of transportation networks. At last, is can be seen that none of the reviewed works is devoted to plan or analyse the bicycle path network, which represents a lack of solutions concerning this important means of transport.

IV. PROPOSED SOLUTION

Considering that the aim of this work is to aid planning bicycle path networks, the proposed method should be able to suggest bicycle paths that leverage the connectivity among the existing bicycle paths. In order to do that, it is assumed that it is necessary to interconnect the clusters of bicycle paths that are not connected yet. Therefore, to fulfill this objective, the proposed method is composed of the following steps:

a) Identification of bicycle path clusters by finding groups of interconnected vertices. Each cluster should be formed by vertices that have at least one edge connecting themselves and none connecting them with other clusters;
b) Selection of pairs of vertices that will be used as source and destination in suggested new bicycle paths in step (c). Each vertex from the pair must belong to a different cluster;
c) Suggestion of new bicycle paths that increase the connectivity between the clusters identified in step (a), use the vertices from each pair selected in step (b). These suggested paths must be the shortest ones that pass through existing streets that do not have bicycle paths.

The following subsections present the main features of the proposed solution.

A. Data Schema

The data schema designed models streets as edges and the intersection among them as vertices. Besides that, each street can also be composed of several parts (edges) connected to each other by intersections as presented in Figure 1. This means that a single street can be formed by the combination of several edges interconnected by intersections. Therefore, the proposed schema is defined as a graph $G = (V, E)$ where V is the set of intersections and E is the set of street parts that connect intersections from V.

Each intersection in V contains the following attributes: geometry (point), cluster identification and betweenness classification. Meanwhile, each street (part) in E has the following attributes: geometry (line), length and the definition whether it has or not bicycle path.

B. Clustering Algorithm

The clustering algorithm designed in this work has been adapted from the one proposed by Girvan and Newman [20], which uses the betweenness centrality metric to identify the edges that represent bridges that connect clusters.

As this metric emphasizes the vertices and edges used in most of the shortest paths, the edges responsible to connect different clusters are identified because they participate in many paths that connect these two clusters.

The clustering algorithm presented in Figure 2 works as follows. First, it is calculated the betweenness centrality of each edge (lines 4-11). After that, the algorithm discards the edge with the highest centrality value (lines 12-13). Then, it is performed a breadth-first search to reorganize the clusters (line 14), attributing for each vertex the cluster id of its neighbourhood. If the neighbourhood do not have cluster id

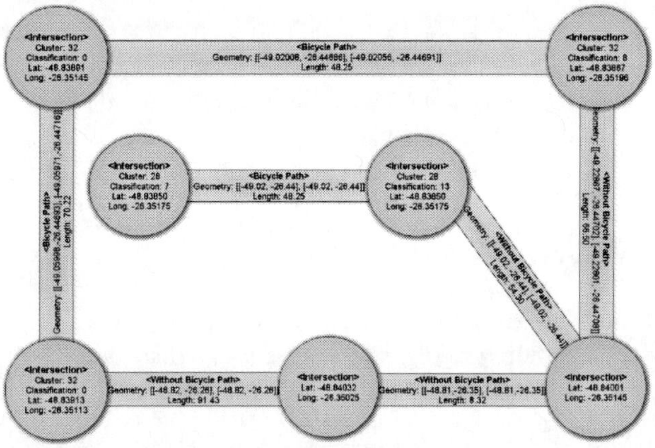

Figure 1. Graph data schema

then a new id is defined. This process is repeated until the stop criterium is fulfilled (line 3). In this work, the stop criterium is the number of clusters formed, defined by the user, previously. Only vertices that have edges with bicycle path are considered in this process.

The algorithm allows to discard only one edge for each iteration. This restriction is imposed due to the fact that it can not be ensure that after removing the edge with highest betweenness score the others will stay at the same position. So, after each discard it is necessary to perform the clustering process again.

The clustering algorithm has been implemented in Gremlin language, using the graph processing library called JUNG.

C. Pair Selection

The selection of vertices to compose the pairs is based on the value of their betweenness centrality metric. Roughly, there will be selected the ones that have the higher betweenness centrality scores. Moreover, both vertices of the pair need to belong to different clusters. Using this approach, it is expected to select the vertices that participate in most of the shortest paths inside the road network and, hence, which allow the highest bicycle network connectivity.

The algorithm starts with the selection of pairs (a, b) by selecting a vertex a from the bicycle path network that belongs to a cluster and that has the betweenness score greater than zero, and that has at least one edge connecting it to any other vertex c, where c must belong either to another cluster or not be part of any cluster. This is performed to ensure that the selected vertex is near to the cluster border. Then, the same process is performed to select the vertex b. After identifying the sets A and B, their elements are combined to form the pair where the betweenness score of $(a_i + b_i)$ is greater than $(a_{i+1}+b_{i+1})$. So, the result is a list of pairs sorted by the value of betweeneess from the highest to the lowest. This algorithm has been implemented using Cypher language in Neo4J.

```
Data:
   G = graph of bicycle path network (only the
edges with bicycle paths);
   min_clusters = minimal number of clusters;
Result:
   clusters = set of vertex grouped by cluster;
begin
    clusters =
     travel_edges_defining_groups(edges(G));
    while quantity(clusters) < min_clusters do
        for v ∈ vertex(G) do
            for v' ∈ vertex(G) where v' ≠ v do
                path = shortest_path(v, v');
                for a ∈ edges(path) do
                    increase betweenness
                      classification of a by 1;
                end
            end
        end
        a' = high-
          est_betweenness_classification(edges(G));

        remove a' from edges(G);
        clusters =
          travel_edges_defining_groups(edges(G));
    end
    return clusters;
end
```

Figure 2. Algorithm of Clustering

```
Data:
   G = graph of road network;
   v' = source vertex of path;
   v'' = destination vertex of path;
Result:
   path = set of edges between source and
destination;
1  begin
2      penalty = 0.2;
3      while penalty <= 1.0 do
4          path = a_star(
5              source: v',
6              destination: v'',
7              cost_function: if edge has bicycle path
             then
8                  cost(edge)*penalty
9              else
10                 cost(edge)
11         );
12         if ∃ path then
13             if ∃ edge ∈edges(path) | edge without
                 bicycle path then
14                 return path;
15             end
16         end
17         penalty = penalty + 0.1;
18     end
19     return ∅;
20 end
```

Figure 3. Algorithm to Calculate Shortest Path

D. New Bicycle Paths Calculation

The last step proposes new paths to connect the existing bicycle paths belonged to the network. The suggested paths should contain at least one street without existing bicycle path. The result should be sorted prioritizing the suggestions with shortest length. This restriction contributes to save costs in building new bicycle paths, as well as helps the cyclists to move around the city faster.

To calculate the suggested paths it has been modified the original A* algorithm to enable it to prioritize the suggestions that present streets without bicycle paths, as presented in Figure 3. Initially, this algorithm applies a penalisation of +20% (line 2) on the length of the streets with bicycle paths. For each interaction the algorithm tries to find a path between the pair of vertices received as input (lines 7-12). If it has succeeded, then it is verified if the path has at least one edge without bicycle path (line 13). If so, then the path is returned as a suggestion (line 14). If not, then the penalty is increased in 10% (line 17) and the process of finding a path is repeated again. This loop is repeated until the length of the streets with bicycle paths has been doubled (line 3). This algorithm has been implemented in Java as an extension inside Neo4J.

The algorithm that suggests new bicycle paths, as seen in Figure 4, uses the other algorithms specified in this work, as follows. First, it executes the clustering (line 2) and the betweenness classification (line 3). Afterwards, it executes the pair selection (line 4) and for every pair it finds the shortest path (line 7) and select the paths with at least on edge without bicycle path (lines 10-11). Finally, it filters the suggestions considered equivalents (lines 14-15). Equivalent suggestions are those that contain a subset of edges without bicycle paths present in another suggestion already calculated.

V. System Development

This section presents the prototype architecture and the data used to build the assessment scenario.

A. System Architecture

The developed prototype has two layers, named front-end and back-end. The front-end encompasses the user interface made with AngularJS framework [21] and Leaflet library [22]. The back-end contains the web service and the extension for Neo4J. The web service processes the requests from front-end, makes requests for either Neo4J or Neo4J extension, and sends back answers to front-end. It has been implemented

```
Data:
    G = graph of road network;
Result:
    suggestions = set of suggested bicycle paths
  between pairs of vertex;
begin
    apply clustering algorithm;
    apply betweenness classification algorithm;
    pairs = select_pairs(vertex(G));
    suggestions = ∅;
    for pair ∈ pairs do
        path = calculate_bicycle_path(pair);
        new_suggestion = ∅;
        for edge ∈ edges(path) do
            if edge does not have bicycle path then
                add edge to new_suggestion;
            end
        end
        if |new_suggestion| > 0 ∧ new_suggestion
          ∉ suggestions then
            add new_suggestion in suggestions;
        end
    end
    return suggestion;
end
```

Figure 4. Algorithm to Suggest Bicycle Paths

using Ruby on Rails framework. The extension for Neo4J was implemented using Java. Figure 5 shows a prototype screenshot identifying the clusters in colours and the suggested bicycle path in black inside the red rectangle.

Figure 5. Prototype suggestions of bicycle paths

B. Assessment Scenario

To perform the experiments it has been chosen the city of Joinville as scenario. This scenario comprises the road network provided by Open Street Map (OSM) database [23] and the bicycle path network provided by the BikeTrails project database [24]. The OSM is a website for collaborative road mapping of any part of the world. The BikeTrails is a project developed by Santa Catarina State University (UDESC) that collects and provides the map of bicycle paths from Joinville city [25].

To extract the data from OSM it was necessary to download a XML with the road network of Joinville. Then, this file was imported to PostGIS using the *osm2po* tool. The bicycle path from BikeTrails was already available in a PostGIS database. The geometries of the OSM database were converted into a graph topology by using the *ST_InitTopoGeo* function from PostGIS [26]. All streets from OSM were included in the topology as "Without Bicycle Path" edges. After that, the bicycle path geometries from BikeTrails were included in this topology by a implemented function called *TopoGeo_AddLineString*. The edges from BikeTrails are labeled as "Bicycle Path". At the end, the topology database has two tables, one with the intersections and another with the streets with and without bicycle paths.

To import this topology from PostGIS to the graph database Neo4J it has been created two JSON files, one containing the intersections (the vertices) and another containing the parts of the streets (the edges). To import these files to the Neo4J it has been implemented a program in Ruby language that makes a REST call to Neo4J containing a statement written in Cypher to insert either a vertex or a edge in the topology.

VI. Result Analysis

This work was evaluated in November 2015 in meetings of the infrastructure working group promoted by IPPUJ (Institute of Research and Planning for Sustainable Development in Joinville). IPPUJ is the public organization in charge of planning Joinville urbanization. This meetings had the participation of cycling groups, universities and the IPPUJ staff, as well.

The assessments made during these meetings comprehend interviews with specialist and environmental observations of the participants. As result, it could be observed that the proposed method, as well as the implemented prototype, may help to improve the discussions about the bicycle path network planning. As main contributions it has been pointed out the possibility to visualize the existing bicycle paths clustered in different colors in a digital map. According to the participants, to distinguish the clusters of connected bicycle paths with colours facilitate considerably the identification of the disrupted points on the network.

Another positive aspect mentioned is related to the classification of the suggested bicycle paths. They are sorted by length prioritising the bicycle paths with shortest length. However, it has been observed as shortcoming that the suggested paths sometimes did not privilegiate straight lines, which is an important aspect mentioned by the cyclists. Also, it has been observed that some suggestions are very similar to each other which restricts the set of applicable suggestions.

Some advises collected during the meetings are regarded to the suggestion criteria. Even considering that length is an important criterium, some participants propose to include as criteria also the direction, inclination and width of the street. Streets less inclined, wider and single directed are preferred.

Regarding the performance, it was observed that the system properly respond to the users with the suggested bicycle paths, even when it is necessary to calculate thousands of path in order to discard paths that are a sub-path of another suggested one. During the experiments, it was observed times between 30 seconds and 1 minute in most of the executions.

VII. CONCLUSION

The bicycle path planning is a complex process that embraces many different geographical, social and economical factors. To help the specialists, this work provides a solution conceived as a decision support system that analyses the road network and offers suggestions for new bicycle paths to improve the connectivity of the existing bicycle path network with the lowest cost possible.

In this work, the problem of suggesting bicycle paths was fitted as a graph analysis. Then, a graph data schema was created to represent the road network topology. This data schema aided in the clusters identification and the betweenness centrality calculation, as well as the implementation of the shortest path algorithm and, hence, the suggestion for new bicycle paths.

Based on the results assessment, it could be seen that the proposed solution helped the specialists on road network planning. Moreover, the prototype showed that the solution is able to promote discussions about the importance of connectivity on bicycle path network planning considering the existence of bicycle path clusters.

As future works, it is possible to consider other road network properties as criteria for suggesting bicycle paths, such as direction, inclination and width. Besides that, it is also possible to consider to change the undirected graph to the directed one in order to evaluate its impacts and benefits.

REFERENCES

[1] Transport Scotland, "Cycling by design 2010," 2010, [Retrieved: Feb., 2017]. [Online]. Available: http://www.transport.gov.scot/system/files/uploaded_content/documents/tsc_basic_pages/Environment/Cycling_by_Design_2010__Rev_1__June_2011_.pdf

[2] P. de B. Cardoso and V. B. G. Campos, "Methodology for defining a bicycle network system," 2013, [Retrieved: Feb., 2017]. [Online]. Available: http://www.anpet.org.br/ssat/interface/content/autor/trabalhos/publicacao/2013/188_RT.pdf

[3] Brazil, "Federal law n.º 12.587, from jan. 3rd of 2012," 2012, urban Mobility Law. [Online]. Available: http://www.planalto.gov.br/ccivil_03/_ato2011-2014/2012/lei/l12587.htm

[4] K. J. Krizek and R. W. Roland, "What is at the end of the road? understanding discontinuities of on-street bicycle lanes in urban settings," *Transportation Research Part D: Transport and Environment*, vol. 10, no. 1, pp. 55–68, 2005.

[5] I. Robinson, J. Webber, and E. Eifrem, *Graph databases*, 1st ed. Beijing, China: "O'Reilly Media, Inc.", 2013.

[6] R. Diestel, "The degree of a vertex," in *Graph Theory*, 3rd ed., ser. Electronic library of mathematics. Hamburg, Germany: Springer, 2006, pp. 3–13.

[7] R. Balakrishnan and K. Ranganathan, "Basic results," in *A Textbook of Graph Theory*, 2nd ed., ser. Universitext (Berlin. Print). New York: Springer New York, 2012, pp. 10–39.

[8] A. Sevtsuk and M. Mekonnen, "Urban network analysis: A new toolbox for measuring city form in arcgis," in *Proceedings of the 2012 Symposium on Simulation for Architecture and Urban Design*, ser. SimAUD '12, San Diego, CA, USA, 2012, pp. 18:1–18:10.

[9] E. Hartuv and R. Shamir, "A clustering algorithm based on graph connectivity," *Information Processing Letters*, vol. 76, no. 4, pp. 175–181, 2000.

[10] S. E. Schaeffer, "Graph clustering," *Computer Science Review*, vol. 1, no. 1, pp. 27–64, 2007.

[11] R. Xu and D. Wunsch, "Survey of clustering algorithms," *IEEE Transactions on Neural Networks*, vol. 16, no. 3, pp. 645–678, May 2005.

[12] J. C. Valverde-Rebaza and A. de Andrade Lopes, *Link Prediction in Complex Networks Based on Cluster Information*. Berlin, Heidelberg: Springer Berlin Heidelberg, 2012, pp. 92–101. [Online]. Available: http://dx.doi.org/10.1007/978-3-642-34459-6_10

[13] DBEngines, "Db-engines ranking - popularity ranking of graph dbms," 2017, [Retrieved: Feb., 2017]. [Online]. Available: http://db-engines.com/en/ranking/graph+dbms

[14] S. Jouili and V. Vansteenberghe, "An empirical comparison of graph databases," in *Social Computing (SocialCom), 2013 International Conference on*, Sept 2013, pp. 708–715.

[15] A. Vaikuntam and V. K. Perumal, "Evaluation of contemporary graph databases," in *Proceedings of the 7th ACM India Computing Conference*, ser. COMPUTE '14. New York, NY, USA: ACM, 2014, pp. 6:1–6:10.

[16] Y. Liu, "A survey of persistent graph databases," Master's thesis, Dept. of Comput. Sci., Kent State University, Columbus, Ohio, 2014.

[17] D. Jun and M. Yikui, "Intelligent decision support system for road network planning," in *ISECS Int. Colloquium on Computing, Communication, Control, and Management*, vol. 4, Aug 2009, pp. 139–142.

[18] S. Mishra, T. F. Welch, and M. K. Jha, "Performance indicators for public transit connectivity in multi-modal transportation networks," *Transportation Research Part A: Policy and Practice*, vol. 46, no. 7, pp. 1066 – 1085, 2012.

[19] S. Porta, P. Crucitti, and v. Latora, "The network analysis of urban streets: A primal approach," *Environment and Planning B: Planning and Design*, vol. 33, no. 5, pp. 705–725, 2006.

[20] M. Girvan and M. E. J. Newman, "Community structure in social and biological networks," *Proceedings of the national academy of sciences*, vol. 99, no. 12, pp. 7821–7826, 2002.

[21] Google, "Angularjs," 2017, [Retrieved: Jan., 2017]. [Online]. Available: https://angularjs.org/

[22] V. Agafonkin, "Leaflet," 2017, [Retrieved: Feb., 2017]. [Online]. Available: http://leafletjs.com

[23] Open Street Map, "Open street map," 2017, [Retrieved: Feb., 2017]. [Online]. Available: https://www.openstreetmap.org

[24] UDESC, "Biketrails," 2017, [Retrieved: Feb., 2017]. [Online]. Available: http://bdes.dcc.joinville.udesc.br:100/ciclo

[25] G. H. R. Costa, F. Baldo, and L. L. Taveira, "A service-oriented platform to map cycling routes," in *Proceedings of the Fifth International Conference on Advanced Geographic Information Systems, Applications, and Services*, ser. GEOProcessing 2013. IARIA, 2013, pp. 1–6.

[26] The PostGIS Development Group, "Chapter 11. topology," 2017, [Retrieved: Jan., 2017]. [Online]. Available: http://postgis.net/docs/Topology.html

[27] D. Abramson *et al.*, "A clustering-based link prediction method in social networks," *Procedia Computer Science*, vol. 29, pp. 432–442, 2014.

Fast Visible Trajectory Spatial Analysis in 3D Urban Environments Based on Local Point Clouds Data

Oren Gal and Yerach Doytsher
Mapping and Geo-information Engineering
Technion - Israel Institute of Technology
Haifa, Israel
e-mails: {orengal,doytsher}@technion.ac.il

Abstract—**In this paper, we present a fast and efficient visible trajectory planning for unmanned vehicles in a 3D urban environment based on local point clouds data. Our trajectory planning method is based on a two-step visibility analysis in 3D urban environments using predicted visibility from point clouds data. The first step in our unique concept is to extract basic geometric shapes. We focus on three basic geometric shapes from point clouds in urban scenes: planes, cylinders and spheres, extracting these geometric shapes using efficient Random Sample Consensus (RANSAC) algorithms with a high success rate of detection. The second step is a prediction of these geometric entities in the next time step, formulated as states vectors in a dynamic system using Kalman Filter (KF). Our planner is based on the optimal time horizon concept as a leading feature ofour greedy search method, making our local planner safer. We demonstrate our visibility and trajectory planning method in simulations, showing predicted trajectory planning in 3D urban environments based on real Light Detection and Ranging (LiDAR) point clouds data.**

Keywords-Visibility; 3D; Urban environment; Spatial analysis.

I. Introduction and Related Work

In this paper, we study a fast and efficient visible trajectory planning for unmanned vehicles in a 3D urban environment, based on local point clouds data. Recently, urban scene modeling has become more and more precise, using Terrestrial/ground-based LiDAR on unmanned vehicles to generate point clouds data for modeling roads, signs, lamp posts, buildings, trees and cars. Visibility analysis in complex urban scenes is commonly treated as an approximated feature due to computational complexity.

Our trajectory planning method is based on a two-step visibility analysis in 3D urban environments using predicted visibility from point clouds data. The first step in our unique concept is to extract basic geometric shapes. We focus on three basic geometric shapes from point clouds in urban scenes: planes, cylinders and spheres, extracting these geometric shapes using efficient RANSAC algorithms with a high success rate of detection. The second step is a prediction of these geometric entities in the next time step, formulated as states vectors in a dynamic system using KF.

Visibility analysis based on this approximated scene prediction is done efficiently, based on our analytic solutions for visibility boundaries. With this capability, we present a local on-line planner generating visible trajectories, exploring the most visible and safe node in the next time step, using our predicted visibility analysis, which is based on local point clouds data from the unmanned LiDAR vehicle. Our planner is based on the optimal time horizon concept as a leading feature ofour greedy search method for making our local planner safer.

For the first time, we propose a solution for the basic limitation of the Velocity Obstacle (VO) search and planning method, i.e., when all the available dynamic velocities for the next time step are blocked in the velocity space and there is no feasible node at the next time step of the greedy search. Computation of the minimum time horizon is formulated as a minimum time problem that generates optimal trajectories in near-real time to the goal, exploring the safest and most visible node in the next time step. We demonstrate our visibility and trajectory planning method in simulations showing predicted trajectory planning in 3D urban environments using real LiDAR data from the Ford Campus Project [1].

II. Visibility Analysis from Point Clouds Data

As mentioned, visibility analysis in complex urban scenes is commonly treated as an approximated feature due to its computational complexity. Recently, urban scene modeling has become more and more exact, using Terrestrial/ground-based LiDAR generating dense point clouds data for modeling roads, signs, lamp posts, buildings, trees and cars. Automatic algorithms detecting basic shapes and their extraction have been studied extensively, and are still a very active research field [2].

In this part, we present a unique concept for predicted and approximated visibility analysis in the next attainable vehicle's state at a one-time step ahead in time, based on local point clouds data which is a partial data set.

We focus on three basic geometric shapes in urban scenes: planes, cylinders and spheres, which are very common and can be used for the majority of urban entities in modeling scenarios. Based on point clouds data generated from the current vehicle's position in state k-1, we extract these geometric shapes using efficient RANSAC algorithms [3] with high success rate detection tested in real point cloud data.

After extraction of these basic geometric shapes from local point clouds data, our unified concept, and our main contribution, focus on the ability to predict and approximate urban scene modeling at the next view point V_k, i.e., at the attainable location of the vehicle in the next time step. Scene prediction is based on the geometric entities and the KF), which is commonly used in dynamic systems for tracking target systems [4],[5]. We formulate the geometric shapes as states vectors in a dynamic system and predict the scene structure the in the next time step, k.

Based on the predicted scene in the next time step, visibility analysis is carried out from the next view point model [6], which is, of course, an approximated one. As the vehicle reaches the next viewpoint V_k, point clouds data are measured and scene modeling and states vectors are updated, which is an essential procedure for reliable KF prediction.

A. Shapes Extraction

1) Geometric Shapes:

The urban scene is a very complex one in the matter of modeling applications using ground LiDAR, and the generated point clouds arevery dense. Despite these inherentcomplications, feature extraction can be made very efficient by using basic geometric shapes. We define three kinds of geometric shapes: planes, cylinders and spheres, with a minimal number of parameters for efficient time computation.

Plane: center point (x,y,z) and unit direction vector from center point.

Cylinder: center point (x,y,z), radius and unit direction vector of the cylinder axis. Cylinder height dimension will be consider later on as part of the simulation.

Sphere: center point (x,y,z), radius and unit direction vector from center point.

2) RANSAC:

The RANSAC [7] is a well-known paradigm, extracting shapes from point clouds using a minimal set of a shape's primitives generated by random drawing in a point clouds set. Minimal set is defined as the smallest number of points required to uniquely define a given type of geometric primitive.

For each of the geometric shapes, points are testedtoapproximate the primitive of the shape (also known as "score of the shape"). At the end of this iterative process, extracted shapes are generated from the current point clouds data.

Based on the RANSAC concept, the geometric shapes detailed above can be extracted from a given point clouds data set. In order to improve the extraction process and reduce the number of points validating shape detection, we compute the approximated surface normal for each point and test the relevant shapes.

Given a point-clouds $P=\{p_1..p_N\}$ with associated normals $\{n_1..n_N\}$, the output of the RANSAC algorithm is a set of primitive shapes $\{\delta_1..\delta_N\}$ and a set of remaining points $R=P\setminus\{p_{\delta_1}..p_{\delta_N}\}$.

B. Predicted Scene – Kalman Filter

In this part, we present the global KF approach for our discrete dynamic system at the estimated state, *k*, based on the defined geometric shapes formulation defined in the previous sub-section.

Generally, the Kalman Filter can be described as a filter that consists of three major stages: Predict, Measure, and Update the state vector. The state vector contains different state parameters, and provides an optimal solution for the whole dynamic system [5]. We model our system as a linear one with discrete dynamic model, as described in (1):

$$x_k = F_{k,k-1}x_{k-1} \tag{1}$$

where x is the state vector, F is the transition matrix and k is the state.

The state parameters for all of the geometric shapes are defined with shape center $\vec{s}$, and unit direction vector $\vec{d}$, of the geometric shape, from the current time step and viewpoint to the predicted one.

In each of the current states *k*, geometric shape center $\vec{s_k}$, is estimated based on the previous update of shape center location $\vec{s}_{k-1}$, and the previous updated unit direction vector $\vec{d}_{k-1}$, multiplied by small arbitrary scalar factor *c*, described in (2):

$$\vec{s}_k = \vec{s}_{k-1} + c\vec{d}_{k-1} \tag{2}$$

Direction vector $\vec{d}_k$ can be efficiently estimated by extracting the rotation matrix T, between the last two states *k, k-1*. In case of an inertial system fixed on the vehicle, a rotation matrix can be simply found from the last two states of the vehicle translations in (3):

$$\vec{d}_k = T\vec{d}_{k-1} \tag{3}$$

The 3D rotation matrix T tracks the continuous extracted plans and surfaces to the next viewpoint V_k, making it possible to predict a scene model where one or more of the geometric shapes are cut from current point clouds data in state *k-1*. The discrete dynamic system can be written as formulated in (4):

$$\begin{bmatrix} \vec{s}_{x_k} \\ \vec{s}_{y_k} \\ \vec{s}_{z_k} \\ \vec{d}_{x_k} \\ \vec{d}_{y_k} \\ \vec{d}_{z_k} \end{bmatrix} = \begin{bmatrix} 1 & 0 & 0 & c & 0 & 0 \\ 0 & 1 & 0 & 0 & c & 0 \\ 0 & 0 & 1 & 0 & 0 & c \\ 0 & 0 & 0 & T_{11} & T_{12} & T_{13} \\ 0 & 0 & 0 & T_{21} & T_{22} & T_{23} \\ 0 & 0 & 0 & T_{31} & T_{32} & T_{33} \end{bmatrix} \begin{bmatrix} \vec{s}_{x_{k-1}} \\ \vec{s}_{y_{k-1}} \\ \vec{s}_{z_{k-1}} \\ \vec{d}_{x_{k-1}} \\ \vec{d}_{y_{k-1}} \\ \vec{d}_{z_{k-1}} \end{bmatrix} \quad (4)$$

where the state vector x is 6×1 vector, and the transition squared matrix is $F_{k,k-1}$. The dynamic system can be extended to additional state variables representing someof the geometric shape parameters such as radius, length etc. We define the dynamic system as the basic one for generic shapes that can be simply modeled with center and direction vector. Sphere radius and cylinder Z boundaries are defined in an additional data structure of the scene entities.

III. FAST AND APPROXIMATED VISIBILITY ANALYSIS

In this section, we present an analytic analysis of the visibility boundaries of planes, cylinders and spheres for the predicted scene presented in the previous sub-section, which leads to an approximated visibility. For the plane surface, fast and efficient visibility analysis was already presented in [6].

In this part, we extend the previous visibility analysis concept [6] and include cylinders as continuous curves parameterization $C_{\text{cInd}}(x,y,z)$.

Cylinder parameterization can be described in (5):

$$C_{\text{CInd}}(x,y,z) = \begin{pmatrix} r\sin(\theta) \\ r\cos(\theta) \\ c \end{pmatrix}_{r=const}, \quad \begin{matrix} 0\le\theta\le2\pi \\ c=c+1 \\ 0\le c\le h_{peds\_\max} \end{matrix} \quad (5)$$

We define the visibility problem in a 3D environment for more complex objects as:

$$C'(x,y)_{z_{const}} \times (C(x,y)_{z_{const}} - V(x_0,y_0,z_0)) = 0 \quad (6)$$

where 3D model parameterization is $C(x,y)_{z=const}$, and the viewpoint is given as $V(x_0,y_0,z_0)$. Extending the 3D cubic parameterization, we also consider the case of the cylinder. Integrating (5) to (6) yields:

$$\begin{pmatrix} r\cos\theta \\ -r\sin\theta \\ 0 \end{pmatrix} \times \begin{pmatrix} r\sin\theta - V_x \\ r\cos\theta - V_y \\ c - V_z \end{pmatrix} = 0 \quad (7)$$

$$\theta = \arctan\left(-\frac{-r - \frac{\left(-vy\,r + \sqrt{vx^4 - vx^2 r^2 + vy^2 vx^2}\right) vy}{vx^2 + vy^2}}{vx}, -\frac{-vy\,r + \sqrt{vx^4 - vx^2 r^2 + vy^2 vx^2}}{vx^2 + vy^2} \right) \quad (8)$$

As can be noted, these equations are not related to Z axis, and the visibility boundary points are the same for each *x-y* cylinder profile, as seen in (7), (8).

The visibility statement leads to complex equation, which does not appear to be a simple computational task. This equation can be efficiently solved by finding where the equation changes its sign and crosses zero value; we used analytic solution to speed up computation time and to avoid numeric approximations. We generate two values of θ generating two silhouette points in a very short time computation. Based on an analytic solution to the cylinder case, a fast and exact analytic solution can be found for the visibility problem from a viewpoint.

We define the solution presented in (8) as x-y-z coordinates values for the cylinder case as Cylinder Boundary Points (CBP). CBP, defined in (9), are the set of visible silhouette points for a 3D cylinder, as presented in Figure 1:

$$CBP_{i=1..N_{PBP\_bound}=2}(x_0,y_0,z_0) = \begin{bmatrix} x_1, y_1, z_1 \\ x_{N_{PBP\_bound}}, y_{N_{PBP\_bound}}, z_{N_{PBP\_bound}} \end{bmatrix} \quad (9)$$

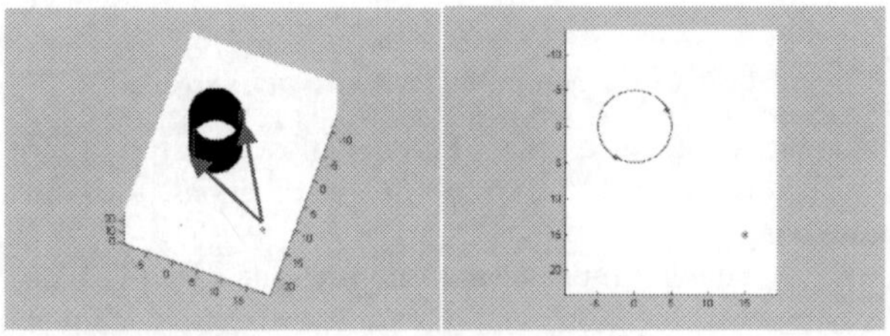

(a) (b)

Figure 1. Cylinder Boundary Points (CBP) using Analytic Solution marked as blue points, Viewpoint Marked in Red: (a) 3D View (Visible Boundaries Marked with Red Arrows); (b) Topside View.

In the same way, sphere parameterization can be described as formulated in (10):

$$C_{Sphere}(x,y,z) = \begin{pmatrix} r\sin\phi\cos\theta \\ r\sin\phi\sin\theta \\ r\cos\phi \end{pmatrix}_{r=const} \quad \begin{matrix} 0\le\phi<\pi \\ 0\le\theta<2\pi \end{matrix} \quad (10)$$

We define the visibility problem in a 3D environment for this object in (11):

$$C'(x,y,z) \times (C(x,y,z) - V(x_0,y_0,z_0)) = 0 \quad (11)$$

where the 3D model parameterization is $C(x,y,z)$, and the viewpoint is given as $V(x_0,y_0,z_0)$. Integrating (10) to (11) yields:

$$\theta = \arctan\left(\frac{r\sin(\phi)}{v\_y} - \frac{1}{v\_y\,(v\_y^2 + v\_x^2)}\left(v\_x\left(r\sin(\phi)\,v\_x - \sqrt{-v\_y^2 r^2 \sin(\phi)^2 + v\_y^4 + v\_x^2 v\_y^2}\right)\right), \frac{r\sin(\phi)\,v\_x - \sqrt{-v\_y^2 r^2 \sin(\phi)^2 + v\_y^4 + v\_x^2 v\_y^2}}{v\_y^2 + v\_x^2}\right) \quad (12)$$

wherer is definedfrom sphere parameter, and $V(x_0,y_0,z_0)$ arechanges from visibility point along Z axis, as described in (12). The visibility boundary points for a sphere, together with the analytic solutions for planes and cylinders, allow us to compute fast and efficient visibility in a predicted scene from local point cloud data, which are updated in the next state.

This extended visibility analysis concept, integrated with a well-known predicted filter and extraction method, can be implemented in real time applications with point clouds data.

IV. FAST VISIBLE TRAJECTORY PLANNING

In this part, we focus on the efficiency of our analytic time horizon solution via classic VO, as demonstrated in simulations.

We use a planner similar to the one presented by [8] with the same cost function, and the Omni-directional robot model mentioned above. For one obstacle, our planner can ensure safety, but the planner is not a complete one. By using an analytic search, the planner computes near-time optimal and safe trajectory to the goal.

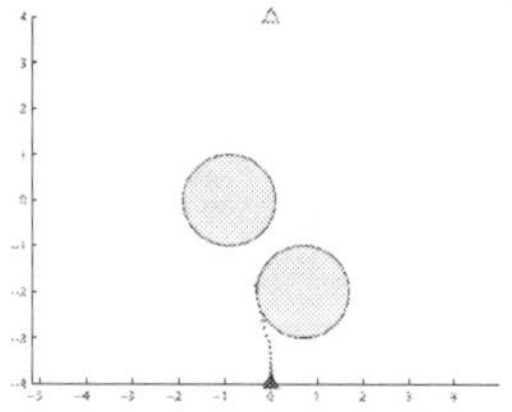

Figure 2. Avoiding Two Obstacles Using Analytic Time Horizon.

As a result, conservative trajectories are computed, althoughin some casesa safe trajectory to the goal cannot be found and collision eventually occurs. In a two-obstacles case, shown in Figure 2, the robot, represented by a point, starts near point (0,-4) at zero speed, attempting to reach the goal at point (0,4) (marked by a yellow triangle) at zero speed, while avoiding two static obstacles. The trajectory is dotted with a red dot representing the current position of the robot. The bounded velocity space, representing VO as yellow cycles and velocity vector (with green triangles), can be seen in Figure 3, relating to the state position in space as shown in Figure 2.

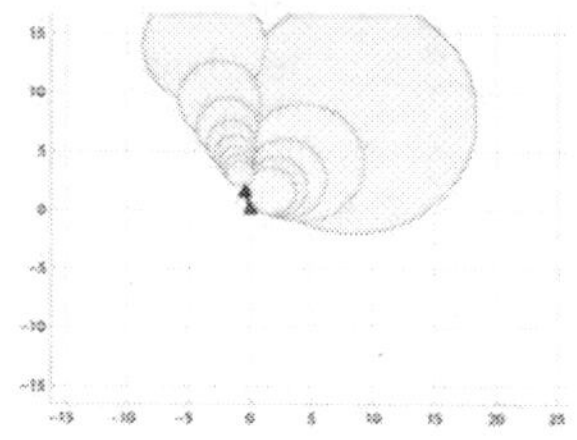

Figure 3. Blocked Velocity Space Avoiding Two Obstacles.

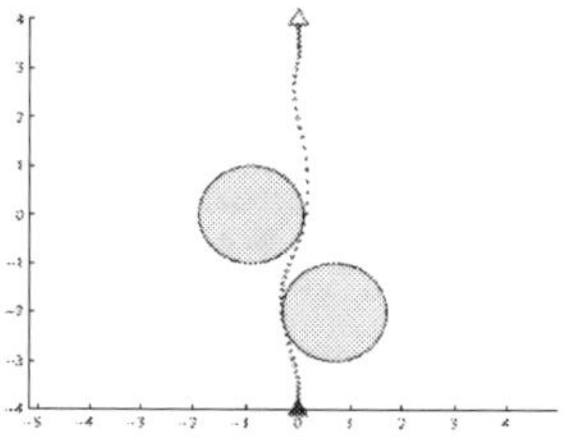

Figure 4. Final Trajectory Avoiding Two Obstacles Using Analytic Time Horizon.

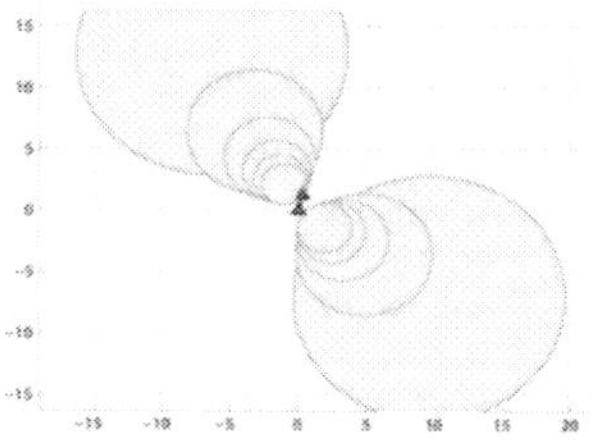

Figure 5. Escaping Blocked Velocity Space Using Analytic Time Horizon.

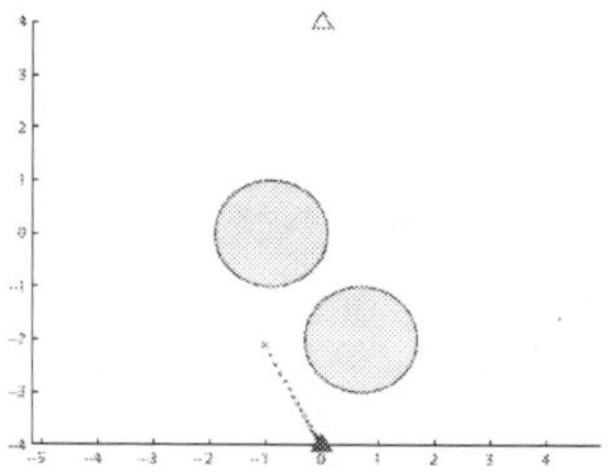

Figure 6. Conservative Solution of Avoiding Two Obstacles.

A. The Planner

As mentioned above, our planner is based on an iterative local planning method. By using RANSAC algorithm, point clouds data are extractedat each time step into three possible objects: plane, cylinder and sphere. The scene is formulated as a dynamic system using KF analysis for objects' prediction. The objects are approximated for the next time step, and each safe attainable state that can be explored is set as candidate viewpoint. The cost for each node is set as total visible surfaces, based on the analytic visibility boundary, where the optimal and safe node is explored for the next time step.

At each time step, the planner computes the next Attainable Velocities (AV). The safe nodes not colliding with objects such as cubes, cylinders and spheres, i.e., nodes outside VO, are explored. Where all nodes are inside VO, a unified analytic solution for time horizon is presented, generating an escape option for these radical cases without affectingvisibility analysis. The planner computes the cost for these safe nodes based on predicted visibility and chooses the node with the optimal cost for the next time step. We repeat this procedure while generating the most visible trajectory.

1) Attainable Velocities

The set of maneuvers that are dynamically feasible over a time step is represented by AV. At each time step during the trajectory planning, we map the attainable velocities that the robot can choose under the effort control envelope.

Attainable Velocities, $AV(t + \Delta t)$, are integrated from the current state (x_1, x_2) by applying all admissible controls $u(t) \in U$. The geometric shape of AV depends on system dynamics. In our case,as described in (13):

$$\dot{x_1} = x_2$$
$$\dot{x_2} = u \tag{13}$$

where $x_1, u \in R^2$.

$$AV(t + \Delta t) = \{v | v = v(t) + \Delta t u, u \in U\}$$

The attainable velocities at time $t + \Delta t$ apply to the position $x(t + \Delta t)$. Thus, the attainable velocities, when intersected with VO that correspond to the same position, would indicate those velocities that are safe if selected at time $t + \Delta t$.

2) Cost Function

Our search is guided by minimum invisible parts from viewpoint V to the approximated 3D urban environment model in the next time step, $t + \Delta t$, set by KF after extracting objects from point clouds data using the RANSAC algorithm. The cost function for each node is a combination of IRV and ISV, with different weights as functions of the required task.

The cost function presented in (14) is computed for each safe node, i.e., node outside VO, considering the robot's future location at the next time step $(x_1(t + \Delta t), x_2(t + \Delta t))$ as viewpoint:

$$w\big(x(t + \Delta t)\big) = \alpha \cdot ISV(x(t + \Delta t)) + \beta \cdot IRV(x(t + \Delta t)) \tag{14}$$

where $\propto, \beta$ are coefficients affecting the trajectory's character, as shown in (14). The cost function $w(x(t + \Delta t)$ produces the total sum of invisible parts from the viewpoint to the 3D urban environment, meaning that the velocity at the next time step with the minimum cost function value is the most visible node in our local search, based on our approximation.

We divide point invisibility value into Invisible Surfaces Value (ISV) and Invisible Roofs Value (IRV). This classification allows us to plan delicate and accurate trajectoriesupon demand. We define ISV and IRS as the total sum of the invisible roofs and surfaces (respectively). Invisible Surfaces Value (ISV) of a viewpoint is defined as the total sum of the invisible surfaces of all the objects in a 3D environment, as described in (15):

$$ISV(x_0, y_0, z_0) = \sum_{i=1}^{N_{obj}} IS_{VP_i^{j=1..N_{bound}-1}}^{VP_i^{j=1..N_{bound}-1}} \tag{15}$$

In the same way, we define Invisible Roofs Value (IRV) as the total sum of all the invisible roofs' surfaces, as described in (16):

$$IRV(x_0, y_0, z_0) = \sum_{i=1}^{N_{obj}} IS_{VP_i^{j=N_{bound}}}^{VP_i^{j=N_{bound}}} \tag{16}$$

Extended analysis of the analytic solution for visibility analysis for known 3D urban environments can be found in [6].

V. SIMULATIONS

We implemented the presented algorithm and tested some urban environments on a 1.8GHz Intel Core CPU with Matlab. We computed the visible trajectories using our planner, with real raw data records from LiDAR as part of the Ford Campus Project.

Point clouds data are generated by Velodyne HDL-64E LiDAR [9]. Velodyne HDL-64E LiDAR has two blocks of lasers, each consisting of 32 laser diodes aligned vertically, resulting in an effective 26:8 Vertical Field Of View (FOV). The entire unit can spin about its vertical axis at speeds of up to 900 rpm (15 Hz) to provide a full 360-degree azimuthal field of view. The maximum range of the sensor is 120 m and it captures about 1 million range points per second. We captured our data set with the laser spinning at 10 Hz.

Due to these huge amounts of data, we planned a limited trajectory in this urban environment for a limited distance. In Figure 7, point clouds data from the start point can be seen, also marked as start point "S" in Figure 10. Planes extracted by RANSAC can be recognized. As part of the Ford Project, these point clouds are also projected to the panoramic cameras' systems, making it easier to understand the scene, as seen in Figure 8.

As described earlier, at each time step the planner predicts the objects in the scene using KF. In Figure 9(a), objects in the scene are presented from a point clouds data set. These point clouds are predicted using KF, and predicted to the next time step in Figure 9(b).

Figure 7. Point Clouds Data set at Start Point.

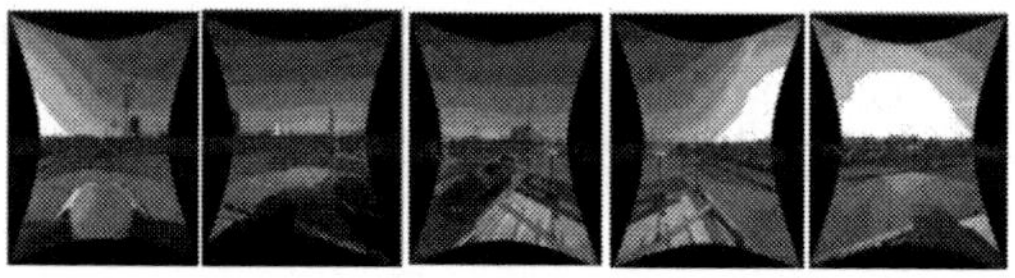

Figure 8. Point Clouds Data Projected to Panoramic Camera Set at Start Point.

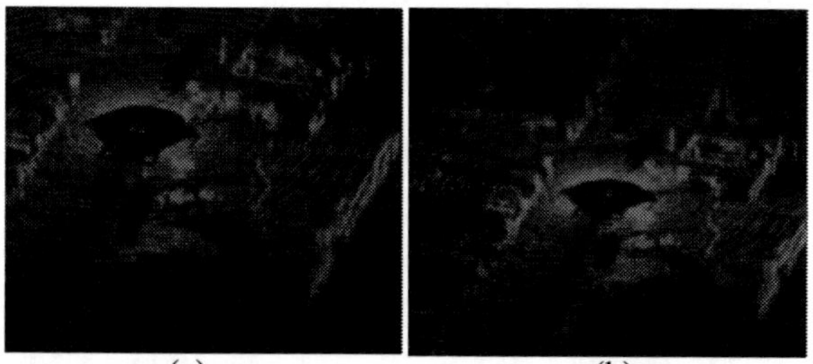

(a) (b)

Figure 9. (a) Objects in point clouds data set. (b) Predicted objects using KF in the next time step.

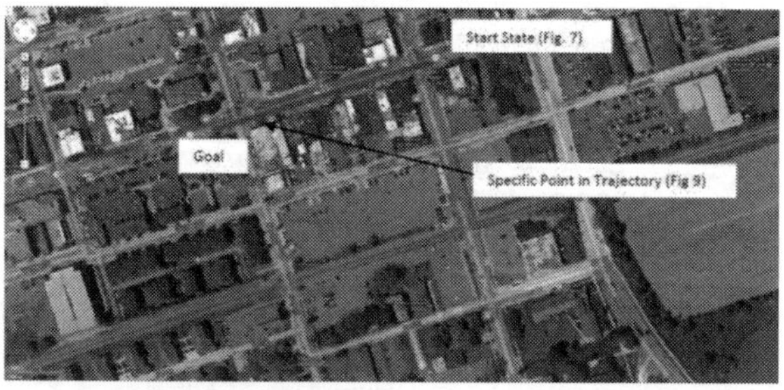

Figure 10. Vehicle Planned Trajectory Colored in Purple.

The planned trajectory is presented in Figure 10 by a purple line. The starting point, marked as "S", is presented in Figure 10, where the cloud points in this state are presented in Figure 8. An arbitrary state during the planned trajectory, which is marked with an arrow, is also presented in Figure 10, where point clouds prediction using KF in this state are presented in Figure 9. For this trajectory, $\propto = 1, \beta = 1$, robot velocity is set to $v_a = 10 \left[\frac{km}{hr}\right]$. In this case, the robot avoided two other cars, without handling cases of analytic optimal time solution for deadlocks with bounded velocity space.

VI. Conclusion and Future Work

In this research, we have presented an efficient trajectory planning algorithm for visible trajectories in a 3D urban environment for an Omni-directional model, based on an incomplete data set from LiDAR, predicting the scene at the next time step and approximating visibility.

We extend our analytic visibility analysis method to cylinders and spheres, which allows us to efficiently set the visibility boundary of predicted objects in the next time step, generated by KF and RANSAC methods. Based on these fast computation capabilities, the on-line planner can approximate the most visible state as part of a greedy search method.

As part of our planner, we extended the classical VO method, where the velocity space is bounded and the robot velocity cannot escape from the VO in the current state. Further research will focus on advanced geometric shapes, which will allow precise urban environment modeling, facing real-time implementation with on-line data processing from LiDAR.

References

[1] G.Pandey, J.R. McBride, R.M. Eustice, "Ford campus vision and lidar data set." International Journal of Robotics Research, 30(13), pp. 1543-1552, November 2011.

[2] G. Vosselman, B. Gorte, G. Sithole, T. Rabbani. "Recognizing structure in laser scanner point clouds.", The International Archives of the Photogrammetry Remote Sensing and Spatial Information Sciences (IAPRS), 2004, vol. 36, pp. 33–38.

[3] R. Schnabel, R. Wahl, R. Klein, "Efficient RANSAC for Point-Cloud Shape Detection," Computer Graphics Forum, 2007, vol. 26, no.2, pp. 214-226.

[4] R. Kalman. "A new approach to linear filtering and prediction problems.", Transactions of the ASME-Journal of Basic Engineering, 1960, vol. 82, no. 1, pp:35–45.

[5] J. Lee, M. Kim, I. Kweon. "A kalman filter based visual tracking algorithm for an object moving," In IEEE/RSJ Intelligent Robots and Systems, 1995, pp. 342–347.

[6] O. Gal, and Y. Doytsher, "Fast Visibility Analysis in 3D Procedural Modeling Environments," in Proc. of the, 3rd International Conference on Computing for Geospatial Research and Applications, Washington DC, USA, 2012.

[7] H. Boulaassal, T. Landes, P. Grussenmeyer, F. Tarsha- Kurdi. "Automatic segmentation of building facades using terrestrial laser data", The International Archives of the Photogrammetry Remote Sensing and Spatial Information Sciences (IAPRS), 2007, vol. 36, no. 3.

[8] O. Gal, Z. Shiller, E. Rimon, "Efficient and safe on-line motion planning in dynamic environment," in Proceedings of the IEEE International Conference on Robotics and Automation, 2009, pp. 88–93.

[9] Velodyne 2007: Velodyne HDL-64E: A high definition LIDAR sensor for 3D applications. Available at: http://www.velodyne.com/lidar/products/white paper. [Accessed 1/23/2017].

Development of the Travel Diary Generating/Printing System (KaDiary) using Geotagged Photos and Extracting Tourists' Behavior from Diaries

Keima Kumano *, Rei Miyagawa *, Satoru Yamada †, Takayuki Kunieda †, Naka Gotoda‡, Masanobu Kii§ and Rihito Yaegashi§,
*Graduate School of Engineering, Kagawa University
Hayashi-cho 2217-20, Takamatsu, Kagawa 761-0396, Japan
Email: s15g463, s16g471@stu.kagawa-u.ac.jp
†Ricoh Company, Ltd., Japan
Ginza 8-13-1, Chuou-ku, Tokyo 104-8222, Japan
Email: satoru.yamada, takayuki.kunieda@nts.ricoh.co.jp
‡ Information Technology Center, Kagawa University
Saiwai-cho 1-1, Takamatsu, Kagawa 760-8521, Japan
Email: gotoda@eng.kagawa-u.ac.jp
§Faculty of Engineering, Kagawa University
Hayashi-cho 2217-20, Takamatsu, Kagawa 761-0396, Japan
Email: kii, rihito@eng.kagawa-u.ac.jp

***Abstract*—Understanding the needs of tourists is important for many areas of tourism. Travel diaries, which include geotagged photos, are becoming popular tools to collect and analyze tourist behavior. We developed a travel diary generating/printing system called KaDiary, which can generate a digital travel diary from geotagged photos taken by tourists, and print the digital travel diary using a printer. This paper describes the development of the KaDiary, the effectiveness of the system and the experiments, which extract tourist behavior from travel diaries on Shodo Island. Results of the experiments identified attractive tourist spots, travel times, including the start times and end times of travel, as well as identified popular travel routes on the island.**

Keywords–Travel diary; Extract tourists' behavior; Geotagged photo.

I. Introduction

Recalling and sharing travel experiences is an important factor for tourism and can inspire tourists to revisit previous locations or invite new tourists to visit travel spots. Collecting and analyzing tourist behavior using geotagged photos has recently attracted a lot of attention and is important to understanding the needs of tourists. By counting the number of photos taken in tourist spots and plotting them to a map using geographical information, we can identify tourist behaviors and easily distinguish which tourist spots are attractive. Of course we can discover the interests of tourists by simply looking at the photos, however, a travel diary using geotagged photos has more advantages because it focuses on the information of tourists as well as the photos. To utilize this information, we developed a travel diary generating/printing system called the KaDiary. The KaDiary generates digital travel diaries (Web-formatted or PDF-formatted) using photos taken by tourists and comments that are given to photos, and prints the digital travel diary using a printer. The travel diary consists of photos, comments, travel behaviors including when and where the tourists visited, the order of tourism spots visited by tourists and the time spent on tourism. Photos and comments are selected using mobile devices by tourists. Travel behaviors are extracted from Exchangeable Image File Formats (EXIF), which are applied to photos. There are many benefits from using our system: (1) Tourists can look back on their experience using a printed travel diary. (2) Tourists can share the digital travel diary with other tourists via the Internet and social media. (3) We can obtain valuable information regarding travel behaviors. This paper describes the development of the KaDiary and confirms the system's effectiveness through experiments conducted to extract tourist behavior on Shodo Island. From the travel diaries we were able to identify the most attractive tourist spots, tourists' travel time, start time of travel, end time of travel and the most popular travel routes on Shodo Island.

This paper is organized as follows. Section II describes related work. Section III describes the development of the KaDiary. Section IV describes the experiment design. Section V describes the result of the analysis. Section VI describes our conclusion and future works.

II. Related Work

Travel behaviors have been recorded for centuries. However, with the popularization of mobile apps and the Internet, travel diaries have become valuable sources of information. Greaves et al.[1] developed and deployed an online seven day travel/activity diary and companion smartphone app to investigate changes in travel behavior and health indicators of residents before and after the construction of a major piece of cycling infrastructure. The smartphone app, which records travel routes on a map can improve both the recall of trips and the accuracy of trip reporting. Safi et al.[2] designed and implemented a smartphone-based travel survey system. Their system provides users with more convenient procedure for recalling and reporting their travel behavior. Our system not only provides a digital travel diary, but can also print travel diaries using a printer. Tourists can access the system using a general camera application and web browser available on most mobile devices without installing a special application.

With the increasing of Global Positioning System (GPS) equipped devices, such as smartphones and tablets, most of photos are having geographical information, which has led to many research projects. Vu et al.[3] explored the activities

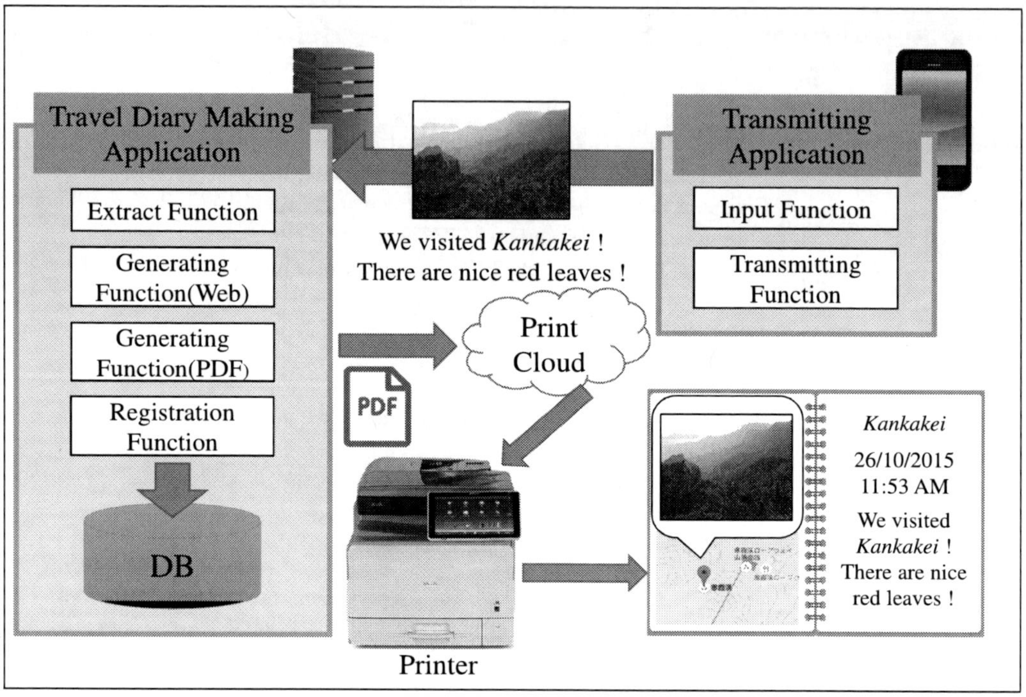

Figure 1. Overview of the Travel Diary Printing/Generating System.

of park visitors in Hong Kong using geotagged photos. They extracted photo locations and photo textual information such as user profiles, photo titles, user-defined photo tags, and content descriptions using text processing, to analyze visitor activity. Kurashima et al.[4] recommended travel route using geotagged photos. They assumed that the collection of each photographer's geotagged photos was a sequence of visited locations, and generated travel routes based on that information. Given that travel information is important for understanding tourist behavior, we tried to extract tourist activities and travel routes from geotagged photos as well.

However, contrary to existing approaches, our system does not require the installation of a special application. Tourists can make travel diaries by taking photos using a general camera application and upload them through a web browser. The system not only creates a digital travel diary, but can also print the travel diary for future recollection and generate a database for tourist behaviors.

III. Development of the KaDiary

This section describes the development of the KaDiary. Section A describes an overview of the system. Section B describes the workflow of the system.

A. System Overview

We developed the KaDiary as a Web application giving tourists the ability to run it on a PC or a mobile device without having to install a special application. Also, we developed the KaDiary using Microsoft Azure[5], which is Cloud Computing Platform that it can be used from any tourist spots. Figure. 1 shows an overview of the KaDiary. The KaDiary includes a transmitting application, a travel diary making application, a print cloud and a printer.

TABLE I. EXAMPLE OF EXIF INFORMATION

Information	*Description*
Maker	ASUS
Model	Nexus7
Date and Time	2014:08:06 10:32:45
Filename	Ritsurin1.JPEG
Latitude	34.3289
Longitude	134.0447
Thumbnail.Height	320px
Thumbnail.Width	480px
MimeType	image/jpeg

The transmitting application has an input function and a transmitting function. The input function allows the user to input a title for the travel diary and add photos and comments for each photo. In order to reduce user anxiety, titles and comments are not necessary to print a diary, however, if no title is detected, the system generates a generic title, for example, “ Shodo Island Travel Diary ” . The transmitting function transmits the title, photos and comments to the travel diary making application.

The travel diary making application creates a digital travel diary as a Web file or a PDF file from the title, photos and comments. The application consists of an extract function, a generating function (Web and PDF) and a registration function. The extract function analyzes the exchangeable image file format (EXIF) and extracts the latitude and longitude as well as the date and time, of each photo. Table I shows an example of EXIF information. The latitude, longitude, date and time in the table can be used for extracting travel behaviors and valuable information about tourism such what are the most popular tourist spots and when's best season to visit. The Web generating function creates a Web formatted travel diary.

However, before generating a Web travel diary, the function edits photos to ensure same size printing on paper. After photo editing, the function generates a Web travel diary using latitude, longitude, date, time and Google Maps APIs[6]. Using Google Maps APIs, the function can extract the order of tourist spots visited as a travel route, and display them on a map, which is also included in the Web travel diary as long as each photo contains geographical information, otherwise the travel route will not appear. The Web travel diary can also be shared with other tourists through the Internet.

The PDF generating function creates a PDF formatted travel diary from the Web travel diary. By generating a PDF travel diary, the application can upload it to a print cloud, which is mentioned below. The registration function registers the EXIF information, comments, title, Web travel diary and the PDF travel diary to a database, which can be used analyze tourist behavior.

The PDF travel diary is registered and saved as a print job in print cloud, and tourists can print it using any printer with print cloud capabilities. Moreover, tourists can print their travel diary without installing specific printer drivers, making it possible to use their own devices.

Figure. 2, 3 and 4 show example pages of a travel diary. Figure. 2 shows an example of a cover page, which includes a map, title, travel date, travel time and travel distance. On the map, there are pins and lines. The pins, ordered in chronological order from A to G, represent locations where the photos were taken using latitude and longitude. The lines represent the travel route from pin to pin. The title is taken from the transmitting application. The travel date is extracted from the date of first photo taken at the beginning of travel. The travel time is the difference between the time of the first photo and last photo taken at the end of travel. The travel distance is automatically calculated from the travel route on the map using Google Maps APIs. Figure. 3 shows an example of a main page. It includes the travel title, travel date, travel time, photos and comments. Photos and comments are uploaded by tourists using the transmitting application. Figure. 4 shows an example of an outline page. It includes a small map, title, travel date, travel time, travel distance and photos. This page is generated based on the idea that some tourists want to see the map and photos on a sheet of paper.

B. Workflow of the KaDiary

The following shows the workflow of the KaDiary.

1) Input the title, photos and comments by using the input function of the transmitting application and transmit them to the travel diary making application from tourist's device.
2) Extract latitude, longitude, date and time from photos using the extract function of travel diary making application.
3) Generate a Web travel diary with a title, photos, comments, latitude, longitude, date, time and Google Maps APIs using the Web generating function.
4) Generate a PDF travel diary from the Web travel diary using the PDF generating function.
5) Register the EXIF information of photos, comments, title, Web travel diary and the travel diary to a database using the registration function.

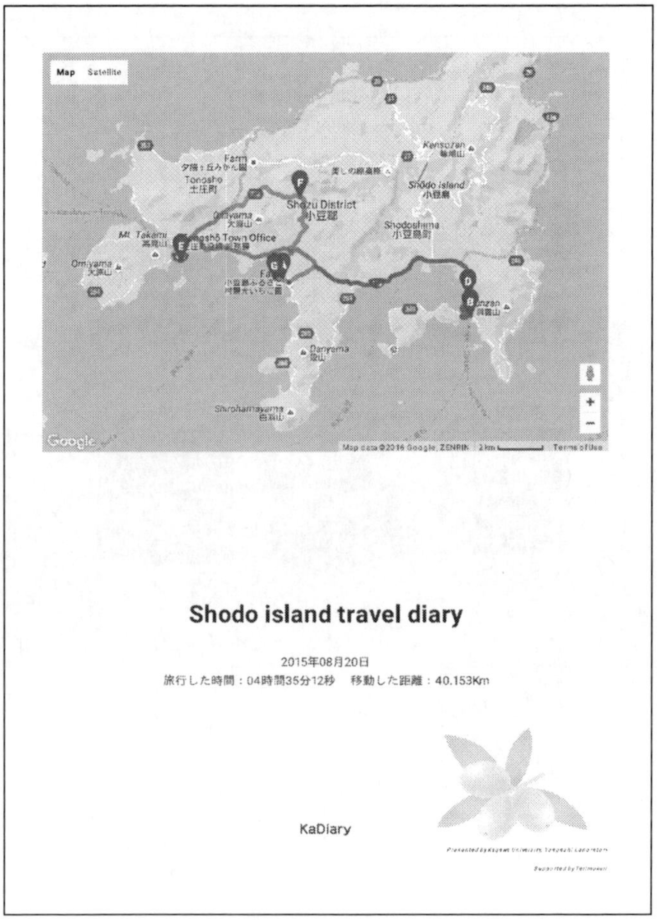

Figure 2. Example of Cover Page.

6) Upload the PDF travel diary to the print cloud.
7) Print a PDF travel diary using a printer with print cloud capabilities.

IV. Experiment Design

We conducted experiments to confirm the effectiveness of the system on Shodo Island. Shodo Island is one of the many islands located in the Seto Inland sea of Japan. The number of tourists who visited Shodo Island were 1,044 in 2003[7]. We added some limitations to the KaDiary system to ensure easy and quick use of the system during peak travel times: First, we limited the number of photos to 9 as tourists often take many photos in tourist spots, and may upload plenty of photos to the system reducing the time to print a diary. Second, we limited the paper size of the diary to A4 only, in order to provide a handy travel diary for tourists. Third, we limited the number of pages to 3, in order to further reduce the time to print a diary.

Finally, we put the Printer, with print cloud capabilities, in a leisure facility. Tourists could upload the photos from anywhere using KaDiary, but could print the diary at the leisure facility only. These experiments were conducted on Oct 21, 22, 23, 29, 30, Nov 5 and 6, 2016 on Shodo Island and tourists could obtain a printed travel diary and digital travel

Figure 3. Example of Main Page.

Figure 4. Example of Outline Page.

diary for free. Figure. 5 shows the printer in the Shodo Island Furusatomura.

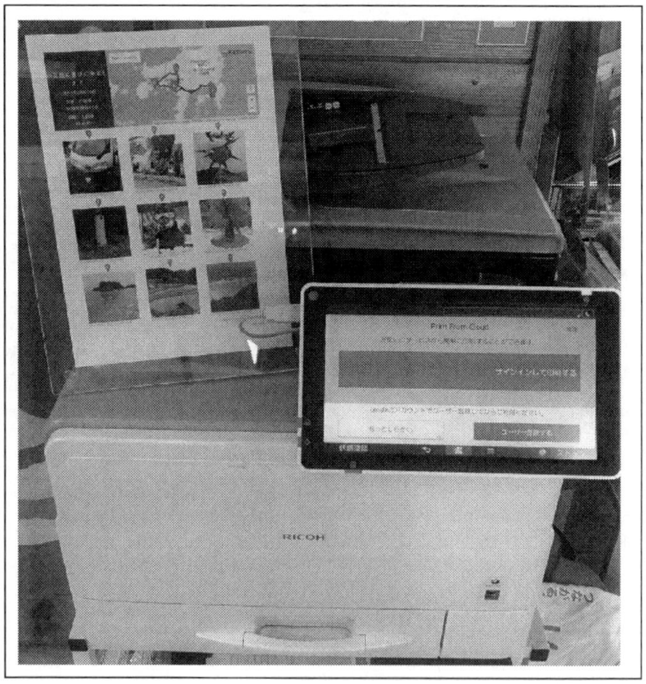

Figure 5. Printer in the Shodo Island Furusatomura.

V. RESULT ANALYSIS

The experiments yielded many photos and diaries. Table II shows the number of diaries and photos, which were extracted by KaDiary. There were a total of 71 diaries of which 18 were route available and a total of 492 photos of which 207 were geotagged.

Figure. 6 shows the location of photos taken on Shodo Island. Many photos were taken in the same places and were focused in the southern part of Shodo Island, making it very useful for identifying attractive tourist spots. Figure. 7 shows the number of travels per travel time. The highest number of tourists was found between 2:00 to 5:00 hours. These results mean that tourists can travel to popular spots in one day without the need to use accommodations on the island. Figure. 8 shows the number of photos per time zone. The highest numbers of photos were taken around noon, leading us to believe that most tourists came to the island around 8:00 am and left the island around 5:00 pm. Figure. 9 shows the travel routes for Shodo Island. This map is includes all the travel routes, which appeared on the diaries. The darker lines are routes more traveled by tourists while the lighter lines are routes less traveled. This map allows us to identify popular

TABLE II. NUMBER OF DIARIES AND PHOTOS WHICH ARE ACQUIRED BY KADIARY

Date	Diaries	Route available diaries	Ratio percentage (diaries)	Photos	Geotagged photos	Ratio percentage (photos)
21/10 Fri	3	0	0%	24	5	20.8%
22/10 Sat	8	3	37.5%	45	23	50.1%
23/10 Sun	13	3	23.1%	92	36	39.1%
29/10 Sat	9	1	11.1%	65	23	35.4%
30/10 Sut	11	2	18.2%	64	18	28.1%
5/11 Sat	9	2	22.2%	60	24	40.0%
6/11 Sun	18	7	38.9%	142	78	54.9%
Total	71	18	25.4%	492	207	42.1%

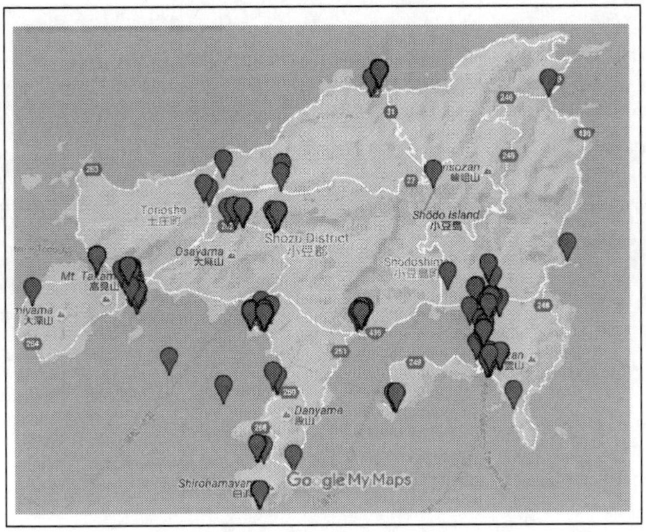

Figure 6. Location of Photos Taken on Shodo Island.

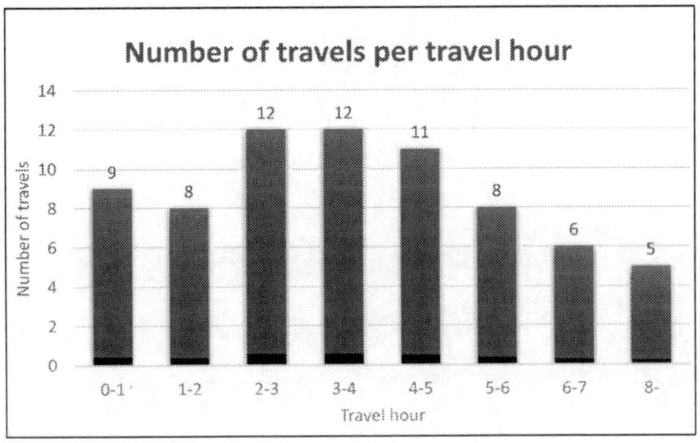

Figure 7. Number of Travels per Travel Hour.

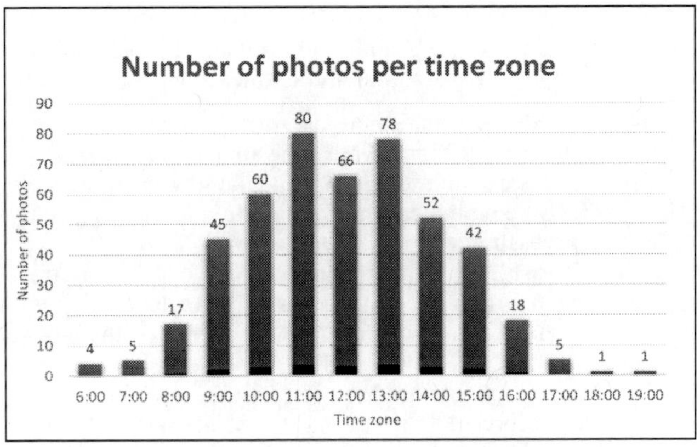

Figure 8. Number of Photos per Time Zone.

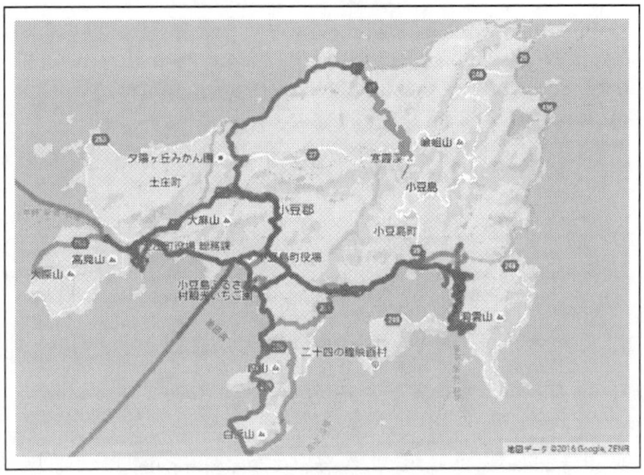

Figure 9. Travel Routes on Shodo Island.

travel routes used by tourists to visit many tourist spots in a short amount of time.

VI. CONCLUSION AND FUTURE WORKS

This paper describes the development of a travel diary generating/printing system called the KaDiary using geotagged photos. The KaDiary generates digital travel diaries (Web-formatted and PDF-formatted) using photos and comments from tourists and prints the digital travel diary using a printer. This system uses the cloud environment and thus can be used in other tourist spots. There are many benefits to using our system: (1) Tourists can look back on their experience. (2) Tourists can share their digital travel diary with other tourists. (3) We can obtain valuable information about tourism in order to learn about travel behaviors. The KaDiary has a transmitting application, a travel diary making application, a print cloud and a printer. The transmitting application runs on devices used by a tourist and can upload selected photos and input titles as well as comments. The travel diary making application can generate digital travel diaries (Web-formatted and PDF formatted) using EXIF data and Google Maps APIs. Tourists can print their own travel diary without installing specific printer drivers using a printer with print cloud capabilities. The results of experiments conducted on Shodo Island show that we can identify attractive tourist spots, travel times, including the start times and end times of travel, as well as identify popular travel routes on the island. Comments from tourists who used the KaDiary, were very positive, for example "I am surprised about the accuracy of the travel route." and "It is nice to have a paper to look back on my travel."

In the future we are planning to implement more functions to enhance tourist satisfaction and extract more information:

1) On Shodo Island there are some indoor tourist spots where GPS signals are unavailable. Therefore, it is necessary to include a function that automatically adds geographical information to photos using image processing.
2) Tourists could not change the layout of the travel diary. Therefore it is necessary to include a function to allow tourists to change the layout of their travel diary.
3) Some tourists took a long time selecting photos. Therefore, it is necessary to include a function that can identify photos tourists want to select, and generate travel diaries automatically from identified photos.

ACKNOWLEDGMENT

Funding from Ricoh Company, Ltd. and Kagawa University are greatfully acknowledged. The authors would also like to thank the staff of the Shodo Island town office and Shodo Island Furusatomura.

REFERENCES

[1] S. Greaves et al. (2015), "A Web-based Diary and Companion Smartphone app for Travel/Activity Surveys.", Transportation Research Procedia, vol. 11, pp. 297-310, 2015.

[2] H. Safi, B. Assemi, M. Mesbah, F. Luis, and H. Mark (2015), "Design and Implementation of a Smartphone-Based System for Personal Travel Survey: Case Study from New Zealand.", In Transportation Research Record: Journal of the Transportation Research Board, vol. 2526, pp. 99-107, 2015.

[3] Q. H. Vu, R. Leung, J. Rong and Y. Miao (2016), "Exploring Park Visitors' Activities in Hong Kong using Geotagged Photos", Information and Communication Technologies in Tourism 2016, pp. 183-196

[4] T. Kurashima, T. Iwata, G. Irie and K. Fujimura (2012), "Travel route recommendation using geotagged photos, Knowledge and Information Systems", vol. 37, No. 1, pp. 37-60, 2012.

[5] MicroSoft Azure, https://azure.microsoft.com/[accessed: 2017.01.29]

[6] Google Maps APIs, https://developers.google.com/maps/[accessed: 2017.01.29]

[7] Transition the number of tourists in Shodo island, http://www.town.shodoshima.lg.jp/oshirase/tyoutyousemi/PDF/shodoshimakankoukyaku-suii.pdf/[accessed: 2017.01.29][in-Japanese]

Development of a GIS-based Spatial Database for the Debris Flow Hazard Assessment of Expressways in South Korea

Min-gi Kim
Institute of Engineering Research
Seoul National University, SNU
Seoul, South Korea
e-mail: beyedsou@snu.ac.kr

Young-woo Song
Department of Civil & Environmental Engineering
Seoul National University, SNU
Seoul, South Korea
e-mail: songyw@snu.ac.kr

Kyung-suk Kim
Expressway and Transportation Research Institute
Korea Expressway Corporation, KEC
Hwaseong, South Korea
e-mail: kskim2k4@ex.co.kr

Kyung-june Lee
Department of Structure & Geotechnical Engineering
Isan Corporation
Anyang, South Korea
e-mail: junk2@hanmail.net

Han-saem Kim
Earthquake Research Center
Korea Institute of Geoscience and Mineral Resources, KIGAM
Daejeon, South Korea
e-mail: adoogen@kigam.re.kr

Choong-ki Chung
Department of Civil & Environmental Engineering
Seoul National University, SNU
Seoul, South Korea
e-mail: geolabs@snu.ac.kr

***Abstract*—In this study, a database based on the geo-information system (GIS) was developed for the debris flow hazard assessment of expressways in South Korea. The debris flow assessment method developed by the Korea Expressway Corporation (KEC) was used for estimating the debris flow hazard grade and for building the database schema. PostgreSQL was selected as a database management system, and PostGIS was used to process the spatial data. The primary information (e.g., expressway, rainfall, digital numerical map, processed information) assess using the KEC method can be standardized and stored in the constructed database. So far, the database was established based on the expressway and debris flow hazard information of 4,478 points along the 22 expressways in South Korea.**

Keywords- Database; debris flow; GIS-based; hazard assessment; expressway.

I. INTRODUCTION

Understanding the mechanism of debris flow is essential for forecasting occurrence and estimating its hazard. There are various factors, however, that affect debris flow occurrence and movement. Many research institutes and national agencies dedicated to mitigating the debris flow hazard have developed their own assessment method [1]-[3]. For instance, Korea Forest Research Institute developed a prediction model for debris flow occurrence and damage, and published a landslide/debris flow hazard map [3]. They highlighted not only the geological, geomorphological, geotechnical, and hydrological factors but also the dendrology factors like the vegetation condition.

Owing to the diversity of the factors affecting debris flow occurrence and movement, developing a debris flow database based on the geo-information system (GIS) has become essential for evaluating the hazard grade in wide regions such as the stations along the expressways. The mapping of the debris flow hazard and the development of a GIS-based database system can be made possible by the use of the constructed debris flow database.

In this study, a debris flow database was developed for the hazard assessment of the mountainous areas near the expressways in South Korea [4]. The database schema was built using the framework for the GIS-based assessment of the debris flow hazard of Korea Express Corporation (KEC). The method developed by KEC focuses on the possibilities of road hazards. The method can be quantitatively and objectively implemented in a simple way by using documents such as numerical maps and expressway design files, minimizing the need for tiresome field investigations on countless potential debris flow occurrence regions in vast areas.

In Section 2, the KEC debris flow hazard analysis method is described. Section 3 describes the database framework for hazard assessment and Section 4 describes the constructed GIS-based database for expressways. Finally the conclusion is provided in Section 5.

II. RESEARCH METHODOLOGY

The KEC debris flow hazard analysis method uses a limited amount of data. Therefore, it is applicable in a national scale. Only digital elevation models (DEMs) and expressway design files of the mountainous area to be assessed are used. The DEMs can be obtained from Korea National Geographic

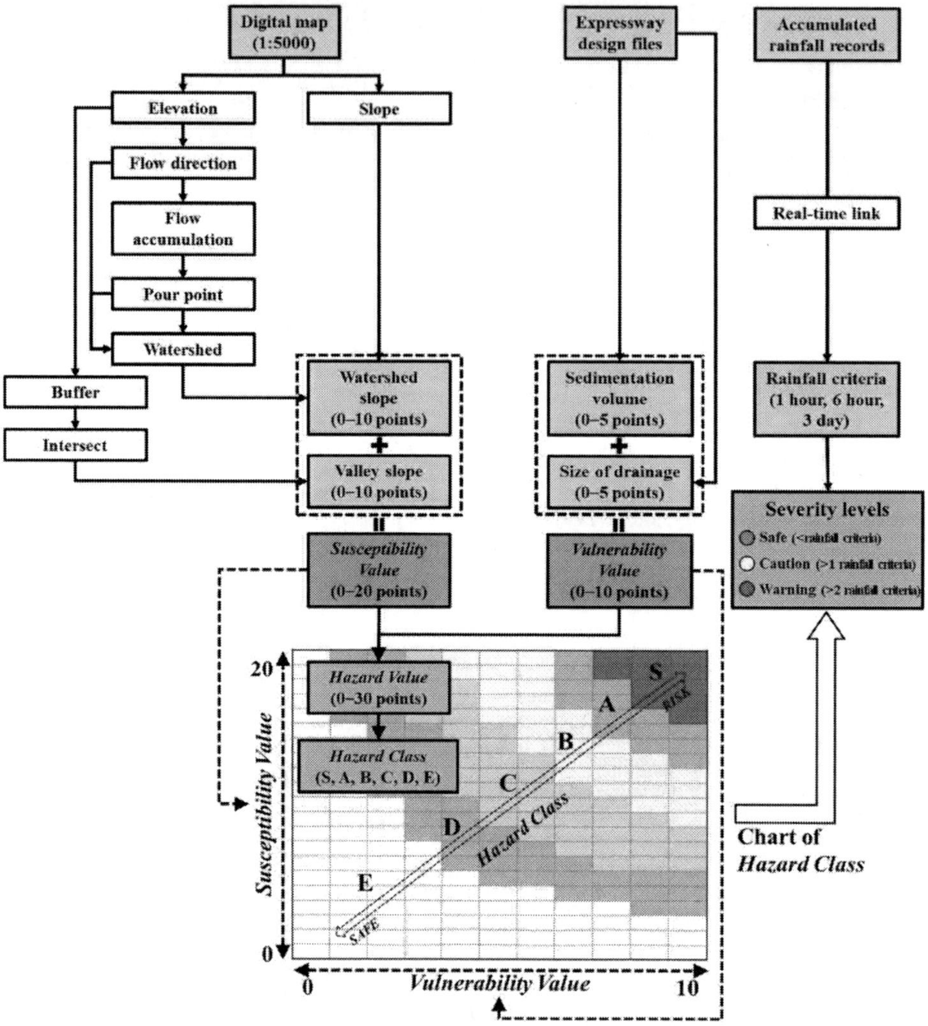

Figure 1. Debris-flow hazard assessment framework for expressways. [5]

Information Institute (KNGII), and the expressway design files can be obtained from KEC.

The debris flow hazard is evaluated using with two indices (Fig. 1): the susceptibility value and vulnerability value. The susceptibility value is the degree of likelihood that a debris flow will occur in the target area whereas the vulnerability value pertains to the degree of likelihood that the occurred debris flow will actually damage or have an impact on the expressway sections.

The susceptibility value is the combination of the debris flow initiation point and the debris flow movement point. For the calculation of the debris flow initiation points, the mean watershed slope degrees and the percentage of watershed over 35° are used. The values of the mean watershed slope degree point and the percentage of watershed over the 35° point are between 0 and 5, respectively. Therefore, the value of the debris flow initiation point is between 0 and 10. For the calculation of the debris flow movement points, the mean valley slope and the length percentage of the valley with slopes over 15° are used. The value of mean valley slope point and the length percentage of valley are between 0 and 5, respectively, and that of the debris flow movement point is between 0 and 10.

In the KEC debris flow hazard assessment method, only the DEMs data are considered for the debris flow possibilities, which are expressed as susceptibility values. The other factors that affect the debris flow possibilities, such as the size and shape of the valley, along with the variations in the slope direction, the properties of the subsoil, and the vegetation, are not used for calculating the susceptibility value for the simplification of the method.

The vulnerability value can be assessed based on the volume of the margin area for depositing debris flow materials before reaching the expressway structures, and the sizes of the drainage facilities running through the expressway. The sedimentation volume attribute, which refers to the volume of the margin area, has a value between 0 and 5, and the size of the drainage attribute is also between 0 and 5. The total vulnerability value can be up to 10 points according to the grading standard.

With the calculated susceptibility and vulnerability values, a hazard class is given for a target expressway section (Fig. 1). The x- and y-axis indicate the vulnerability and susceptibility values, respectively. Based on the results of the investigations of the past debris flow occurrences, the hazard classes were separated by rainfall reoccurrence period for expressway design purposes. Hazard class S indicates the likelihood of debris flow occurrence in areas with 2- to 5-year rainfall reoccurrence periods. Hazard classes A, B, C, and D have 5- to 20-year, 20- to 50-year, 50- to 100-year, and over-100-year rainfall reoccurrence periods, respectively. Hazard class E indicates an area with a very low likelihood of debris flow damage [4]-[6].

III. DEBRIS FLOW HAZARD ASSESSMENT DATABASE FRAMEWORK

For data storage and debris flow hazard management, a database was developed. The developed database can be called "geodatabase (GDB)" because it is a container for spatial and attribute data. PostgreSQL (Ver. 9.5) was chosen for the database management system (DBMS), and PostGIS was used to assign the spatial attributes of the expressways. PostGIS is a specified extension function of PostgreSQL for storing GIS objects. It provides spatial objects for the PostgreSQL database, allowing the storage of and query on information about location and mapping [7][8].

Fig. 2 shows the structure of the geodatabase for debris flow hazard assessment. The database basically contains information on two information classes: primary information and processed information. Primary information stores not only general expressway, and rainfall information but also digital numerical-map data. The basic topographical information, which is used for calculating the susceptibility value of the hazard assessment system, is derived from the digital numerical-map data. The expressway information is composed of organization information used to manage the

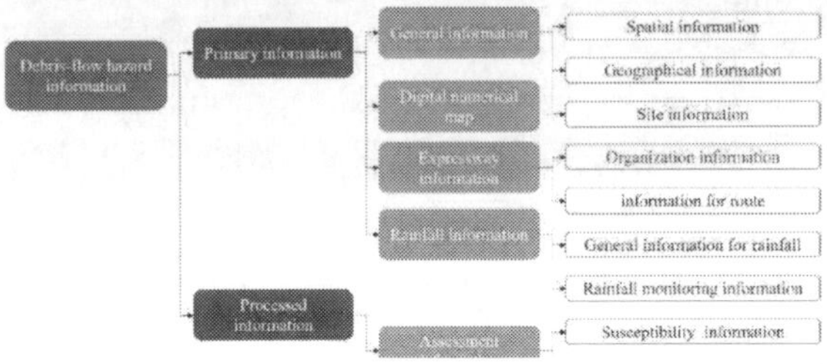

Figure 2. Structure of the database for debris flow hazard assessment.

South Korean expressway route data and spatial information. The rainfall information data format has also been standardized. The rainfall data from automatic weather station (AWS) is essential to the real-time debris flow warning system combined with the hazard assessment system.

Using the standardized primary information data, hazard assessment of the target area can be performed. After that, the results of the hazard assessment, such as the hazard class, susceptibility value, and vulnerability value, should again be stored in the database.

IV. GIS-BASED DATABASE CONSTRUCTION FOR THE EXPRESSWAYS IN SOUTH KOREA

The database construction procedure consists of four parts.

Figure 3. Data collection from the field survey.

First, a field survey is conducted (Fig. 3). The susceptibility value of the hazard assessment system can be computed with only the topographic data from the digital numerical map. A field survey should be conducted, however, to calculate the vulnerability value.

Moreover, it is possible to confirm the factors that need to be considered when calculating the susceptibility value with the naked eyes in the field survey. This helps confirm the accuracy of the susceptibility assessment result.

After the field survey, the result should be reported in a fixed form. The report includes not only the field survey result but also the debris flow hazard class, which was determined

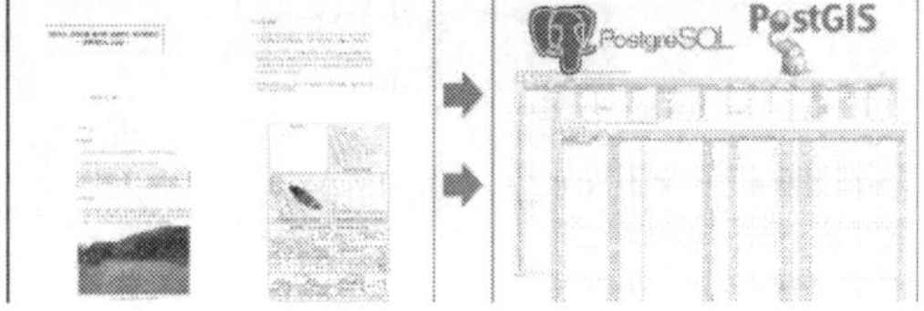

Figure 4. Reporting of results and building of the database.

using the KEC debris flow hazard assessment method. The spatial data, field survey data, and hazard assessment results of the target point were standardized to construct a database using PostgreSQL and PostGIS (Fig. 4).

The data stored in the debris flow hazard database can be inquired about and visualized with the GIS system. In this study, the representative open-source GIS system Quantum GIS (QGIS, version 2.14.3-Essen) desktop was utilized for visualization (Fig. 5) [9]. The green dots indicate the target points for the debris flow hazard assessment along the expressways in South Korea. The information on the debris flow hazard assessment results and field survey results of 4,478 debris flow risk sites along the 22 expressways is being stored in the developed debris flow hazard database up to now. The blue dots mark the 676 AWS points for collecting rainfall data.

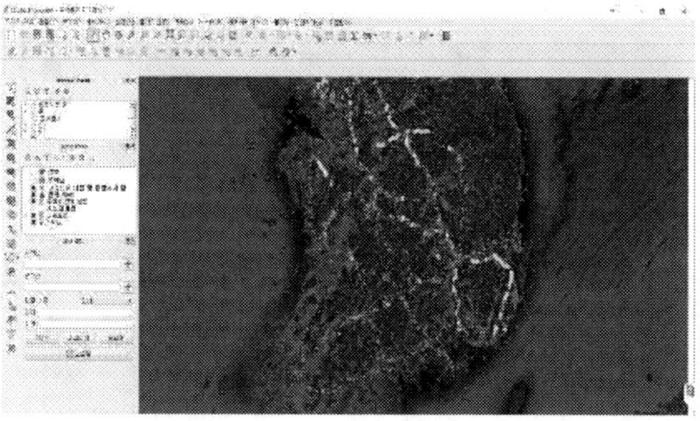

Figure 5. Visualization of the constructed database using Quantum-GIS.

Then, the QGIS plugin was developed to display the picture of the target site and the countermeasurement plan of the debris flow hazard areas (see Fig. 6 and Fig. 7). The

Figure 6. The QGIS plugin for displaying local pictures.

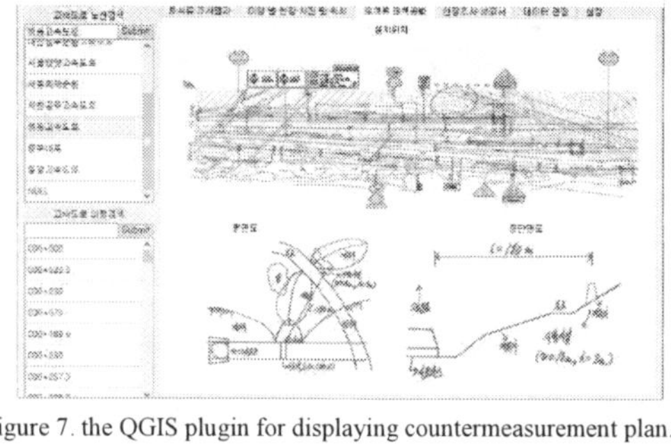

Figure 7. the QGIS plugin for displaying countermeasurement plan.

programming language Python was used to develop the plugins [9][10].

V. CONCLUSIONS

For the effective debris flow hazard management of the expressways in South Korea, a database based on the geo-information system was constructed. To assess the debris flow hazard of the target points along the expressways, the Korea Express Corporation (KEC) method was adapted. The database schema and structure were based on the factors that need to be considered when estimating the hazard grade with the KEC method.

The general information, digital numerical map, expressway information, and rainfall information were standardized. Then the processed information, such as the susceptibility information, vulnerability, and the hazard class information, of a target point were again stored in the database.

Various open-source GIS tools were utilized to construct the database. PostgreSQL and PostGIS provided a database frame for handling the spatial attributes. Moreover, QGIS provided a visualization platform for mapping and inquiring about the information.

The constructed database was used for debris flow assessment on 4,478 points along the 22 expressways in South Korea. Various countermeasurements were applied to the sites estimated to be hazardous among them.

ACKNOWLEDGMENT

This research was supported by a National Research Foundation of Korea grant funded by the South Korean government's MSIP (No.2015R1A5A7037372)

REFERENCES

[1] P. Lin, J. Lin, J. Hung, and M. Yang, "Assessing debris-flow hazard in a watershed in Taiwan. Engineering Geology 66, pp. 295-313, 2002.

[2] D. Park, N. V. Nikhil, and S. Lee, "Landslide and debris flow susecptibility zonatino using TRGRS for the 2011 Seoul landslide even, Nat. Hazards Earth Syst. Sci., no. 13, pp. 2833-2849, 2013.

[3] H. Yun, et al., "Development of prediction model for the occurrence and damage of debris flow", Korea Forest Research Institute. Research Report 09-20: pp. 92-107, 2009 (In Korean)

[4] Expressway & Transportation Research Institute, Korea Expressway Corportation, "Development of debris flow hazard analysis method and its application", Korea Expressway Corporation Report, 2009 (In Korean)

[5] H. Kim, C. Chung, S. Kim, and K. Kim, "A GIS-Based Framework for Real-Time Debris-Flow Hazard Assessment for Expressways in Korea", Int J Disaster Risk Sci 7: pp. 293-311, 2016.

[6] S. Kim, H. Kim, G. Kim, and C. Chung, "Debris-flow Risk Assessment along Expressways in Korea using GIS", Geohazards 2014, Kathmandu, Nephal, pp. 159-163, 2014

[7] "PostgreSQL: The world's most advanced open source database", http://www.postgresql.org [6, 2016]

[8] "PostGIS: Spatial and Geographic Objects for PoestgreSQL", http://www.postgis.net [6, 2016]

[9] "QGIS(Quantum GIS version 2.14.3-Essen): A free and open source geographic information system", http://www.qgis.org [4, 2016]

[10] "PyQGIS Developer Cookbook": http:www.docs.qgis.org/testing/en/docs/pyqgis_developer_cookbook/ [6, 2016]

A Markov Chain Monte Carlo Cellular Automata Model to Simulate Urban Growth

Ahmed Mustafa[1,2,*], Gen Nishida[2], Ismaïl Saadi[1], Mario Cools[1], Jacques Teller[1]
[1]Local Environment Management & Analysis, ArGEnCo, University of Liège, Belgium
[2]Computer science department, Purdue University, USA
*Email: a.mustafa@ulg.ac.be, a-mustafa@purdue.edu

***Abstract*— This paper investigates the potential of a cellular automata (CA) model based on logistic regression (logit) and Markov Chain Monte Carlo (MCMC) to simulate the dynamics of urban growth. The model assesses urbanization likelihood based on (i) a set of urban development driving forces (calibrated based on logit) and (ii) the land-use of neighboring cells (calibrated based on MCMC). An innovative feature of this CA model is the incorporation of MCMC to automatically calibrate the CA neighborhood transition rules. The MCMC based CA model is applied to Wallonia region (Belgium) to simulate urban growth from 1990 to 2000 using Corine Land Cover data (CLC). The outcome of logit model is evaluated by the relative operating characteristic (ROC). The simulated map of 2000 is then validated against 2000 actual map based on cell-to-cell location agreement. The model outcomes are realistic and relatively accurate confirming the effectiveness of the proposed MCMC-CA approach.**

Keywords- cellular automata; Markov chain Monte Carlo; logistic regression.

I. INTRODUCTION

Among the various urbanization modelling approaches, the cellular automata approach has gained popularity for urban modelling. Since the pioneering work of Tobler [1], there has been considerable interest in modifying standard CA models to make them more suitable for urban modelling [2]–[4]. Key challenges in CA are calibrating the transition rules. Early methods for CA calibration were based on trial and error [5] and/or a visual test, to determine the model's parameters. Recently, a variety of automated methods based on statistics [6], machine learning [7], artificial neural networks [8] and optimization algorithms [9] have begun to be widely employed. This paper contributes to such automated calibration methods by using MCMC to calibrate CA neighborhood transition rules.

In this paper, CA model is employed to simulate urban growth based on urbanization probability of a cell according to a number of driving forces of urban growth and state of the cell and its neighbors. Logit method is used to calibrate the driving forces parameters whereas MCMC is used to calibrate neighborhood rules.

This paper is structured as follows. Section II presents the study area. Section III describes the CA model. Section IV gives and discusses the results. Finally, Section V presents our conclusions.

II. STUDY AREA

The study area is located in southern Belgium (Wallonia region). It accounts for 55% of the territory of Belgium with a total area of 16,844 km². The main metropolitan areas are Charleroi, Liège, Mons, and Namur (Fig. 1). They are all characterized by a historical city-center, around which the urban development expanded.

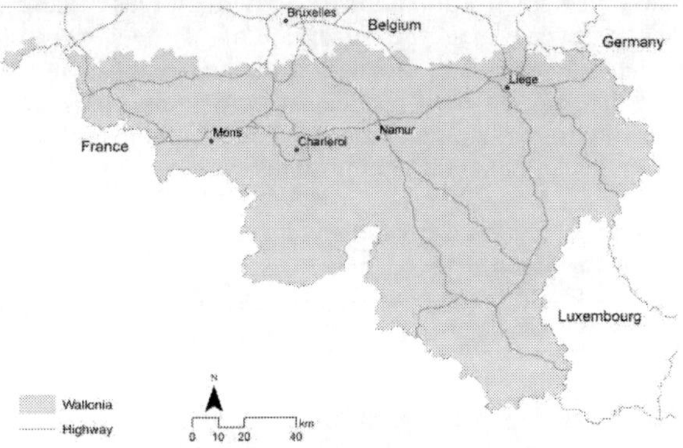

Figure 1. Study area.

The total population in 2010 was 3,498,384 inhabitants that makes up a third of Belgium population.

III. METHODS

The initial state of the simulation starts from land-use in 1990 and proceeds to simulate an urban growth of 2000. The analysis of land-use change is based on the CLC with resolution of 100×100m for the years 1990 and 2000. The 44 classes of CLC datasets have been reclassified into 7 classes (urban lands, arable lands, grasslands, forests, wetlands, water bodies and others). The quantity of change was constrained to the actual quantity of new urban cells in 1990-2000 divided evenly by 10 (the number of years).

The quantity of change is spatially allocated based on two decision rules. The first rule set concerns the main urban growth driving forces, using logit. The second decision rule deals with the neighborhood interactions, using MCMC. The input dependent variable (Y) for logit model is a binary map of the actual non-urban/urban changes within 1990-2000. The independent variables (Xn) are distance to roads, distance to major cities, slope, access to jobs, and zoning. All Xn do not take into account neighboring regions or states.

All Xn are standardized and show a very low degree of multicollinearity (variance inflation factors ranging from 1.01 to 2.76). Logit is calibrated using a random sample of 50,000 cells in order to minimize spatial autocorrelation. MCMC is used to calibrate neighborhood interaction which is arranged in five square distances from the cell. We use the most popular MCMC formulation based on the Metropolis-Hastings algorithm that yields a sequence of samples whose stationary distribution eventually converges to a specified probability density function. The objective function of the MCMC is the maximization of cell-to-cell (CTC) location agreement. The sample with higher score is sampled more than the sample with lower score. In this manner, the algorithm smartly samples from a parameter space, and the global optimal solution can be obtained in a relatively small number of runs.

IV. Results and Discussions

Table I lists logit calibration of driving forces. These coefficients reveal that the location of a new urban development is strongly correlated with the zoning status. Distances to different road classes and cities also play an important role in explaining urban development at a specific location but far less than the zoning status.

TABLE I. COEFFICIENT VALUES OF THE DRIVING FACTORS.

Driving factor	*Coefficient*
Intercept (constant)	-0.9816
Slope	0.0002
Dist to cities	-0.1982
Dist to highway	-0.1962
Dist to major roads	-0.2292
Dist to secondry roads	-0.3185
Dist to local roads	-0.5677
Access to jobs	0.0004
Zoning	2.6809

The weights calibrated by MCMC that defines the neighborhood interactions are illustrated in Fig. 2. The calibration shows that the impact of existing urban lands on new urban development is extremely significant, whereas other land-uses have far less effect than urban land in the immediate neighborhood of the cell. The neighborhood effect is strongest in the immediate neighborhood of the cell, decreases and becomes neutral at a distance of around 5 cells.

The ROC value of the probability map, generated by logit, is 0.78. The cell-to-cell location agreement is 32.75%.

V. Conclusion

This paper presents a CA model based on MCMC. The MCMC allows to automate the calibration of the model without losing flexibility and analysis capability. The model is calibrated based on the observed urban growth in 1990–2000 and used to simulate 2010 urban growth in Wallonia.

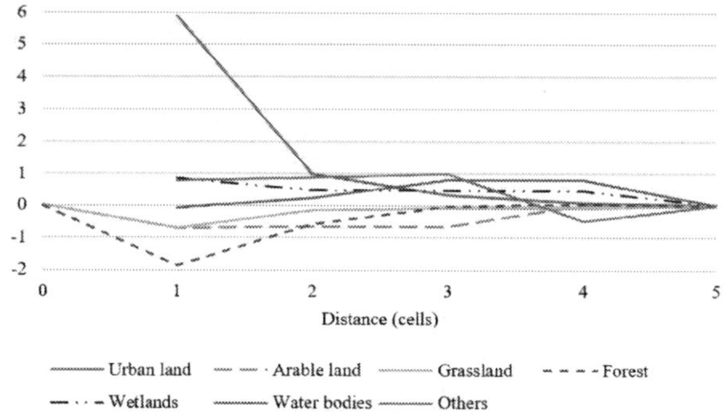

Figure 2. Weighting parameters (Y axis) that represent the interaction between an urban cell and other land-uses

The cell-to-cell location agreement, which measures for the new urban cells in the 1990-2000, is similar to the numbers reported for the best performing CA urban models. The results confirm that MCMC is a method with great potential for urban CA calibration.

Acknowledgment

The research was funded through the ARC grant for Concerted Research Actions, financed by the Wallonia-Brussels Federation.

References

[1] W. R. Tobler, "Cellular Geography," in *Philosophy in Geography*, S. Gale and G. Olsson, Eds. Springer Netherlands, 1979, pp. 379–386.

[2] K. C. Clarke and L. J. Gaydos, "Loose-coupling a cellular automaton model and GIS: long-term urban growth prediction for San Francisco and Washington/Baltimore," *Int. J. Geogr. Inf. Sci.*, vol. 12, no. 7, pp. 699–714, 1998.

[3] D. Guan, et al., "Modeling urban land use change by the integration of cellular automaton and Markov model," *Ecol. Model.*, vol. 222, no. 20–22, pp. 3761–3772, 2011.

[4] A. Mustafa, M. Cools, I. Saadi, and J. Teller, "Urban Development as a Continuum: A Multinomial Logistic Regression Approach," in *Computational Science and Its Applications -- ICCSA 2015*, O. Gervasi, B. Murgante, S. Misra, M. L. Gavrilova, A. M. A. C. Rocha, C. Torre, D. Taniar, and B. O. Apduhan, Eds. Springer International Publishing, 2015, pp. 729–744.

[5] R. White and G. Engelen, "Cellular Automata as the Basis of Integrated Dynamic Regional Modelling," *Environ. Plan. B Plan. Des.*, vol. 24, no. 2, pp. 235–246, 1997.

[6] A. M. García, I. Santé, M. Boullón, and R. Crecente, "Calibration of an urban cellular automaton model by using statistical techniques and a genetic algorithm. Application to a small urban settlement of NW Spain," *Int. J. Geogr. Inf. Sci.*, vol. 27, no. 8, pp. 1593–1611, 2013.

[7] A. Rienow and R. Goetzke, "Supporting SLEUTH – Enhancing a cellular automaton with support vector machines for urban growth modeling," *Comput. Environ. Urban Syst.*, vol. 49, pp. 66–81, 2015.

[8] S. Berberoğlu, A. Akın, and K. C. Clarke, "Cellular automata modeling approaches to forecast urban growth for adana, Turkey: A comparative approach," *Landsc. Urban Plan.*, vol. 153, pp. 11–27, 2016.

[9] K. Al-Ahmadi, L. See, A. Heppenstall, and J. Hogg, "Calibration of a fuzzy cellular automata model of urban dynamics in Saudi Arabia," *Ecol. Complex.*, vol. 6, no. 2, pp. 80–101, 2009.

Towards Smart Urban Planning through Knowledge Infrastructure

Robert Laurini
LIRIS – INSA Lyon, University of Lyon, France, and Knowledge Systems Institute, USA.
e-mail: Roberto.Laurini@gmail.com

***Abstract* — In companies, the use of the so-called business intelligence and knowledge engineering is more and more commonly found. By essence, companies are using computer tools, which tends to include them in the knowledge society; from a mathematical point of view, knowledge representation is made through rules and logics. And then comes the question: what could be done in this direction for urban planning? The big challenge is to deal with urban and environmental features which are usually described, stored and manipulated via computational geometry and spatial analysis. But those disciplines cannot easily be combined with logics. The goal of this position paper is to show how knowledge engineering can be the foundation of a new type of urban planning, *i.e.*, urban planning based on knowledge. Geographic knowledge bunches are usually described through geographic objects, relations, structures, ontologies, gazetteers, rules and mathematical models. After having explained those bunches of knowledge, the structure of a geographic inference engine is sketched so to renovate urban planning. Then beyond Spatial Data Infrastructure, we explain that some geographic knowledge infrastructure could be the basis of a new generation of tools for urban planning.**

Keywords — Smart City, Territorial Intelligence; Geographic Knowledge; Knowledge Infrastructure; Geographic Rules; Smart Planning; Geographic Reasoning.

I. INTRODUCTION

In many domains, it is more and more common to speak about knowledge and even the expression "knowledge society" was coined. Several definitions have been proposed to outline this new type of human society. According to a 2005 UNESCO report [21], "Knowledge societies are about capabilities to identify, produce, process, transform, disseminate and use information to build and apply knowledge for human development. They require an empowering social vision that encompasses plurality, inclusion, solidarity and participation". Starting from this definition, it could be interesting to examine how knowledge can improve not only the management of a city but also urban planning at large. The goal of this position paper is to give a few directions for renovating urban planning through knowledge engineering especially by modeling geographic rules.

Of course, humans are at the center of smart city, but the use of knowledge technologies can help amplify human reasoning not only by studying alternatives of urban development, but also evaluating the consequences in various terms, human, societal, financial, etc. When we say humans, we do not only mean experts in urban planning but also lay-citizens who can influence decisions (public participation or participatory democracy).

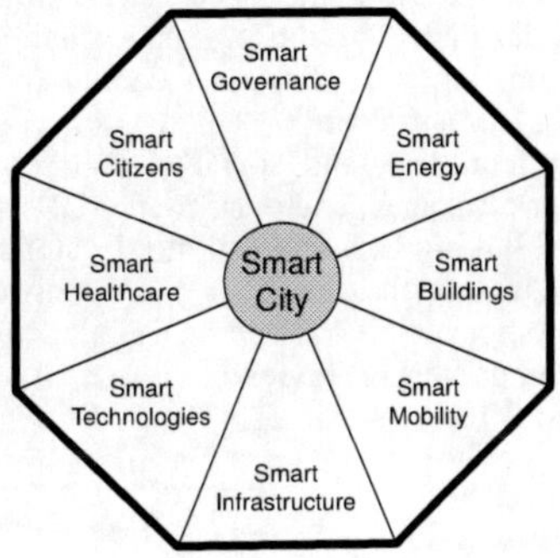

Figure 1. The Smart City components according to Mathew's diamond (2013) [26].

From practically half a century, information technology has profoundly transformed urban planning. Initially, it was only for some statistics and mathematical modeling of cities [6] and then for map-making. During a few years, the expression "computer-assisted cartography" was used, emphasizing how computers could help the automatic creation of maps. At the end of 70s, it became obvious that automatic cartography must be seen differently, and geographic or urban data must be stored into databases. Then the expression "GIS" was coined for software systems able not only to store geographic data, to make maps but also integrating tools devoted to spatial analysis. As a consequence, urban planning has gradually been renovated [14], first by data then by information and now by knowledge [17].

The paper will by organized as follows; first, several definitions will be analyzed in order to sketch smart urban planning [7]. Then, we will examine the promises of knowledge engineering technologies for renovating urban planning.

II. DEFINITIONS REGARDING SMART CITIES AND TERRITORIAL INTELLIGENCE

Many definitions have been proposed to define both smart cities and territorial intelligence. They have in common the integration of sustainable development.

About Smart Cities

Carlo Ratti, director of the MIT Senseable City Lab, claims that an intelligent or smart city is technological, interconnected, clean, attractive, comforting, efficient, open, collaborative, creative, digital and green. The European Union considers six components: economy, mobility, environmental, people, living, governance to shape a Smart City. This latter definition was extended by Mathew [18] illustrated Fig. 1 as a form of a diamond connecting Smart Governance, Smart Citizens, Smart Healthcare, Smart Energy, Smart Buildings, Smart Technology, Smart Infrastructures and Smart Mobility.

According to [13], "Smart cities are the result of knowledge-intensive and creative strategies aiming at enhancing the socio-economic, ecological, logistic and competitive performance of cities. Such smart cities are based on a promising mix of human capital (e.g., skilled labor force), infrastructural capital (e.g., high-tech communication facilities), and social capital (e.g., intense and open network linkages) and entrepreneurial capital (e.g,. creative and risk-taking business activities". Notice that the last definition stresses the importance of knowledge in a smart city. For other definitions and analysis, please refer to [1] for a very comprehensive review.

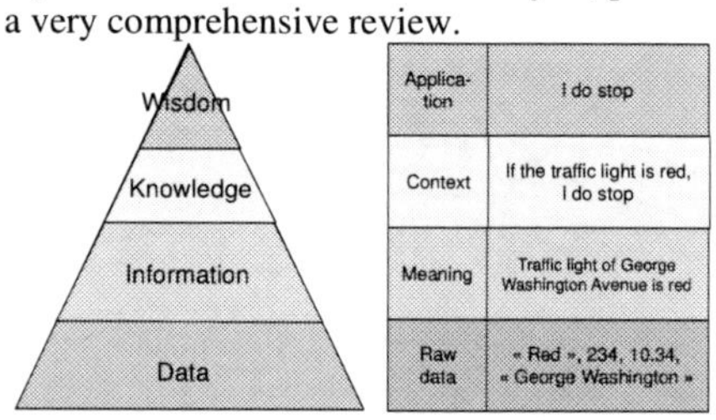

Figure 2. Data, information, knowledge and wisdom.

In order to plan and manage a city, a novel way is through knowledge engineering [15] which require the design and implementation of a knowledge infrastructure. Remember (Fig. 2) that "data" are raw measures, "information" concerns data with their meaning and "knowledge" an information which can be useful to solve a problem. Moreover by applying knowledge, a sort of wisdom can be reached. Fig. 3 illustrates the role of this knowledge infrastructure in a smart city which is based on a physical layer integrating communications, sensors and data.

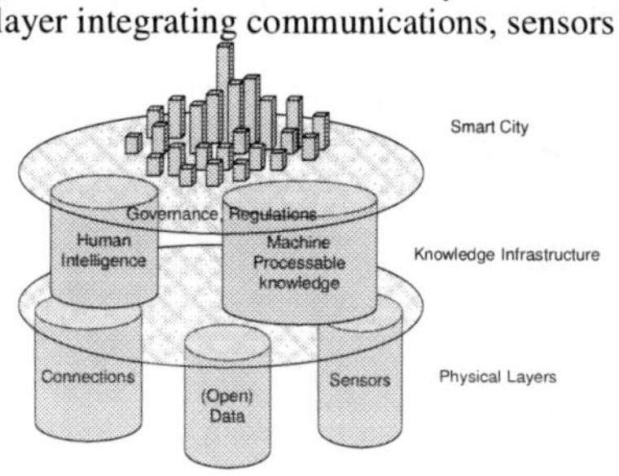

Figure 3. Position of a knowledge infrastructure in a smart city.

For years, in companies business rules are been a common way to encode knowledge. According to Graham [9] and Morgan [19], rules (business rules) should be considered as first-class citizens in computer science. In enterprises, the "craft" of expert know-how is capitalized in a computer system in the form of so-called "business rules". These rules can then be explained and implemented in applications, such as business intelligence in software architectures often named ERP (Enterprise Resource Planning). Two forms are common IF-THEN-Fact or IF-THEN-Action. For instance, let us consider a newly-designed building. In order to check whether it must comply with the local Master Plan, several rules must be followed as exemplified Fig. 4.

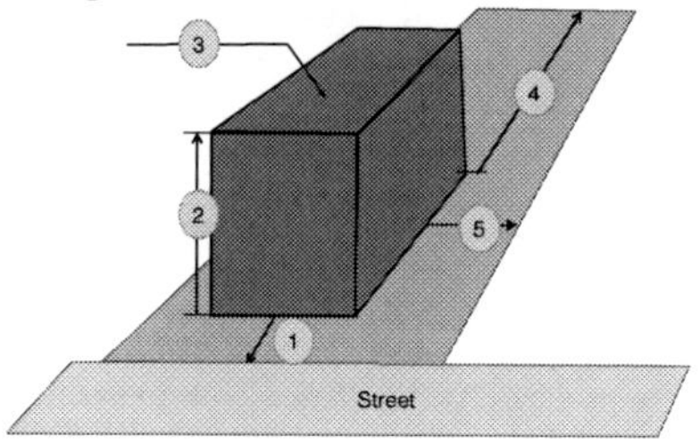

Figure 4. Example of building-related planning rules.

In Fig. 4, Rule 1 gives the minimum distance to the road, Rule 2, the maximum height of the building, Rule 3 the volume of the building, Rule 4 the distance to the end of plot and the 5, the distance with neighbors. Here, to be valid (accepted according to the meaning of the regulation), the building project must comply with this complete set of rules.

About Territorial Intelligence

As the concept of "Smart Cities" focuses on cities, "the concept of "Territorial Intelligence" has a larger meaning. Considering it, also several definitions can be quoted. According to [5], "Territorial Intelligence can be compared with the territoriality which results from the phenomenon of appropriation of resources of a territory; it consists in know-how transmissions between categories of local actors of different cultures." this definition was extended later [8] by specifying that territorial intelligence innovations must include: (*i*) use of multidisciplinary knowledge, (*ii*) dynamic vision of territories, (*iii*) involvement of communities and practitioners, (*iv*) sharing, co-constructing and (*v*) cooperating and participatory territorial governance.

For our part, let me propose the following definitions [17], "**Territorial intelligence can be defined as an approach regulating a territory (maybe a city) which is planned and managed by the cross-fertilization of human collective intelligence and artificial intelligence for its sustainable development**".

And now the question is "how artificial intelligence and especially knowledge engineering can help not only local decision-makers to plan city but also lay citizens to give their opinion about the future of their city [15], [17]?"

Smart Urban Planning

Smart Urban Planning can be seen as a possible answer. Similarly several visions are possible, among others [2] and [7], by having all three facets, sustainable development, greater involvement of citizens and major use of technologies. By examining the difference between the words smart and intelligent, the authors of [7] explain that the adjective intelligent seems to imply the capability of developing actions in order to solve a problem by using methods and information contained into a knowledge base whereas the word smart seems to have, apart from the cognitive heritage (even if not organized in analytical way), also the power of solving the problem "operatively", showing which are the "tools" to be used for the specific purpose. Summing up, while the intelligent thinks, works out and suggests the models to adopt in order to find a solution, the smart shows also the operative way and the devices to use.

Let us examine rapidly an introductory example. In [22], an example of rule encoding is given concerning road naming in Australia in order to automate the process. Rules are defined in the form of ontological vocabularies using SWRL. However they have some limitations. For instance in one rule, the road length which must be taken into account, is given as an attribute, not computed from road coordinates. In another, a panoramic view is also given as an attribute, not calculated taken terrain morphology into account by 3D computational geometry.

III. PROMISES OF GEOGRAPHIC KNOWLEDGE

As previously told, geographic knowledge must be multidisciplinary. One of the ways to represent knowledge is by using rules. In planning, the rules have the following origins, physical (water, floods, vegetation, landslides, etc.), societal (economy, etc.), administrative (laws, decrees, etc.) or even from best practices. In addition, other rules can be extracted from spatial data mining [17], [18].

One of the difficulties is the fact that among the urban actors, some have different "logics". With regard to industry creation, an environmentalist or an industrialist may have different ideas on the possible implications of this or that choice. Similarly, some groups may have different priorities: before an empty space, athletes imagine a stadium; pupil's parents a school; and a realtor a building, etc. From a formal point of view, these aspects will occur in multi-actor and multi-criteria decision support systems.

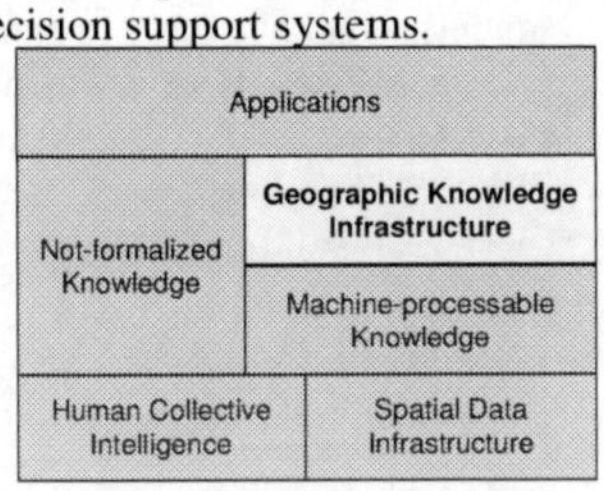

Figure 5. Geographic Knowledge Infrastructure.

After the book edited by Kim *et al.* (1989) [12], in their paper, Batty and Yeh (1991) [3] exposed the promises of so-called expert systems for urban planning. In that period, those systems were only built on logics characterized by the difficulty to use them and by limited interfaces. Now, 25 years after, with the evolutions of information technologies, artificial intelligence and geovisualization, new approaches can be integrated to design new kinds of intelligent systems especially devoted to geographic applications and overall urban planning. Let us call them geographic inference engine which will be able to make reasoning about geographic knowledge. Whereas a conventional inference engine is only based on logics, such a system must integrate topology, computational geometry, statistics and spatial analysis because geographic rules necessitate those aspects to be modeled.

Advocacy for Geographic Knowledge Infrastructure

Based on this background, it is possible to define a Geographic Knowledge Infrastructure I17]. From decades, governments, national or local, have developed spatial data infrastructures. Similarly, it is possible to envision geographic knowledge infrastructure (Fig. 5) as bunches of knowledge necessary to developed higher level applications, those bunches coming either from data mining over the spatial data infrastructure or from human collective intelligence able to be formalized in a machine-processable format. Of course, many bunches cannot be yet formalized.

Chunks of low level knowledge will be directly detailed into chapters dealing with geographic objects and relations whereas high level knowledge more studied in the geographic rule chapter as a basis for territorial intelligence, and smart city planning and governance.

Requirements for Geographic Knowledge Systems

In order to get a well-done geographic system, there are some requirements to follow: (*i*) offering a relevant and complete representation of reality, (*ii*) offering a robust and accurate representation for any granularity of interest, (*iii*) storing consistent and validated knowledge, (*iv*) updating regularly, (*v*) supporting geographic reasoning, (*vi*) representing any shareholder's logics, (*vii*) combining GKB coming from different sources, and (*vii*) defining planning projects and assessing them.

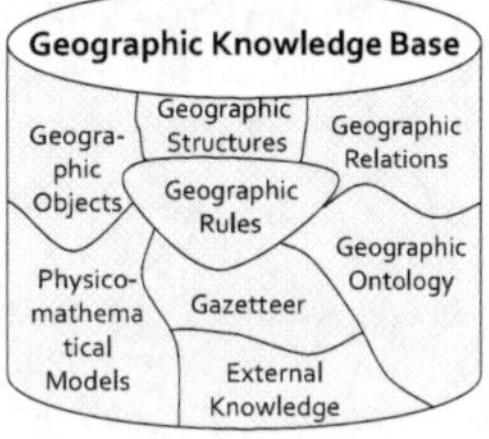

Figure 6. Contents of a geographic knowledge base

GKS Components

In consequence, any geographic knowledge base will consist of Fig. 6 a set of geographic objects, a set of geographic relations, an ontology, a gazetteer, a set of geographic structures, a set of physico-mathematical models and a set of rules; in addition, external knowledge can also be very useful; let us explain those components. For more details, please refer to [17].

Geographic Objects: Features existing in the real world (rivers, roads, parcels, buildings, engineering networks, etc.) can be modeled with types, names, attributes and geometric coordinates by points, lines and areas. Often 3D information can be taken into account. Often fuzzy sets can be invoked to model objects with undefined boundaries, such as mountains or deserts. One of the big problems is that the same geographic object can have different geometric representations (Fig. 7).

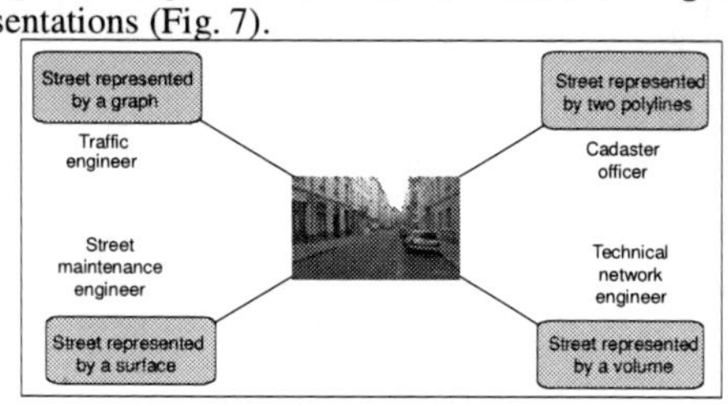

Figure 7. Various geometric representations of a street.

Geographic Relations: Between geographic objects, the majority of relations can be defined based to topological relations (overlapping, etc.) such as Egenhofer relations [6]. But some others can be defined (administrative relations, twinning relations, etc.).
Geographic ontologies: An ontology is a semantic network or a graph between concepts. For us, essentially, geographic ontologies are organizing geographic types. More and more geographic ontologies integrate geographic relations; for instance, an example in urban planning integrates 254 concepts organized into five levels [20].

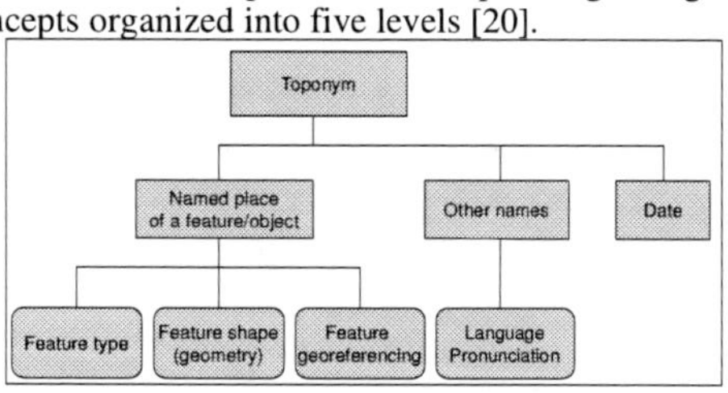

Figure 8. Example of structure of a gazetteer after [10].

Gazetteers: Initially a gazetteer is a dictionary of placenames (toponyms). Since there are complex many-to-many relationships between names and places, since places can change names over time, can change their shape (compare Rome in Romulus' time and now), can absorb other places, etc. And the same name can be assigned to different places. See Fig.8 for an example of gazetteer's structure [10]. Now gazetteers tend to become databases of names with links with ontologies. See [11] for more details concerning gazetteers.
Sets of geographic structures: Two types of structures are common, tessellations and networks, which have specific relations between their components. A country is divided in regions, provinces, etc. which form a tessellation and city into quarters. Often hierarchical tessellations must be considered. The structure of networks is very common. Among them, let mention, road networks, river networks and engineering networks such as for electricity, gas, telephone, sewerage and for the management of traffic lights. In addition, several urban structures can derived from shape grammars such as the organization of city blocks, allotments, etc.
Physico-mathematical models: A lot of knowledge regarding environmental planning, transportation planning and demography is encapsulated into models. It is important to use this already-existing knowledge into this novel system. In addition, there could be added more sophisticated models for multi-criteria decision-making and spatial analysis.
Geographic Rules: As rapidly explained, rules are the key-element for knowledge management since due to rules, new objects can be created, new values can be assigned to attributes, new relationships can be set, etc. Moreover, since often rules can be applied successively, they can represent a sort of chain of causality (*A=> B*, *B => C*, etc.). More details can be found in [24, 25]. In fact, let us look at some of them:

- in the United Kingdom, we drive on the left;
- in Canada, the majority of the population lives along the border with the United States;
- each capital city has an international airport nearby;
- between the two capital cities, in general, there are direct flights;
- in the Northern Hemisphere, the more you are going to the north, the colder (but locally this is not always true);
- the more you climb a mountain, the colder;
- heavy rain upstream, downstream flooding;
- mosques are oriented towards Mecca;
- if a zone is a swamp, it is necessary to prohibit construction;
- if there is unemployment, the creation of companies or industrial areas must be encouraged;
- if a plot is adjacent to an airport, it is necessary to limit the height of buildings;
- it is forbidden to open a new tobacco shop within 500 meters of an another already existing;
- when you want to install a metro-line under a street, please move underground networks to another place;
- a good practice in Mexico is to use a bus to go from Puebla to Oaxaca City.

$\forall B \in PROJECT, \exists P \in GO$ $\Omega\text{-}Type(B) =$ "Building", $\Omega\text{-}Type(P) = $ "Parcels", $Contains\ (Geom(P), Geom(B))$: $Height(B) < 10$ $\wedge Street\_distance(B, P) > 3$ $\wedge Neighbor\_distance(B, P) > 3$ $\Rightarrow$ $UP\text{-}Allowed\ (B, P)$	Rule 1

Back to Fig. 5, the following [Rule 1) rule can be written. For instance, suppose that the building in project is described with BIM (Building Information Management) language from which procedures can be applied to compute *Height*, *Street_distance* and *Neighbor_distance*. In this rule, *GO* means the set of stored geographic objects with the knowledge base, and *PROJECT*, the set of currents projects.

Ω-Type means the ontological type and *Contains* corresponds to the Egenhofer relation [6].

Another example of rule is given in Fig. 9 illustrating the case of a city in a country in which a rule stipulates that it is forbidden to open a new tobacco shop within less than 500 meters from another one. In this case, some buffer zones around the existing tobacco shop must be defined. And the places where it is possible to open a new pharmacy are given via a set of geometric operations.

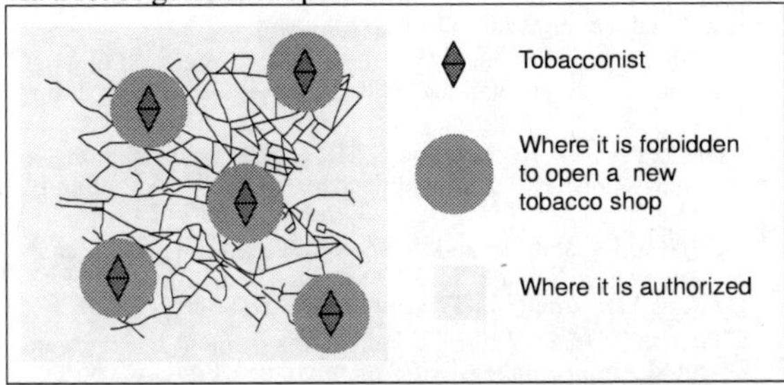

Figure 9. Example of administrative rule: "it is forbidden to open a new tobacco shop within 500 meters from another existing one".

This rule can be formalized as follows:

$\forall F_i \in OG, \exists Z \in Terr,$ $G\text{-}Type(F_i)=Point,\ G\text{-}Type(Z)=Area,$ $\Omega\text{-}Type(F_i)$ = "Tobacco_Shop", $Geom\ (F_i) \in Terr$ $\Rightarrow$ $Geom(Z)= Terr - Union(Buffer(F_i,\ 500))$	Rule 3

In which in addition, *Terr* is a territory; G-*Type* is the geometric type; *Geom* the geometry of an object; *Union* and *Buffer* respectively geometric operations for determining union and buffer; and Z, the zone in which it is allowed to open a new tobacco shop.

The rules can have several origins; the more important are given by experts and some of them can be extracted from spatial data mining under the name of association rules. Various categories can be distinguished: (*i*) Geodetic rules relative to North, South, East and West; (*ii*) Physical geography (sun, flood, winds, vegetation, etc.); (*iii*) Rules coming from laws (see building example given Figure 5, or such as "in UK, one drives left"); (*iv*) Rules coming from sociology or economy such as "along the edges of sea, the greater the distance from the sea, the lower are prices of homes", "the more children, the more schools", or "all big cities have an international airport"; (*v*) Rules relative to flows (transportation of humans, freight); (*vi*) Rules coming from best practices; (*vii*) Rules linked to quality control, mutation of topological relations due to scales (for instance, depending of the scale, a road touches or not a lake); (*viii*) Facing the same situation, some shareholders can have different rules; see an example in Rule 4; (*ix*) Some local rules can supersede global rules, for instance when municipal level rules different from state rules, Etc.

$\forall P \in GO, \forall B \in PROJECT,$ $\Omega\text{-}Type(P)$ = "Parcels", *P.Landuse* = "Vacant": $Area(P) > 1000$		Rule 4
For an environmentalist	$\Rightarrow \Omega\text{-}Type(B)$ = "Recreational_Park"	
For a sportsman	$\Rightarrow \Omega\text{-}Type(B)$ = "Stadium"	
For parents of pupils	$\Rightarrow \Omega\text{-}Type(B)$ = "School"	
For The Chamber of Commerce	$\Rightarrow \Omega\text{-}Type(B)$ = "Start_up_Facility"	
For a land developer	$\Rightarrow \Omega\text{-}Type(B)$ = "Residence"	

All those geographic rules use the vocabulary of the ontology and place names described in the gazetteer and sometimes some mathematical models.

External knowledge: In practically all GIS, only data inside the jurisdiction of the entity in charge of planning activities are stored. But often "external knowledge" or "*extra muros* knowledge" could be of importance, in contrast with "internal knowledge" or "*intra muros* knowledge". External geographic knowledge means knowledge the location of which is outside the jurisdiction: it includes neighboring knowledge located at the vicinity of the jurisdiction and outside knowledge coming from everywhere else. For instance outside knowledge can model experiments and good practices in other cities.

Neighboring knowledge represents knowledge located at the vicinity of the jurisdiction, for instance within an out-buffer. It must include main geographic objects, relationships between those objects and the objects located inside the jurisdiction and especially cross-border rules if any.

Especially from technology and urban sociological watching, interesting experiments made in other territories or cities can be modeled and stored as external good practices. Let us call those bunches of knowledge, external outside knowledge. However, the primary step will be to analyze the semantics of this knowledge and to propose a way or a language to be machine-processable, for instance by a variant of case-based reasoning.

Other types of knowledge: In this list, we can add documents which can be considered as storing geographic information giving in natural language.

IV. CONCLUSION: RESEARCH AGENDA TOWARDS URBAN KNOWLEDGE BASES

The benefit of this novel approach will be to simplify the study of consequences and the assessment of urban projects by means of rules and inference engines.

The knowledge society will shape the city of the future. Now that the background of a knowledge infrastructure for smart urban planning is sketched, several questions emerge. Let us precise some of them.

The main question is not to create a smart city from scratch, but rather to "smartify" a city, *i.e.*, to define a methodology to pass from an existing city (whatever is its level of development) to a real living smart city. And knowledge engineering and infrastructure could be considered as the key issue for this transformation.

In the previous section, even if a model of knowledge infrastructure was argued and presented, some validation must be launched by creating operational systems of urban planning based on knowledge engineering. Among the key-problems we have to solve is the discovery of socio-economic rules.

The second aspect concerns citizen participation. Since each citizen or groups of citizens have different interests, this issue has two sides. The first side concerns nimbies who can have divergent interests. But there are citizens who are aware of global interest; but what is general interest and what could be the entity really in charge of global interests? Nevertheless from a computing point of view, we need a robust model to describe citizen's opinions, to analyze them and to synthetize them. Existing multi-actor multi-criteria decision support systems are often very naïve and cannot integrate various forms of knowledge.

Supposing that such a system exists, an important issue is to evaluate the efficiency of generated smart urban plans. But this is a very long task since the efficiency or limitations can often be discovered decades after.

From the knowledge engineering side, various problems must be solved. Among them, let us mention urban and environmental rule encoding, robustness vis-à-vis measurement errors and scaling effects, the combination of knowledge coming from different sources, encoded with different languages and different levels of trust. Do not forget also the integration of external knowledge. And finally, we have to give the complete specifications of a future geographic inference engine.

As those research topics will be carried out and implemented in robust systems, real experiences of knowledge-based smart urban planning will be launched. Indeed, in our society, knowledge is THE infrastructure as the philosopher Michel Serres recently told. Now, since knowledge-based economy is common in businesses, why not in local authorities?

However the main barrier is not technological, but rather political: are politicians really ready to empower citizens?

REFERENCES

[1] V. Albino, Berardi U., and Dangelico R.M (2015) "Smart Cities: Definitions, Dimensions, Performance, and Initiatives", Journal of Urban Technology, 2015, Vol. 22, No. 1, 3–21, http://dx.doi.org/10.1080/10630732.2014.942092.

[2] L. Anthopoulos and Vakali A. (2012) "Urban Planning and Smart Cities: Interrelations and Reciprocities". In "Future Internet Assembly, from Promises to Reality" ed. by Álvarez F., *et al.* LNCS, Springer-Verlag 7281, pp. 178-189, 2012.

[3] M. Batty M and Yeh T. (1991) "The promise of expert systems for urban planning". In "Computers, Environment and Urban Systems", Volume 15, Issue 3, 1991, pp. 101–108.

[4] R. Baxter (1976) "Computer and Statistical Techniques for Planners"; Methuen Press 1976, 336 pages.

[5] Y. Bertacchini Y., Rodriguez-Salvador M. and Souari W. (2007) "From territorial intelligence to competitive & sustainable system Case studies in Mexico & in Gafsa University". Second International Annual "Conference of Territorial Intelligence", Oct 2007, Spain pp. 37-54.

[6] M. Egenhofer M. and Franzosa R.D. (1991) "Point-set topological spatial relations", Int'l J. of GIS, vol.5, no.2, pp. 161-174.

[7] R. Fistola and La Rocca, R.-A. (2013) "Smart city planning: a systemic approach", 6th Knowledge Cities World Summit, September 9-12, 2013, Istanbul, Turkey, pp. 520-529.

[8] J.-J. Girardot and Brunau E. (2010) Territorial Intelligence and Innovation for the Socio-Ecological Transition. 9th Int'l Conf. of Terr. Intel., ENTI, Nov 2010, Strasbourg, France.

[9] I. Graham (2006) "Business Rules Management and Service Oriented Architecture: A Pattern Language". London, Wiley.

[10] Ž. Jakir, Hećimović, Ž. and Štefan, Z. (2011) "Names Ontologies". In Advances in Cartography. Lecture Notes in Geoinformation and Cartography edited by Anne Ruas, Ed.; Springer Verlag: Heidelberg, Germany, 2011; pp. 331–349.

[11] C. Kessler, Janowicz, K., and Bishr, M. (2009) "An Agenda For The Next Generation Gazetteer: Geographic Information Contribution and Retrieval". In Proceedings of the 17th ACM Int'l Conf. on Advances in Geographic Information Systems, New York, NY, USA, 4–6 November 2009; pp. 91–100,

[12] T.J. Kim, Wiggins, Lyna L., and Wright, J.R. (Eds.) (1989) "Expert Systems: Applications to Urban Planning", Springer-Verlag, New York.

[13] K. Kourtit and Nijkamp P. (2012), "Smart Cities in the Innovation Age, Innovation: The European Journal of Social Science Research 25: 2 (2012), pp. 93–95.

[14] R. Laurini (2001) "Information Systems for Urban Planning: A Hypermedia Cooperative Approach", Taylor and Francis, 308 p. February 2001.

[15] R. Laurini (2014) "A Conceptual Framework for Geographic Knowledge Engineering", Journal of Visual Languages and Computing (2014), Volume 25, pp. 2-19,

[16] R. Laurini, Servigne S., and Favetta F. (2016) "An Introduction to Geographic Rule Semantics". 22nd International Conference on Distributed Multimedia Systems, DMS 2016, Salerno, Salerno, Italy, November 25-26, 2016, Published by Knowledge Systems Institute, ISBN: 1-891706-40-3, pp. 91-97.

[17] R. Laurini (2017) "Geographic Knowledge Infrastructure for Territorial Intelligence and Smart Cities". Wiley-ISTE-Elsevier. To be published in April 2017.

[18] J. Mathew (2013) "City as a Customer". Can be downloaded from http://www.frost.com/c/10046/blog/blog-display.do?id=2377335. Visited March 4, 2017.

[19] T. Morgan (2008) "Business Rules and Information Systems: Aligning IT with Business Goals". Addison-Wesley. 384 p.

[20] J. Teller (2007) "Ontologies for an Improved Communication in Urban Development Projects. In "Ontologies for Urban Development", edited by J. Teller, Springer, 2007, pp. 1-14.

[21] UNESCO (2005) "Towards knowledge societies". Published in 2005 by the United Nations Educational, Scientific and Cultural Organization, Paris.

[22] P. Varadharajulu, West G., McMeekin D. Moncrieff S. and Arnold L. (2016), "Automating Government Spatial Transactions". Int'l Conf. GISTAM Conf., Roma, April 2016.

3D Visualization and Simulation Module based on Virtual Geographic Environments for Sea Level Rise on Ponta da Areia Beach - São Luís, Maranhão, Brazil

David Silva e Silva*, Karla Donato Fook†, André Luís Silva dos Santos†, Hélder Pereira Borges†,
Denilson da Silva Bezerra‡ and Dario Vieira Conceição§
*State University of Maranhão
São Luís, Maranhão, Brazil
Email: davidsilva.silva@outlook.com
†Federal Institute of Education, Science and Technology of Maranhão
São Luís, Maranhão, Brazil
Email: {karladf, andresantos, helder}@ifma.edu.br
‡Ceuma University
São Luís, Maranhão, Brazil
Email: denilson_ca@yahoo.com.br
§Engineering School of Information and Digital Technologies
Villejuif, Paris, France
Email: dario.vieira@efrei.fr

Abstract—**The growing concern about sea level rise leads to the study of vulnerability to coastal flooding due to extreme events. Therefore, the need for simulation studies on this topic, including the ground altimetry, distribution of buildings, environmental, social and economic impacts, lead to the development of this work. The Virtual Geographic Environments are proposed as support systems for specific studies of simulation and analysis of geographic phenomena, being then presented as accurate and significant tools for this study. This work proposes the application of concepts of Virtual Geographic Environments for the development of a 3D module for visualization and simulation of sea level rise in Ponta d'Areia region, in São Luís, Maranhão.**

Keywords–three-dimensional visualization; geoprocessing; sea level rise.

I. Introduction

Sea level rise is a persistent effect related to climate change and is one of the significant events discussed in the Intergovernmental Panel on Climate Change (IPCC). In terms of resulting impacts, a 1-meter rise in sea level would result in the loss of approximately 0.3% of mainland and would affect approximately 56 million people in 84 developing countries [1]. In Brazil, there are 395 municipalities located in the coastal zone where approximately 24% of the native population resides [2]. In 2000, 12 million people in Brazil lived in low-lying areas at risk to sea level rise, and forecasts indicate that this number can reach 18.7 million people in 2060 [3]. Face to the risks to sea level rise, the need for simulation studies on the topic, including the ground altimetry, distribution of buildings, environmental, social and economic impacts, lead to the development of this work.

Virtual Geographic Environments (VGEs) are a mix of geographic knowledge, computational technology, virtual reality, and geographic information technologies, which aim to provide a multidimensional representation similar to the real-world geographical environment (in representation and scale), giving users an ability to explore, perform experiments and simulate phenomena [4], being therefore presented as accurate and significant tools for this study.

Based on the concept of VGEs, this work presents the development method of a display and simulation module of sea level rise through a 3D virtual environment (web platform), based on the four Representative Concentration Pathways (RCPs) estimatives for 2100 appointed by the IPCC [5].

The paper is organized as follows: Section II presents the characterization of the study area, Section III describes the process of data acquisition, Section IV describes the development method, Section V presents the preliminary results, and Section VI presents the conclusions.

II. Study Region

The study area is Ponta d'Areia Beach, located in San Marcos Bay, west of São Luís Island, with a lenght of 2.5 km (Fig. 1), from Ponta d'Areia Pontal (29'17 S Latitude and 44° 09'19 W Longitude) to San Marcos Lighthouse (2° 29 '04 S Latitude S and 44° 08 '22 W Longitude) [6].

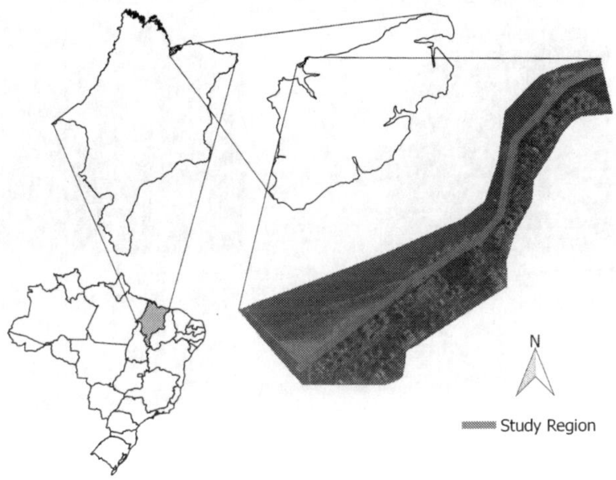

Fig. 1. Study Region.

This area receives the action of semidiurnal tides that can reach 7 meters in periods of equinoctial spring tides [6], being a vulnerable region to extreme events mainly related to a set of erosion actions.

Considering the problem of the coastal areas vulnerability related to the sea level rise phenomenon, especially the one in Ponta d'Areia area, this work is leaded by the questioning about the impacts that this phenomenon will produce in the study area and if the knowledge of these effects will predict ecologically, socially or economically harmful events.

III. Data Acquisition

The input data used to generate the 3D terrain model was the Shuttle Radar Topography Mission (SRTM) satellite image with 1 arc second spatial resolution (30 meters), provided by the United States Geological Survey.

In order to estimate the beach range, two World-View 3 satellite images captured from Google Earth, one for high tide and one for low tide, were used to generate values between 0.1 and 1m. With the tools of the QGIS, three vector files (shapefiles) were obtained from the images: a point grid with lat / long coordinates and SRTM pixel altimetry, contour lines, and a polygon mesh representing the buildings, with exported data in GeoJson format (Fig. 2).

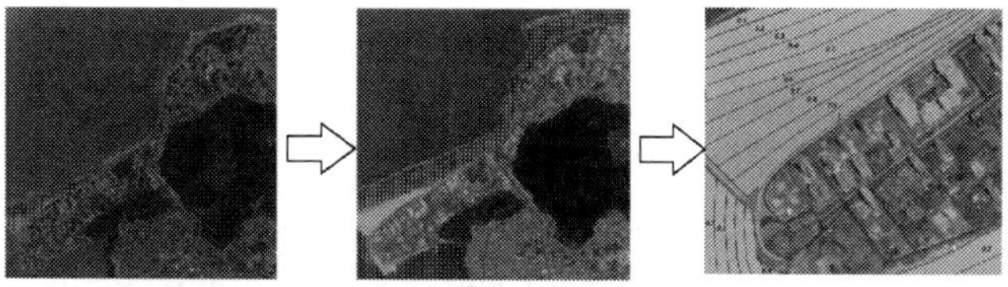

(a) Estimating Beach Range

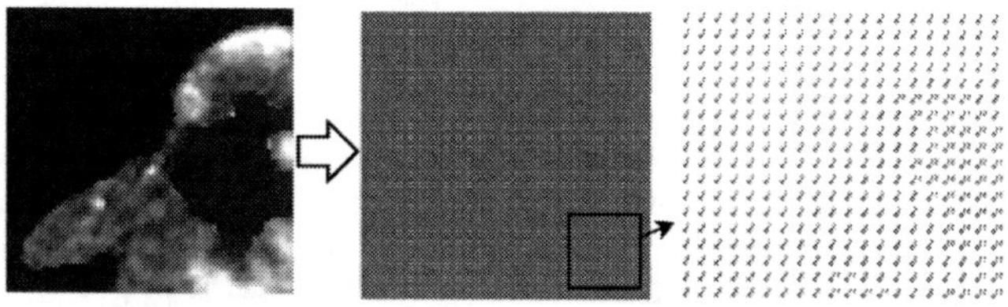

(b) Acquiring Point Grid

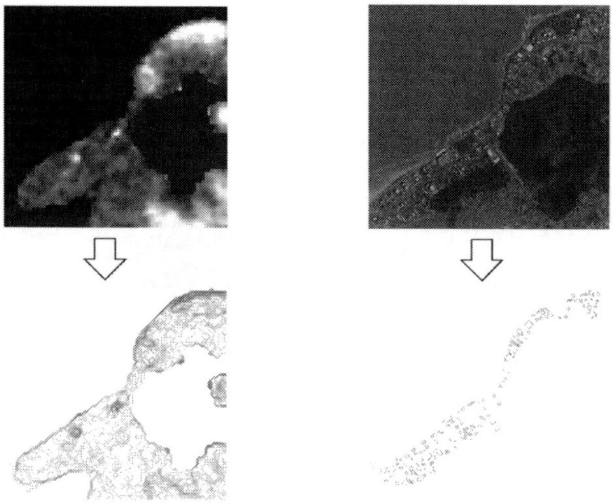

(c) Acquiring Contours Lines and Buildings Features

Fig. 2. Aquisition of Contour Lines, Building Features and Point Grid.

The data in a GeoJSON file are organized into "features" and a feature has fields such as: "geometry", which store the vector structure of geometry and "properties", which store descriptive information related to geometry. The basic types of geometries used were point, line, and polygon representing respectively the grid of points, contour lines, and buildings.

IV. Implementation

The module was developed with Threejs (JavaScript Library 3D / API for WebGl), trhough which the algorithm reads the GeoJson files and transforms them into 3D structures (Fig. 3).

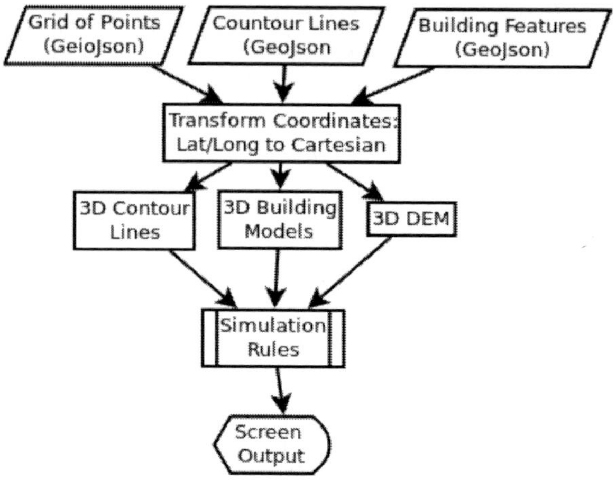

Fig. 3. Flow of Transformation.

For 3D representation of the terrain, the GeoJson dotted file was used to create the Digital Elevation Digital Model (DEM). The contour lines were transformed into a 3DLine type geometry, and they are used as a feature to display terrain altimetry in the virtual environment. The polygons representing the buildings were transformed into models of 3D buildings (with detail level 1, blocks without roof structures), with each building having as attribute its elevation in relation to sea level and its estimated height (Figs. 4, 5 and 6).

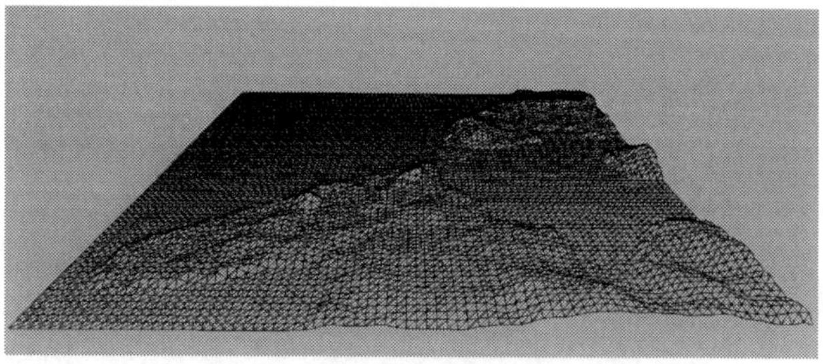

Fig. 4. DEM.

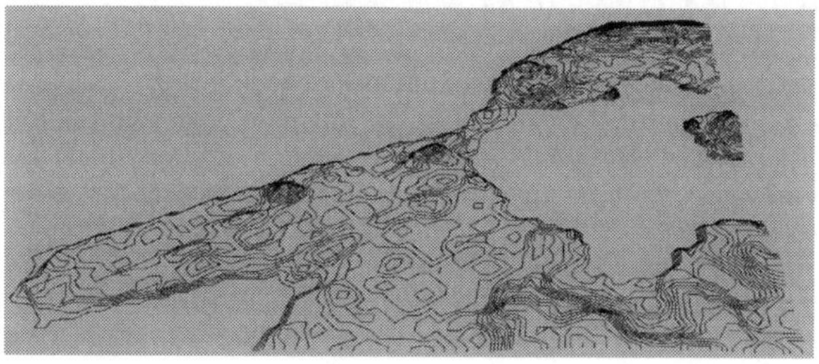

Fig. 5. 3D Contour Lines.

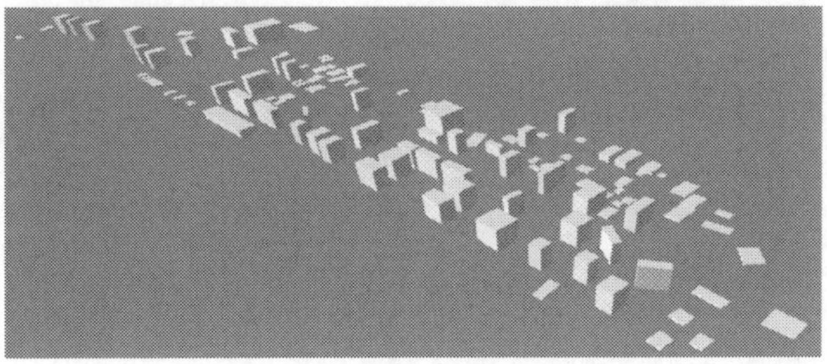

Fig. 6. 3D Buildings.

The water body (represented by a flat geometry) increases with sea level increments. The simulation of sea level rise is defined by (1) [7].

$$E = C_a + (Ev \times R) \tag{1}$$

E is the sea level, C_a is the water body rise at each step, Ev is the elevation step related to one year, R is the incremental rate at each elevation step. In this work, 85 elevation steps (Ev) concerning to 2015 - 2100 period were adopted. The incremental rate R is defined by the $\frac{RCP\,estimate}{85}$ ratio.

For the total land loss estimative, a vertices scan is performed on the DEM at each elevation step using the rule shown in in Fig. 7, where each vertex represents an area of $30m^2$.

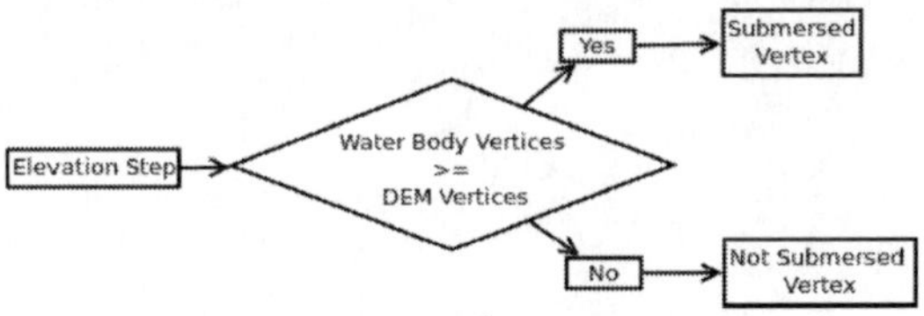

Fig. 7. Land Loss Identification Rule.

In order to identify buildings at risk, a building matrix scan is performed at each elevation step, using the rule shown in Fig. 8. When a building at risk is identified it is marked with red color (Fig. 9).

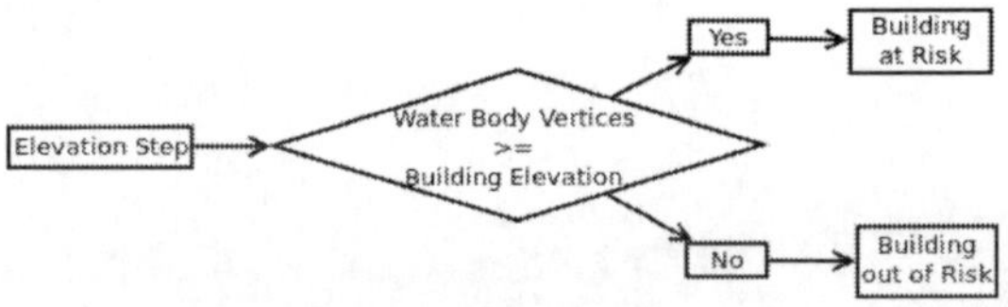

Fig. 8. Building Identification Rule.

Fig. 9. Module Interface.

The virtual environment is displayed in the web browser and the menu has controls to display the 3D terrain model, contour lines, surface satellite image, buildings, water body elevation animation, as well as total land loss per year.

V. Results and Discussion

Table I shows the total land loss in the study area for each PCR estimate appointed by the IPCC.

TABLE I. Total Land Loss.

RCP	Estimate by 2100	Terrain Loss
2.6	0.61m	$63.960m^2$
4.5	0.71m	$74.520m^2$
6.0	0.73m	$74.520m^2$
8.5	0.98m	$87.240m^2$

With the elevation data used (SRTM) any sea level rise estimated at the IPCC will directly affect residential buildings, however, in the sites where the elevation reaches 0.98 cm (RCP 8.5), loss of entire beach area was observed (Fig. 10). Consequently, sea breakthrough will intensify the erosion process by modifying the geomorphology of the region, endangering other structures such as marina, boardwalks, kiosks, first aid stations and restaurants along the waterfront , directly bringing social impacts such as loss of leisure area and economic impacts as potential loss for tourism.

Fig. 10. Sea Level by 2100.

VI. Conclusion and Future Work

The method developed in this study presents a simplified process for the implementation of a visualization and simulation module using GIS data as input. The module automates data reading in GeoJson format and transforms it into 3D models, as well as performs the simulation of sea level rise over the study area. This module is part of a larger project focused on developing a virtual web environment based on the concept and proposal of the VGEs, with the aim of supporting the study of sea level rise phenomenon and its impacts in the study area. In the future one intends to add: data storage and retrieval module, improved simulation models of the phenomenon including erosion and updated altimetry data, resulting in a web simulation and display tool open to the public.

Acknowledgment

The authors thank to the Foundation for Support to Research and Scientific and Technological Development of Maranhão (FAPEMA) and to the Federal Institute of Education, Science and Technology of Maranhão (IFMA) for their financial support.

REFERENCES

[1] S. Dasgupta, B. Laplante, C. Meisner, D. Wheeler and J. Yan, "The impact of sea level rise on developing countries: a comparative analysis." World Bank policy research working paper, n. 4136, 2007, DOI: 10.1596/1813-9450-4136.

[2] T. M. Strohaecker, "Natural Risk Potential." In: Ademilson Zamboni & Joao Luiz Nicolodi (org.), Macrodiagnosis of the Brazilian Coastal and Marine Zone, pp.93-120, Ministry of the Environment, Secretariat of Climate Change and Environmental Quality. Federal District, Brazil. 2008.

[3] B. Neumann, A. T. Vafeidis, J. Zimmermann and R. J. Nicholls, "Future coastal population growth and exposure to sea-level rise and coastal flooding-a global assessment." PloS one, vol. 10, n. 3, pp. 1–34, 2015, DOI: 10.1371/journal.pone.0131375.

[4] H. Lin et. al, "Virtual geographic environments (VGEs): a new generation of geographic analysis tool." Earth-Science Reviews, vol. 126, pp. 74–84, 2014, DOI: 10.1016/j.earscirev.2013.08.001.

[5] P. P. Wong et. al, "Coastal Systems and Low-Lying Areas." In: Climate Change 2014: Impacts, Adaptation, and Vulnerability. Part A: Global and Sectoral Aspects. Contribution of Working Group II to the Fifth Assessment Report of the Intergovernmental Panel on Climate Change, Cambridge University Press, Cambridge, United Kingdom and New York, USA, pp. 361–409, 2014.

[6] F. P. Correia, L. S. Silva, S. R. Alves, M. N. Gatinho and L. J. B. S. Dias, "Characterization of the Landscape of the Northern Coastal Zone of the Island of Maranhão: The Case of Ponta d'Areia Beach." In: VI National Symposium on Geomorphology/Regional Conference on Geomorphology, Goiânia, pp. 1-10, Brazil, 2006.

[7] D. da S. Bezerra, "Modeling of Mangrove Dynamics in the Face of Sea Level Rise." Doctoral thesis, National Institute for Space Research - INPE, São José dos Campos, Brazil, 2014.

Web Processing Services to Describe Provenance and Geospatial Modelling

Guillem Closa, Joan Masó, Núria Julià, Lluís Pesquer
Grumets Research Group, CREAF
g.closa@creaf.uab.cat, joan.maso@uab.cat,
n.julia@creaf.uab.cat, l.pesquer@creaf.uab.cat
Edifici C, Universitat Autònoma de Barcelona
Bellaterra, Catalonia, Spain

Alaitz Zabala
Grumets Research Group, Dep de Geografia
alaitz.zabala@uab.cat
Edifici B, Universitat Autònoma de Barcelona
Bellaterra, Catalonia, Spain

***Abstract*— There are still some gaps regarding the complete geospatial provenance description. These gaps prevent the use of provenance information for replication and reproducibility task. In addition, the lack of automated tools for capturing the provenance is an obstacle to a widely generation of provenance information. In this sense, we present a tool that captures and represents provenance information based on the combined use of Web Processing Service (WPS) standard and the ISO 19115 lineage model. The tool, developed in the frame of the MiraMon GIS & RS software, shows a graphical visualization of provenance and allow users to edit provenance information by adding or deleting process steps or sources to a geospatial workflow. The automatic capture of lineage information is a step forward in the development of a model constructor tool. It will allow reproducing previous process workflows and applying them to other similar situations.**

Keywords- Provenance; WPS; Modelling

I. INTRODUCTION

Buneman [1] defines provenance information as the description of data origins and the processes by which a dataset is created. This includes also the description of the algorithms used, the processing steps, the inputs and outputs, the computing environment where the process runs, the organization/person responsible for the product, etc [2][3]. In the context of scientific models, data provenance records the workflow processing steps and their inputs/outputs that contribute to the production of the final data products [4].

The scientific community is interested in provenance information because it provides important information to determine the fit for purpose and the reliability of a product. In the geospatial domain data provenance plays a significant role in data quality and usability assessment [5], among others qualities. Moreover, if data provenance information is complete and points to real data and metadata, it can be used as a source for a workflow replication (with other inputs) or for data replication (reproducibility purposes) [2].

As a result of web-technology improvements that have reduced the data volume, computing steps, and resources required by the end-user, geospatial data and geoprocessing tools are available as services [6]. More recently, *Model as a Service* (MaaS) approach has been defined [7][8]. In this paradigm, where the origin of data has a high level of heterogeneity, several authors [9][10] see that provenance information is even more important for inspecting and verifying quality, usability and reliability of data.

Although that the importance of provenance in the geospatial community is documented, its complete description in geospatial metadata is still scarce [11]. Usually, most of the geodata come with some provenance information but in many cases only as a simple textual description, thus having a negative impact on its automated usage [12]. According to *Di* et al. [5], there are two main obstacles that generate this situation: the lack of standards that fully describe provenance information models ensuring reproducibility, and the lack of automated tools for capturing the provenance information.

To exchange and share geospatial data provenance in a distributed information environment, an interoperable model for provenance is needed [13]. The geospatial community has traditionally used the ISO 19115 [14] and 19115-2 standards to encode metadata and provenance [15]. However, there are still some gaps in the ISO models, such as the concrete model initialization, its basic assumptions and parameters values. These deficiencies prevent the complete description of provenance and blocks it use in workflow replication and data reproduction tasks.

Besides representation, provenance applications also need to ensure provenance capture, management and retrieval [16]. In addition, automatic tools that capture and store provenance as a part of metadata information are needed. Most of the work has focused on analysing and capturing provenance information that was created during execution, rather than on metadata generated before execution [17]. However, tools that document provenance before and after the execution are needed too.

In this regard, we have implemented a provenance engine tool that automatically captures and represents provenance information based on the combined use of Web Processing Service (WPS) standard and ISO 19115 lineage model. The tool, developed in the framework of the MiraMon Geographic Information System (GIS) and Remote Sensing (RS) [18], presents a graphical visualization of provenance and allow users to edit provenance information of a geospatial workflow before and after the execution. This automatic acquisition of geospatial provenance represents a step forward in the development of a model constructor tool in the context of MiraMon software.

This paper is structured as follows. Section II introduces related work, then sections II and III present the use of WPS to capture provenance and the developed tool. Following section IV introduces the efforts done in generating geospatial models from the captured provenance information. Finally, the conclusions are presented in the last section.

II. RELATED WORK

When selecting a standard for describing provenance in the geospatial domain, some requirements should be taken into account [3]. For Di et al. [5] ISO 19115 and ISO 19115-2 templates are enough to record the complete geospatial lineage. Alternatively, He et al. [14] combines ISO 19115 with W3C PROV [19] to better describe provenance. Others, such as Lopez-Pellicer et al. [20] propose to adapt and extend the W3C PROV model to geospatial community requirements.

Beyond the models used to capture and store provenance, an effective visualization of provenance is also necessary to understand and evaluate data [21]. There are different types of visualization proposals [22], namely:

- Provenance as node-links: data is represented as points and processes as lines. [23][24].
- Provenance as a radial plots: Brings a visual focus to the relationships rather than the relative spatial locations [25].
- Tree diagrams: This technique displays a tree-form diagram starting from the data that is being analysed. Most provenance data have hierarchical properties or attributes [26][27]. Thus we found this type a suitable one to describe provenance.

When generating a geospatial model from concrete executions, a generalization process have to be carried out to standardise and reference the common processing functions. Yue et al. [28] use three levels of encapsulation to reduce the difficulty of sharing and use geo-analysis models in the web. Otherwise, Müller [29] proposes a hierarchical approach to process definitions with different abstraction levels. WPS process profiles [30] are also useful to determine which information from the concrete execution needs to be added to the model to ensure it reusability. An Application Profile is essentially the same as the ProcessDescription document obtained in response to a *DescribeProcess* request [31] (Fig. 1). This approach is in line with our approach of using the WPS standard to capture provenance, consequently we will use *DescribeProcess* documents to generalise models.

III. WPS TO CAPTURE GEOSPATIAL PROVENANCE

A. DescribeProcess documents to capture Provenance

The Web Processing Service (WPS) Interface provides rules for standardizing inputs and outputs (requests and responses) for geospatial processing services [32]. WPS instances are exposed via HTTP-GET, HTTP-POST and SOAP [33] Internet protocols. The potential of geoprocessing applications supported by the WPS allows to apply it in a wide range of fields [34]. Its main properties are: remotely execution, chain of several processes and standardized encodings for data and metadata. WPS is applied in many different fields and sectors that need geoprocessing applications; in particular it is successfully implemented for environmental models [35][36] and in combination to other standards: WPS+OpenMI [37], WPS+WCS [38], WPS+WFS [39]. WPS has three main operations: *getCapabilities, describeProcess and Execute.*

The *describeProcess* is the operation that allow a client to request and receive back detailed information about the processes that can be run on the service instance, including the inputs required, the allowable formats, and the outputs that can be produced [32]. The *describeProcess response* documents use the eXtensible Markup Language (XML). The information described in the WPS describeProcess documents(Fig 1) is the following:

- Process Description: A description of the process and an Identifier.
- Inputs: The input description, the dataType (*ComplexData*, *BoundingBox*, *LiteralData)*, the MIME type, an identifier and the name.
- Outputs: The output description, the dataType (*ComplexData*, *BoundingBox*, *LiteralData)*, the MIME type, an identifier and the name.

Considering that provenance information is the description of processes and sources, *describeProcess* documents could also be used to document provenance information. In addition, *describeProcess* operation can be requested in a local environment. This provides a magnificent opportunity to capture provenance automatically in a GIS local instance. In our case, we have used the *describeProcess* documents to describe all the MiraMon Applications (App), and capture its provenance information when executed. This permits the system to reference sources as a complex data, bounding box or capture the values of the *LiteralData* type.

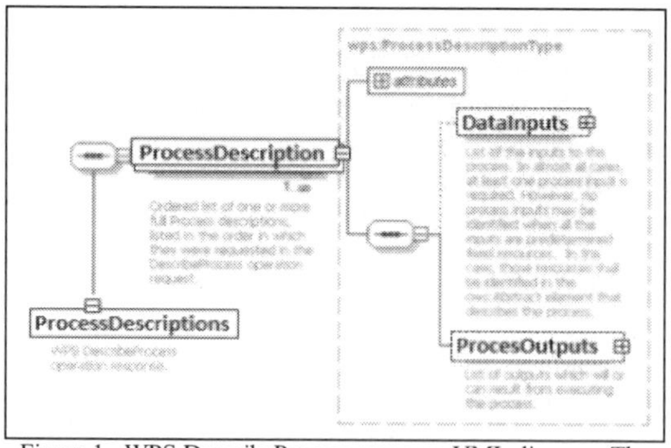

Figure 1. WPS DescribeProcess response UML diagram. The DescribeProcess schema is composed by a processDescription tag that includes a list of DataInputs and ProcessOutputs.

WPS is enough well known for the geospatial community, and this allows to jump the interoperability wall. More detail about the use WPS *describeProcess* documents in the context of MiraMon GIS & RS software are provided in Section III.

B. *Combining WPS and ISO to describe provenance*

As mentioned, we have detected some limitations in the ISO 19115 models that prevents the reproducibility of geospatial data using provenance information. In order to overcome this issue we propose the combination of the ISO provenance schemas (LI_Lineage and LE_ProcessStep) with *WPS describeProcess* documents (Fig. 2) presented in the previous section. Combining these two models allows to describe provenance as an ordered list of processes with ISO, including a WPS description of sources and outputs of each process step.

The ISO 19115 and 19115-2 can be described using the *eXtensible Markup Language* (XML). In fact, the ISO 19115-3 provides the XML implementation schema for ISO 19115 and 19115-2 and may be used to describe, validate, and exchange geospatial metadata. The lineage models of ISO (LI_Lineage and LE_ProcessStep) allow to describe the provenance information in three different ways:

- A list of process steps and a list of sources separately.
- A list of all the sources used and then add the description of all the processes as a child.
- A list of all the process steps that use some sources.

Describing provenance with a list of processes that use some sources provides the better way to report a complete record of provenance [12], because it follows the workflow execution. Thus, we use ISO in this way because permits the full description of provenance of a workflow as an ordered succession of different process steps. ISO model describes for each intermediate step the sources used and the outputs generated.

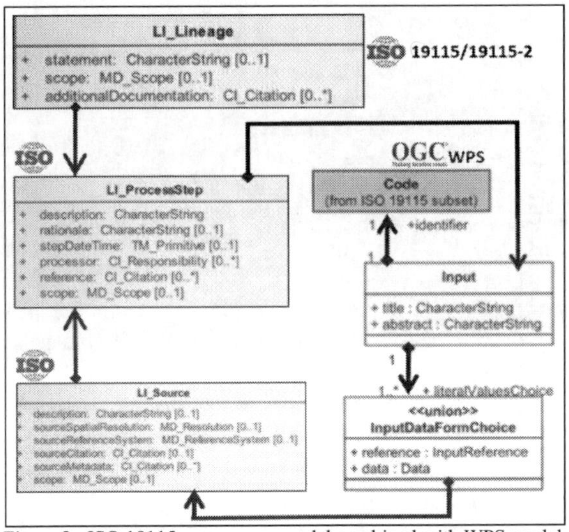

Figure 2. ISO 19115 provenance model combined with WPS model.

However, when describing sources, there is no place to indicate the data type or the value used (for literal data). In this context, to improve the description of the sources and the outputs of each step we introduce the use the *WPS DescribeProcess* to capture, among others characteristics, the data type and the literal data values. The sources and outputs used in each process step of the WPS are connected via identifiers to the ISO schemas.

The combination of ISO provenance schemas with WPS permits the automatic description of the algorithms used, the processing steps, the execution dates, the data type, the units (when necessary) and data values or data location.

The detected gap (no place to define the data type or the value used for literal data) has been introduced as a request for the revision of ISO 19115-2 and we are working with the editors to extend the standard to include this information.

IV. PROVENANCE ENGINE TOOL

A. *Provenance capturation in the context of GEMM*

MiraMon is a Geographic Information System (GIS) and Remote Sensing (RS) software [18]. The main characteristic of MiraMon software is that metadata are carefully managed and completely integrated with the dataset, which allows, at every processing step, to program automatic decisions based on quality information from the previous steps in the process chain [40]. MiraMon incorporates a Metadata Manager (GeMM) to ensure maximum documentation of layers. GeMM allows generating, editing and saving metadata, including the description of the data model and the relations with databases for several hierarchical levels (dataset to several dataset series). The metadata information is stored in REL format documents, which are the native format of MiraMon to document and store metadata information. These files store metadata about identification, extent, related databases, responsible party, technical specification and quality information [41][42]. In addition, as a part of quality information, there is also place for documenting provenance information. REL documents conform to INSPIRE ISO 19115 and FGDC standards and. moreover, metadata can be exported to HTML or XML (ISO 19139) files. Unlike others purely documentary applications, GeMM maintains the dependencies and consistency by checking coherence between metadata and datasets.

MiraMon software has more than 90 applications. In order to capture provenance information automatically, the main task has been the generation, for each App, of a *DescribeProcess response* template that describes the process and its allowed input and output data types. In addition, we use the optional tag *ows:metatada* to define the exact syntax and order of the parameters.

The provenance engine, using the WPS *DescribeProcess* templates, captures provenance of each process carried out and stores it in the metadata files as a part of the quality information of the dataset.

The provenance engine is a piece of code that is shared by the visual interface of the GeMM and the MiraMon Apps. It is encoded as a library of C functions that can be linked to each module. Each App uses these functions to read metadata of the source datasets, load it, integrate it, and add the current App process step in the provenance information of the resulting dataset.

The provenance engine writing function can select between two alternatives: a) include all lineage details: complete sequence and description of process steps and previous data sources; or b) write only the last process step and link to the metadata sources. To save space, the generic purpose of each process step and its parameters is not stored. Instead, only identifiers are recorded. The reading function supports the two alternatives described before, being able to read the provenance information by following the links to previous sources recursively if needed. The graphical interface of GeMM requires a more elaborated set of functions to enrich the presentation of provenance information extracted from a *DescribeProcess* response template.

This allows the GeMM to capture, concurrently to an App execution, provenance information using the *DescribeProcess response* templates of each App (Fig. 3).

The system captures the exact parameters and values involved in an execution (that can be numbers, text strings, or bounding box data) and references to datasets or to data services. The system updates metadata information at every intermediate step maintaining the dependencies between the datasets and metadata files during all the workflow execution. The tool keeps track of the dependencies to source datasets and can browse to their metadata too.

B. *Provenance editing and visualization*

In complex environments, scientists rely on visualization tools to help them understand large amounts of data that are generated from experiments [24].

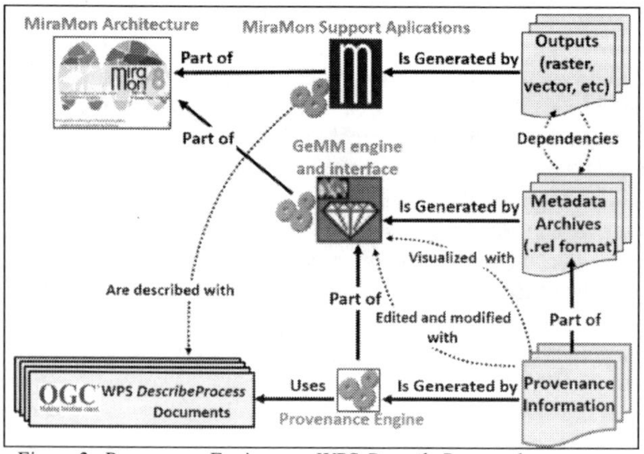

Figure 3. Provenance Engine uses WPS *DescribeProcess* documents to extract provenance information and then the GeMM interface allows users to edit and modify provenance.

According to Steele et al. [43], there are two categories of data visualization *Exploratory*, designed to support researcher who has not certain what is in it; and *Explanatory*, when a researcher is trying to explain the data to someone else. This differentiation remits also to the contraposition of the "*data user needs*" in front of "*data producer needs*", where the user needs more exploratory visualization ways, while producers more explanatory. The graphical interface of our provenance engine fits for both, exploratory and explanatory data visualization approaches.

The provenance engine presented in this paper helps data users to navigate and interpret provenance. The tool represents provenance information as a succession of processes. Each process has an indented list of all parameters used and outputs generated. At the same time, some parameters of the workflow are derived by previous processes (child process), which have, in a deeper level, its own indented list of parameters used, and so on. Thereby, the structure of the provenance schema is progressively increasing its profundity reminding a hierarchical indented form (Fig. 4). From our point of view, this tree-like provenance structure is a suitable way to visualise the provenance information because can easily represent the flow of a specific chain of processes.

The graphical interface of GeMM allows also editing provenance information by adding or deleting child processes or child sources to a geospatial workflow. Moreover, the algorithm description, the processing steps carried out, the execution dates, the responsibility of the product and the processes order can be edited and adapted to each scenario if necessary. This allows data producers to complete the provenance description automatically captured during the process or workflow execution.

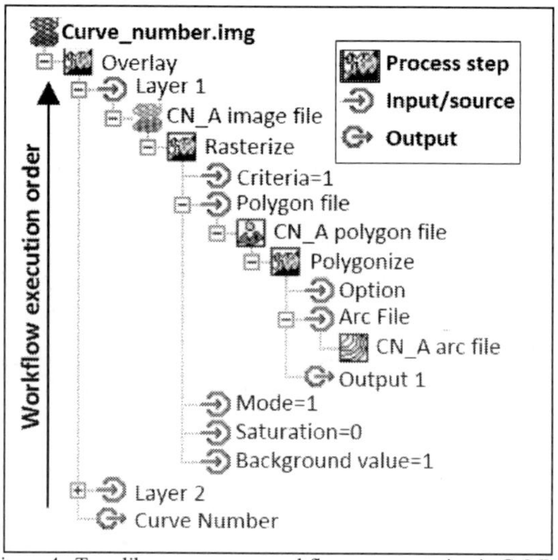

Figure 4. Tree-like provenance workflow representation in GeMM. The example shows processes and sources used in the layer (Curve_Number.img) generation.

V. GEOSPATIAL MODELLING

The automatic acquisition of geospatial provenance provides the complete recipe of the geospatial data generated. This supposes an opportunity to develop a model constructor tool in the MiraMon architecture. A model constructor allows the reproduction of previous chains of processes in different scenarios and applying them to similar situations using the provenance captured from previous executions.

Models, as a general representation of a system, are used to understand and simulate a geospatial phenomenon. Thus, a model have to provide enough information to enable the model users to apply it in different scenarios. As pointed in section II there are different approaches in order to generalize specific workflows. In our case, to document models we use the same WPS *DescribeProcess* templates generated to capture provenance. The WPS templates provide the necessary information of each App (process description, process syntax, algorithm location and parameters data type) to allow users to understand each individual process that conforms the model.

The provenance tool (presented in Section III) provides the specific order of the process chain and allows browsing the data inputs of each intermediate step, if necessary.

Finally, all captured information can be automatically exported as a batch file. The generated batch files points to processes and sources used to run workflows. Thus, this allows users to easily reproduce a workflow, or replicate it with different conditions (scope, data, parameters, algorithm options, etc). In addition, the collection of MS-DOS command lines permits automatize executions and ease the use of loops to process large volumes of data.

VI. CONCLUSIONS

Geospatial provenance facilitates geospatial data evaluation for reuse, and brings us closer to the replication of process chains and geospatial modelling. We have detected that there still some gaps regarding to the complete geospatial provenance description, affecting the provenance usefulness. Some gaps detected in the ISO 19115 lineage model has been introduced as a request for the revision of ISO 19115-2.

In this paper, we have shown that the combination of WPS *DescribeProcess* documents with ISO model provides a more complete provenance description. As a proof of concept, we have presented a provenance engine in the framework of MiraMon GIS and Remote Sensing software. The tool allows automatically capturing provenance information and its manually edition if needed. In addition, the automatic description of provenance information is a step forward in the development of a model constructor tool in the context of MiraMon software.

The near future efforts should point to enhance the process chaining and model generation in a distributed environment using provenance information.

ACKNOWLEDGMENT

This work has been conducted within the framework of the Geography PhD program of the Universitat Autònoma de Barcelona, and was supported by the European Commission [grant agreements H2020-641538: ConnectinGEO, H2020-641762: ECOPotential and H2020-689744: Ground Truth 2.0], Spanish Ministry of Economy and Competitiveness [ACAPI (CGL2015-69888-P MINECO/FEDER)] and Catalan Government [SGR2014-1491]).

REFERENCES

[1] P. Buneman, S. Khanna,W and Chiew Tan. Why and Where: A Characterization of Data Provenance. In Database Theory—ICDT. *Springer Berlin Heidelberg.* pp. 316-330, 2001.

[2] L. Di, P. Yue, H. Ramapriyan and R. King. Geoscience Data Provenance: An Overview. Geoscience and Remote Sensing, IEEE Transactions on, 51(11). pp. 5065-5072, 2013.

[3] D. Garijo, Y. Gil and A. Harth. Challenges in Modelling Geosaptial Provenance. Proceedings of the Fifth 24 International Provenance and Annotation Workshop (IPAW), Cologne, Germany, June 9-13, 2014.

[4] A. Chebotko, S. Chang, S. Lu, F. Fotouhi, and Yang, P. Scientific workflow provenance querying with security views. In Proceedings of the 2008 The Ninth International Conference on Web-Age Information Management (Washington, DC, USA), WAIM '08, IEEE Computer Society, pp. 349–356, 2008.

[5] L. Di,Y. Shao and L. Kang.Implementation of geospatial data provenance in a web service workflow environment with ISO 19115 and ISO 19115-2 lineage model. Geoscience and Remote Sensing, IEEE Transactions on, 51(11). pp 5082-5089, 2013.

[6] L. Di and McDonald, K. Next generation data and information systems for earth sciences research, in: 10 Proceedings of the First International Symposium on Digital Earth, vol. I. , Science Press, Beijing, 11 China, pp. 92–101, 1999.

[7] G. Geller and W. Turner. The model web: a concept for ecological forecasting. In IEEE International Geoscience and Remote Sensing Symposium. Pp. 2469-2472, 2007.

[8] S. Nativi, P. Mazzetti, and G. Geller. Environmental model access and interoperability: The GEO Model Web initiative. Environmental Modelling & Software, 39. pp. 214-228, 2013.

[9] S. Bechhofer, D. De Roure, M. Gamble, C. Goble and I. Buchan. Research objects: Towards exchange and reuse of digital knowledge. In, *The Future of the Web for Collaborative Science,* Raleigh, NC, USA. *2010.*

[10] Z. Xu, Y. Wang,Y. Li., F. Ma, F. Zhang and C. Ye. Sediment transport patterns in the eastern Beibu Gulf based on grain-size multivariate statistics and provenance analysis. Acta Oceanologica Sinica, 32(3). pp. 67-78, 2010.

[11] P. Díaz, et al. Analysis of Quality 19 Metadata in the GEOSS Clearinghouse. International Journal of Spatial Data Infrastructures Research, 20 7. pp. 352-377, 2012.

[12] P. Yue, J. Gong and L. Di. Augmenting geospatial data provenance through metadata tracking in 28 geospatial

service chaining. Computers & Geosciences, 36(3). pp. 270-281, 2010.

[13] L. He, P. Yue, L. Di, M. Zhang and L. Hu. Adding Geospatial Data Provenance into SDI—A Service-Oriented Approach. Selected Topics in Applied Earth Observations and Remote Sensing, IEEE Journal of, 8(2).pp. 926-936, 2015.

[14] ISO 19115-1:2014 (2014). "Geographic Information-Metadata- Part 1: Fundamentals".

[15] J. Masó, G. Closa, Y. Gil and B. Prob. OGC® Testbed 10 Provenance Engineering Report OGC Public Engineering Report (pp. 1-87): Open Geospatial Consortium. 2013.

[16] S. Miles, et al. The requirements of using provenance in e-science experiments. Journal of Grid Computing, 5 (1).pp. 1–25, 2007.

[17] J. Kim, Y. Gil and V. Ratnakar. Semantic metadata generation for large scientific workflows, Proceedings of the 5th International Semantic Web Conference, Athens, Georgia, USA, Lecture Notes in Computer Science (LNCS) 4273. Springer, Berlin, Germany, pp. 357–370, 2006.

[18] X. Pons. (2004). MiraMon. Geographical information system and remote sensing software. Centre de Recerca Ecològica i Aplicacions Forestals (CREAF).

[19] P. Groth, and L. Moreau. PROV-Overview: An Overview of the PROV Family of Documents. Working group note, W3C. 2013.

[20] F. Lopez-Pellicer and J. Barrera. D16.1 Call 2: Linked Map VGI Provenance Schema. In Linked Map subproject of Planet Data. Seventh Framewok Programe, 2014.

[21] M. Kunde, H. Bergmeyer and A. Schreiber. Provenance and annotation of data and processes. In J. Freire, D. Koop, and L. Moreau, editors, IPAW '08, chapter Requirements for a Provenance Visualization Component. p.p. 241–252, 2008

[22] M.Borkin et al. Evaluation of filesystem provenance visualization tools. IEEE Transactions on Visualization and Computer Graphics, 19(12). pp. 2476-2485, 2013.

[23] N. Del Rio and P. Da Silva. Probe-it! visualization support for provenance. In International Symposium on Visual Computing. Springer Berlin Heidelberg .pp. 732-741,2007.

[24] G. Salton, J. Allan, C. Buckley, and A. Singhai. Automatic analysis, theme generation, and summarization of machine-readable texts. Science, 264. pp. 1421–1426, 1994.

[25] C. Scheidegger, et al. Tackling the provenance challenge one layer at a time. *Concurrency and Computation: Practice and Experience*, *20*(5). Pp. 473-483, 2008.

[26] G.Closa and J. Masó. A provenance visualization tool for global earth observation system of systems. In EGU General Assembly Conference Abstracts (Vol. 15, p. 8266). April, 2013.

[27] L. Gou and X. Zhang. Treenetviz: Revealing patterns of networks over tree structures. IEEE TVCG, 17(12), December 2011.

[28] S. Yue, M. Chen, Y. Wen and G. Lu. Service-oriented model-encapsulation strategy for sharing and integrating heterogeneous geo-analysis models in an open web environment. ISPRS Journal of Photogrammetry and Remote Sensing, 114. pp. 258-273, 2016.

[29] M. Müller. Hierarchical process profiles for interoperable geoprocessing functions. In Proceedings of the 16th AGILE Conference on Geographic Information Science, Leuven, Belgium. 2013.

[30] OGC® WPS 2.0 Interface Standard. OGC 10-59r2, 2010 14-065

[31] WPS concepts (November, 2016) Retrieved from:http://geoprocessing.info/wpsdoc/Concepts

[32] OGC® WPS 2.0 Interface Standard. OGC 10-59r2, 2010 14-065

[33] D. Box et al. Winer, Simple Object Access Protocol (SOAP) 1.1, W3C Note. Retrived: November, 2016. http://www.w3.org/TR/SOAP

[34] C. Michaelis and D. Ames. Evaluation and implementation of the OGC web processing service for use in client-side GIS. Geoinformatica, 13(1). pp. 109-120, 2009.

[35] A. Castronova, J. Goodall and M. Elag. Models as web services using the Open Geospatial Consortium (OGC) Web Processing Service (WPS) standard Environmental Modelling and Software Volume 41, pp. 72-83, 2013.

[36] L. Granell, S. Díaz, N. Schade,J. Ostländer and J. Huerta. Enhancing Integrated Environmental Modelling by Designing Resource-Oriented Interfaces. Environmental Modelling & Software, 39.pp. 229-246, 2013.

[37] J. Goodall, B. Robinson and A. Castronova. Modeling water resource systems using a service-oriented computing paradigm. Environmental Modelling & Software, 26(5). pp. 573-582, 2011.

[38] G. Yu, P. Zhao, L. Di, A. Chen, M. Deng and Y. Bai. BPELPower-A BPEL execution engine for geospatial web services Computers and Geosciences Volume 47. pp. 87-101, 2012.

[39] X. Meng, Y. Xie and F. Bian. Distributed geospatial analysis through web processing service: A case study of earthquake disaster assessment Journal of Software Volume 5, Issue 6, pp. 671-67, 2010.

[40] L. Pesquer, J. Masó, G. Moré, X. Pons, J. Peces and E. Doménech. Servicio interoperable (WPS) de procesado de imágenes Landsat. Teledetección, 37. pp. 51-56, 2012.

[41] A. Zabala, J. Masó, L. Bastin and L. Bigali. Increasing dataset quality metadata presence: Quality focused metadata editor and catalogue queriables. . Inspire Conference. Florence, Italy, June 23-27, 2013.

[42] A. Zabala, J. Masó and X. Pons. Quality and user feedback metadata: theoretical aspects and a practical implementation in the MiraMon metadata editor. Inspire Conference. Barcelona, Spain, Setember 26-30, 2016.

[43] J. Steele and N. Iliinsky. Beautiful visualization: looking at data through the eyes of experts. "O'Reilly Media, Inc.", 2010.

A Method for Identifying Patterns of Movement of Trajectory Sets by Using the Frequency Distribution of Points

Vanessa Barbosa Rolim
Computer Science Department
Santa Catarina State University (UDESC)
Joinville, Santa Catarina, Brazil
E-mail: nessabrolim@gmail.com

Marilia Ribeiro da Silva
Felipe Flamarion da Conceição
Cláudio César Gonçalves de Faria Filho
Fernando José Braz
Informatic Department
Federal Institute Catarinense (IFC)
Araquari, Santa Catarina, Brazil
E-mail: {marilia.ribeirods, felipeflamari, claudio.cesar.faria.filho}@gmail.com
E-mail: fernando.braz@ifc-araquari.edu.br

***Abstract*—This work aims to provide a method to identify movement patterns of trajectory sets. The proposal, considering the frequency distribution of points, identifies a set of frequent regions, which can be used to compose a global frequent region. This region represents the area where the set of trajectories executes its movements. Besides, the set of central points, for each individual frequent area, composes the reference trajectory.**

Keywords–trajectory; cluster; movement patterns; similarity.

I. Introduction

A trajectory can be comprehended as a set of points — represented by latitude, longitude and the time it was recorded. Studies about trajectories of mobile objects have assisted on understanding behaviors and patterns of people and animals mobility, transportation facilities, nature phenomena, and even sports.

One of the areas of study of trajectory is the similarities. That is, when different trajectories share common characteristics or are very close to an established pattern, we say they are similar. Some of characteristics looked on analysis of similarities between trajectories are: length, shape, speed, acceleration, movement, distance between different trajectories, semantic.

Therefore, tasks like clusters of data are useful and can generate knowledge on pattern discovery. In terms of trajectories, the patterns of movement are classified like: moving together pattern, sequential pattern and, periodical patterns [1][2].

According to Zheng [1] a group of objects that move together by a determined period of time show a moving together pattern. Also, if trajectories have a moving together pattern, then, they have shape similarity too.

Several works, like described in Section II, describe methods to find trajectories' similarities using data mining concepts. Besides that, the main approach about these methods is to find frequent trajectories, based in algorithm of association rules like the Apriori, and find clustering patterns based on Density-Based Spatial Clustering of Applications with Noise (DBSCAN) and K-means.

Therefore, this paper proposes a method (*TRAJREF*) to find clusters of trajectories considering frequent coordinates, which generate a reference trajectory.

This work is organized as follows: Section II shows a revision of related works. Section III shows concepts and definitions. Section IV describes the methodology adopted. Section V relates the experiments. Section VI presents the results. Section VII concludes the article and presents perspective of future works.

II. Related Work

Distance functions are important to manage and manipulate trajectories data. They are presented in steps that involve the preprocessing, like the compression and the trajectory discretization. Also they can be used as measures of similarity.

A comparative study made by Wang et al. [3], presents a quantitative analysis of six distance functions used in similarity measurement. The functions are based in measures like Euclidian Distance, Dynamic Time Warping, Edit Distance and Longest Common Subsequence.

Hung et al. [4] proposes an algorithm of clustering trajectories to identify routes and movement behaviors together of an user. The propose consists in a framework of trajectory pattern mining, called *Clustering and Aggregating Clues of Trajectories (CACT)*.

Trajectory Community Discovery using Multiple Information Sources (TODMIS) [5] is a mining framework to discover trajectories communities. According to the author, a group is different of a community. A group is one set of related objects by spatial proximity. A community is a set of objects that have a interaction or a relationship shared by proximity or resemblance.

Shaw and Gopalan [6] developed a method that find frequent trajectories using clustering based sequential patterns mining, called *Clustering Based Sequential Mining* (CBM).

Trajectory Clustering (TRACLUS) is an algorithm that transforms a trajectory in a set of segments [7]. This algorithm is used by *partition-and-group* framework that groups trajectories or similar segments. After the segmentation, the framework groups the trajectories or the segments that have a together movement pattern similar.

Aung et al. [8] proposes two algorithms of frequent routes discovery, based in data mining algorithm *Apriori*. These algorithms are called *Apriori Based Approximate Frequent Route Miner (A-1)* and *Divide and Conquer Frequent Route Miner (A-2)*. Besides, he used the function of Fréchet distance like similarity measure. This measure is used in curve measures and in the resolution of computation problems.

Considering that if trajectories have similar forms, they also have similar deflection angles between their segments, Melo et al. [9] proposes a method to find shape similarity between trajectories applying statistics correlation in deflection angular vectors. The deflection angle is measured between the extension of previous trajectory segment and the relation of the next segment. This way, to find the deflection angle, it is used the difference between azimuths. Thus, by considering geodesic angles measures, this method shows that even if the trajectories are in totally distinct geographic positions, the shape similarity can be detected.

The previous proposals present methods and algorithms to find sets of similar trajectories. Segmentation, distance and shape matching are the tools to discover the cluster of similar trajectories.

This paper presents a proposal to find similar trajectories considering distance between coordinates points and a trajectory reference composed by a set of frequent points.

III. BASIC CONCEPTS AND DEFINITIONS

This section presents the definitions related to the proposal. The concepts are based in Zheng et al. [10], Fontes and Bogorny [11].

Coordinate *(c): is a tuple* (x, y)*, such that* x *is a latitude and* y *is a longitude.*

Point *(p): is a tuple* (c, t)*, such that* c *is a coordinate and* t *represents the instant of time when the coordinate was captured.*

Trajectory *(T): is made by a vector of points and can be defined by* $T = [p_1, p_2, \ldots, p_n]$*, such that* p_1 *is the initial point,* p_n *is the final point and* n *is the number of points.*

Sub-trajectory *(S): is a vector* $S = [p_i, p_{i+1}, p_{i+2}, \ldots, p_f]$ *, such that* p_i *is the initial point of segment and* p_f *is the final point of segment, and* $0 < p_i < p_f$ *e* $p_i < p_f < p_n$*,* n *is the number of points of trajectory, that is,* $S \subset T$*.*

Frequent Point *(*fp*): is a tuple* (p, n)*, such that* p *is a point and* n *is its sample rate, that is, the point repetitions* p *in a set of trajectories.*

Frequent Area *(*FA*): is a vector that contains the frequent points* fp *delimiters for a radius with a distance d, defined as the input parameter of the algorithm and recalculated after the points frequent distribution. Therefore, the* FA *is a cluster of frequent points. So, a* $FA = [fp_i, fp_{i+1}, fp_{i+2}, \ldots, fp_{i+n}]$*.*

Candidate Points *(*cp*): is the frequent point* fp *that represent the center of a frequent area* FA*, so a* $cp \in FA$*. In this way, the candidate point* cp *is the frequent point* fp *with higher sample rate and the larger amount of neighbors, therefore the* cp *represents the cluster geometric center. A candidate point can be represented as* $cp = \max\{(fp_i) | fp_i \in FA \text{ and } 0 < i < n)\}$*, where* n *is the vector length* FA*.*

Reference Trajectory *(*RT*): is a virtual trajectory* T*, that is a building trajectory with a set of candidate points* cp*. Like this, a reference trajectory to be can represented as* $TR = [cp_i, cp_{i+1}, cp_{i+2}, \ldots, cp_{i+n}]$*.*

IV. PROPOSED METHOD

The clusterization of similar trajectories can be realized according to various parameters, such as distance between points, trajectories, trajectories segments, and others [12]. This work aims to propose a trajectories clustering method based in frequency of points in a given area.

The proposal considers that a set of similar trajectories describes a movement into a neighborhood of a reference trajectory. The reference trajectory can be defined considering the frequency of coordinate points into a given radius.

The reference areas are determined according to the frequency that the points in the neighborhood of a reference point occurs. To reduce the computational cost of various trajectories, all points outside an existing area — that are not inside the neighborhood of a candidate point according with a predetermined distance — it is considered a new candidate point.

When a point is inside of two or more areas, it should analyze if this point could be a better candidate point than the points that were previously selected. This analysis occurs only in areas where the point is located. If this area has more points, it is considered a frequency area. Those points that are not in this area are grouped in new areas.

Once every point has been analyzed, and there are not points into two different areas, one reference trajectory is built by using the candidates points.

In order to find the set of reference areas and the trajectory reference, this work proposed the algorithm *TRAJREF*. The algorithm receives a set of trajectories *trajs*, and the maximum distance *d* that a point *p1* of a trajectory *a* must have from another point *p2* of a trajectory *b*. The algorithm returns the areas with higher frequency of points through a list of tuples, in which the first element of the tuple is the *cp*, and the second element is the list of next points that are into the area that encircles the *cp*. Also, the algorithm returns a reference trajectory compose by *cp*'s.

Figure 1 presents the steps proposed in order to find the reference trajectory.

1) **Identify frequent areas:** Go through every points of *trajs*, noting its relations with the *cp*'s that were already identified. The first point contained in *trajs* will be the first *cp*. Each new analyzed point must calculate the distance from *cp*, if this distance is smaller than *d*, this point must be concatenated in the list of near points from *cp*. If the distance is bigger than *d*, this point turns in *cp*. Figure 1(a) presents a set of trajectories (*trajs*), and Figure 1(b) shows the set of *cp*'s, and their neighborhood areas defined by the radius *d*.
2) **Verify *cp* auxiliary list:** Once that every points have been covered, it must analyze the points contained in *cp* auxiliary list. This verification intent to identify

the existence of a *cp* with more near points than the already known *cp*. Therefore, it must compare the distance *d* between the auxiliary list point with the frequency area points that this point is already contained. In case the area of auxiliary point has more points than frequency areas already known, then it must create a new area, which the center is the auxiliary CP. All points that aren't contained in the new frequency area must be inserted in new frequency areas centered in the first point that isn't contained in previous frequency area. Figure 1(c) represents two frequency areas that contain the same point. That point remains to both areas, and is recorded in an auxiliary list.

3) **Exclusion of irrelevant areas:** After verifying all points of the trajectories and identifying the best *cp*'s, the goal is to exclude areas that doesn't have frequent points into a distance *d*. The result of this process is presented by the Figure 1(e).
4) **Building a reference trajectory:** The reference trajectory is composed of a set of *cp*'s.
5) **Return:** The algorithm must return the frequency areas found and the reference trajectory.

V. Experiments

This section presents the tools and materials used to develop the methodology. It also details the framework *partition-and-group* and the implementation of algorithm TRACLUS to compare and analyze the results.

A. *Trajectories Data*

To realize the experiments, one of the goals was reducing the capture and pre-processing cost of trajectories. This way, it was used simulated trajectories on MyMaps. MyMaps is a platform of Google that allows creating and sharing customized maps. Besides, it allows importing and exporting files on *kml* format, compatible formats of Quantum GIS.

The simulated trajectories represent routes in a region of Itaum neighborhood in the city of Joinville - Santa Catarina - Brazil. Figure 2 shows the simulations on MyMaps; it contains 7 trajectories with starts and finals points close to each others.

B. *Proposed Method*

The environment to execute the experiments includes the programming language Python 2.7, the packages 'numpy' version 1.12.0rc2, 'utm' version 0.4.1 and 'heapq' version 8.4. The experiments consider three different values to distance (d): 15, 20 and 30 meters. Those values represent the radius that define the neighborhood area around the *cp* points. The reference trajectories were represented in a map in order to compare with the results obtained by using the TRACLUS proposal.

C. *TRACLUS Proposal*

Experiments were made using the framework *partition-and-group* [7] to compare the results of purposed method in this article. The framework consists in two phases. In the partitioning phase, the trajectories are segmented using the minimum description length principle (MDL). The clustering phase considers the density to group similar segments in a cluster.

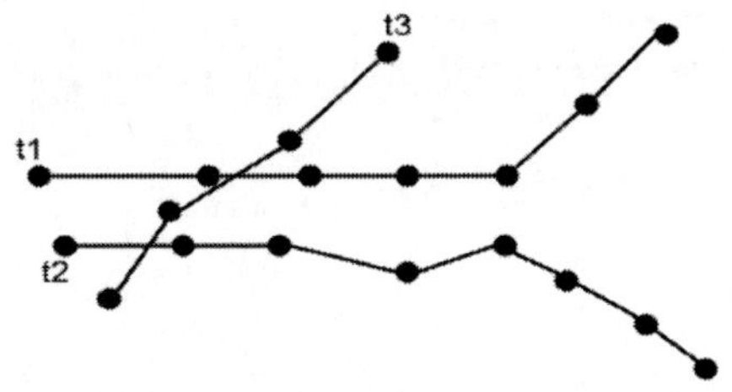

(a) Set of trajectories {t1, t2, t3}.

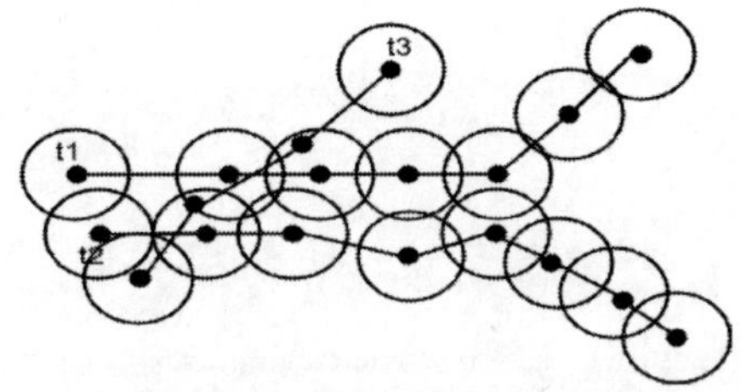

(b) Given a distance d, the points are grouped.

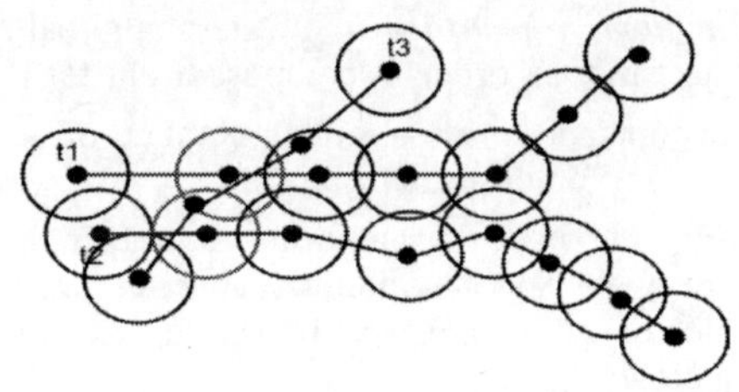

(c) If a point is in two areas, it must be considered a candidate point, and a new area is calculated.

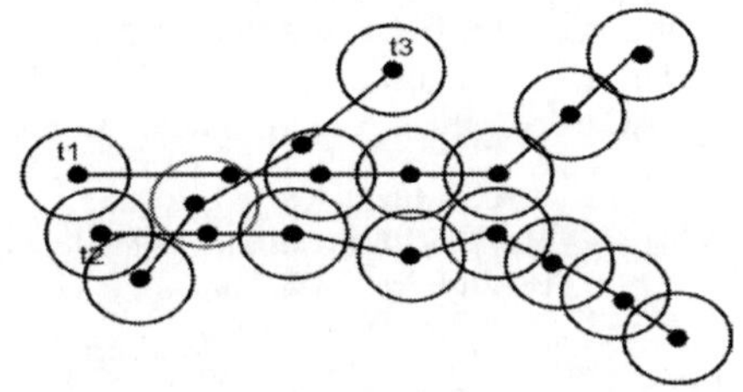

(d) If the new area has more points, it is a frequent area.

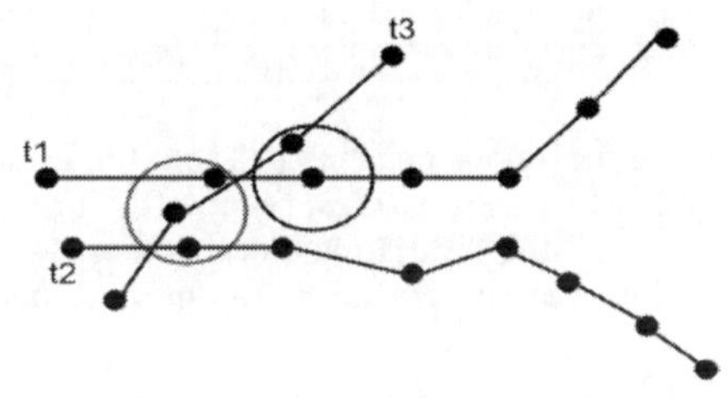

(e) All areas without neighbors are discarded.

Figure 1. An example of the proposed algorithm.

The TRACLUS proposal was implemented using the package 'traclus_impl' version 0.999 [13] of python language. Besides the set of trajectories, TRACLUS considers another input values:

- ϵ: radius cluster [14][15];
- *min_neighbors*: minimal number of neighbor segments [7];

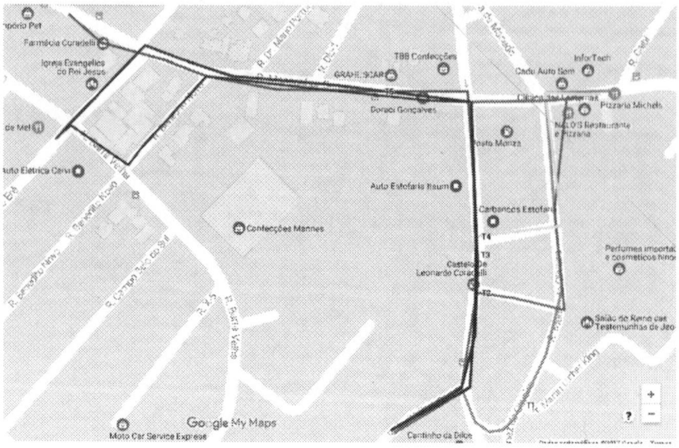

Figure 2. Simulated trajectories from Itaum neighborhood in Joinville - Santa Catarina - Brazil using MyMaps

- *min_num_trajectories_in_cluster*: minimal number of trajectories in order to compose a cluster [7];
- *min_vertical_lines*: minimal number of segments in order to compose a cluster [14].
- *min_prev_dist*: is a smoothing parameter, described by Lee et al. [7], in order to generate a representative trajectory, this concept is similar to the reference trajectory.

The experiments of the TRACLUS proposal were executed considering three values of ϵ 0.00015, 0.00020 and 0.00030. Table I presents the values. The ϵ values are the same to the d values of TRAJREF proposal, however, in a different scale. The other TRACLUS values remain stable during the three experiments.

TABLE I. VALUES VARIATIONS FOR THE INPUT PARAMETERS OF TRACLUS ALGORITHM.

	Experiments		
	1	2	3
ϵ	0.00015	0.00020	0.00030
min_neighbors	2	2	2
min_num_trajectories_in_cluster	2	2	2
min_vertical_lines	2	2	2
min_prev_dist	0.0002	0.0002	0.0002

Considering the values presents in Table I, a cluster will be formed by at least two trajectories, segments with two or more neighbors. Besides, the ϵ variations, in this work, will be used to identify differences in the points sample rate belonging to a cluster.

VI. Result Analysis

The analysis of the experiments considers the quantity of frequent points areas and the trajectory composed by those areas.

The variables considered to analyze the results of TRACLUS algorithm were the quantity of representative trajectories obtained, the clusters number and the segments belonging to each cluster number.

Three experiments were conducted considering three different values of d (15, 20 and 30), and ϵ — TRACLUS — (0.00015, 0.00020 and 0.00030). The obtained results were plotted in a map in order to facilitate the visualization and comparison (see Figures 3, 4 and 5) The reference trajectories are represented by the lines with *map icons*.

The Figure 3(a) shows the result of the proposed method, with 9 frequency areas (clusters) which form the reference trajectory. Figure 3(b) represents the TRACLUS results, with two representative trajectories, which segments are represented by yellow and red lines. TRACLUS proposal can not identify the cluster in the left side of the Figure 3(a), considering ϵ = 0,00015.

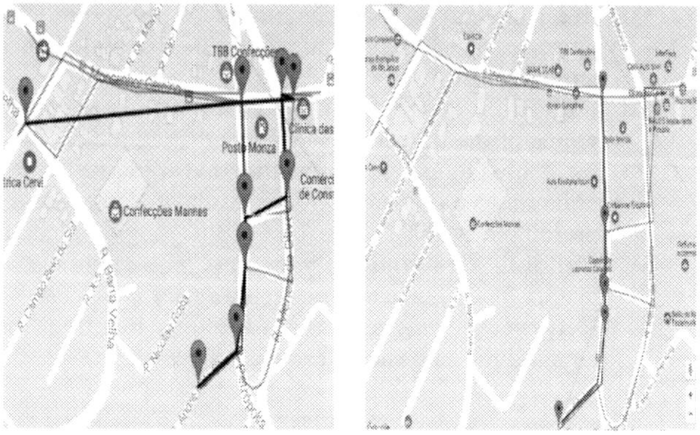

(a) (b)

Figure 3. Experiment 1 (d = 15 and ϵ = 0,00015) - (a) reference trajectory resulting by the proposed algorithm, and (b) representative trajectories by TRACLUS.

Figure 4(a) shows the result of the proposed method, with 10 frequency areas. Figure 4(b) shows the three representative trajectories of TRACLUS. The results are similar. The increase of ϵ value implies an increase in the number of clusters and representative trajectories. Besides, it is possible to verify that when the d value increase, the accuracy of the proposed method increases too.

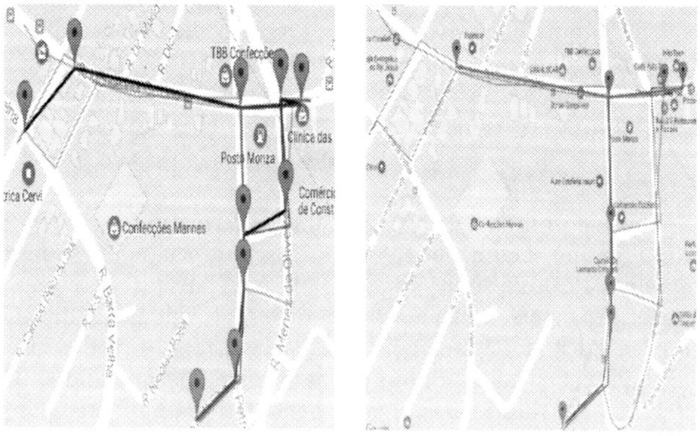

(a) (b)

Figure 4. Experiment 2 (d = 20 and ϵ = 0,00020) - (a) reference trajectory resulting by the proposed algorithm, and (b) representative trajectories by TRACLUS.

Figure 5(a) represents the result of the proposed method, with 12 frequency areas. The Figure 5(b) shows the three representative trajectories of TRACLUS, similar to the previous experiment. In this case, TRACLUS proposal identifies a new segment, represented by a pink line in the figure.

In order to compare the quantitative results, Tables II and III are presented.

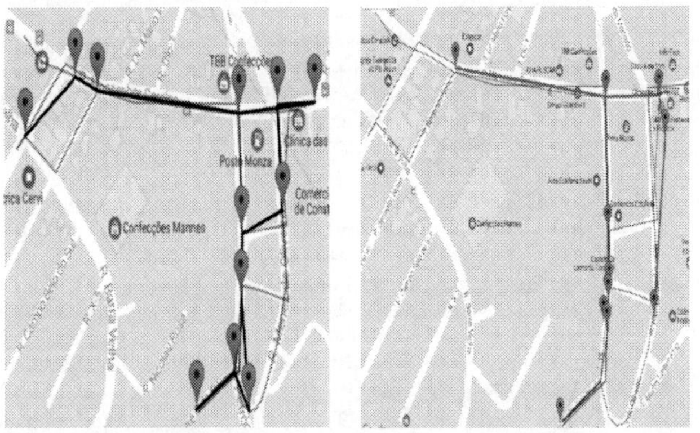

(a) (b)

Figure 5. Experiment 3 (d = 30 and ϵ = 0,00030) - (a) reference trajectory resulting by the proposed algorithm, and (b) representative trajectories by TRACLUS.

TABLE II. VALUES OF INPUT PARAMETERS - PROPOSED ALGORITHM.

	Experiment		
	1	2	3
n^o of reference trajectories	1	1	1
n^o of clusters	9	10	12

TABLE III. VALUES BY INPUT PARAMETERS - TRACLUS.

	Experiment		
	1	2	3
n^o of representative trajectories	2	3	3
n^o of points of the representative trajectories	2, 4	4, 2, 4	5, 3, 4
n^o of clusters	2	3	3
n^o of segments in clusters	3, 5	7, 3, 5	3, 5, 6

Figures 6(a) and 6(b) represent a *zoom* of the further south point of trajectories. It is a candidate point in all experiments, and will be named by $p1$.

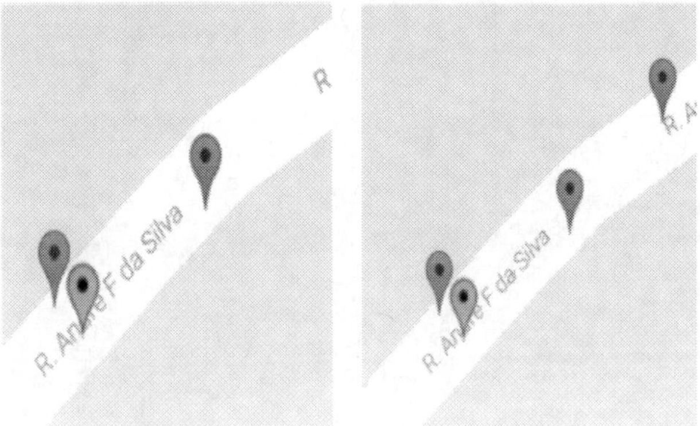

(a) (b)

Figure 6. Zoom in a candidate point - (a) frequent area where d = 20 - (b) frequent area where d = 30

It is possible to verify that when the maximal distance between points decreases, the quantity of points that belong to the frequent area $p1$ also decreases. It is an expected behavior of the proposed algorithm and contributes to certify the results.

Figure 7 presents the results of the experiments considering two identical trajectories. The proposed algorithm (TRAJREF) finds several frequency areas. Those areas are overlapping the original trajectories, as expected.

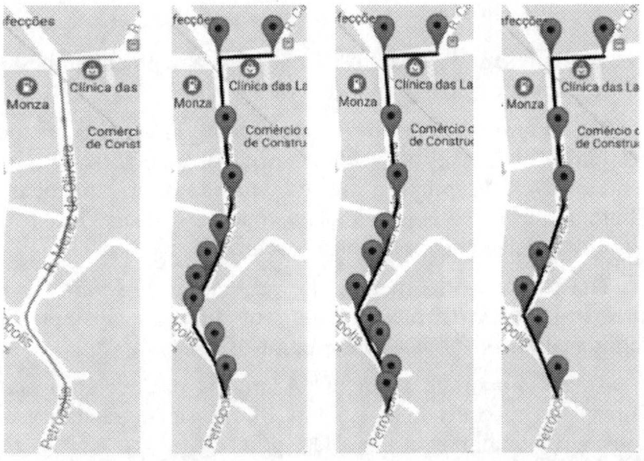

(a) (b) (c) (d)

Figure 7. Experiment with identical trajectories - (a) original trajectory (b) (d = 15) (c) (d = 20) (d) (d = 30).

Figure 8 shows the result of the experiment with TRACLUS proposal considering two identical trajectories. It is possible to note that the proposal returns a representative trajectory over a segment of the original trajectory. The algorithm does not find a representative trajectory matching the complete original trajectory. The partitioning step of the TRACLUS could be a reason for that.

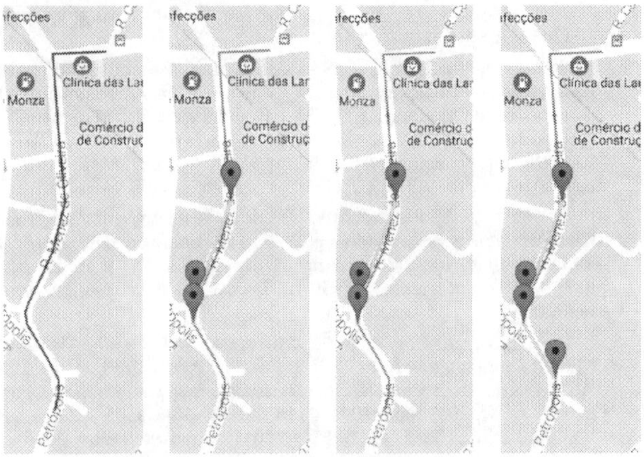

(a) (b) (c) (d)

Figure 8. Experiment with identical trajectories - (a) original trajectory (b) ($\epsilon = 0.00015$) (c) ($\epsilon = 0.00020$) (d) ($\epsilon = 0.00030$).

It is possible to note that the proposed algorithm (TRAJREF), is efficient to find the reference trajectory with precision and fidelity to the original trajectories presents in the database. Besides, found a greater sampling of points along the reference trajectory.

VII. Conclusion

The prime goal of this work was to present a method to find clusters of trajectories considering the frequency of occurrence of points based in an area defined by a given radius. After finding the clusters, the method returns a reference trajectory, based in the set of clusters.

Experiments allowed to conclude that the proposal (TRAJREF) presents similar results with TRACLUS proposal. However, the present proposal does not have a segmentation step, an expensive computational process.

The reference trajectory obtained by TRAJREF method presents a high level of fidelity to original trajectories of cluster. However, the propose method, still is not able to identify diferent clusters along reference trajectory, like TRACLUS algorithm. Like this, additional research is necessary.

The future works include the generation of several reference trajectories to representation of different clusters. The segmentation is another future point of research.

A very important point of research is to develop a additional step to prevent that points of the same trajectory are considered neighbor of candidate point.

Finally, it is possible to affirm that this method is suitable to be used in contexts where frequent points in a set of trajectories are a preponderant factor, as urban planning and public transportation.

REFERENCES

[1] Y. Zheng, "Trajectory Data Mining: An Overview," ACM Transactions on Intelligent Systems and Technology, vol. 6, no. 3, may 2015, pp. 29:1 – 29:41, URL: http://dx.doi.org/10.1145/2743025 [retrieved: out, 2016].

[2] Z. Feng and Y. Zhu, "A Survey on Trajectory Data Mining: Techniques and Applications," IEEE Access, vol. 4, apr 2016, pp. 2056 – 2067, ISSN:2169-3536, URL: http://ieeexplore.ieee.org/document/7452339/ [retrieved: out, 2016].

[3] H. Wang, H. Su, K. Zheng, S. Sadiq, and X. Zhou, "An Effectiveness Study on Trajectory Similarity Measures," in Proceedings of the Twenty-Fourth Australasian Database Conference, vol. 137. Australian Computer Society, Inc., 2013, pp. 13 – 22, ISBN: 978-1-921770-22-7, URL: http://dl.acm.org/citation.cfm?id=2525416.2525418 [retrieved: out, 2016].

[4] C.-C. Hung, W.-C. Peng, and W.-C. Lee, "Clustering and Aggregating Clues of Trajectories for Mining Trajectory Patterns and Routes," The VLDB Journal, vol. 24, no. 2, apr 2015, pp. 169 – 192, ISSN: 1066-8888, URL: http://dx.doi.org/10.1007/s00778-011-0262-6 [retrieved: out, 2016].

[5] S. Liu, S. Wang, K. Jayarajah, A. Misra, and R. Krishnan, "TODMIS: Mining Communities from Trajectories," in Proceedings of the 22Nd ACM International Conference on Information & Knowledge Management. ACM, 2013, pp. 2109 – 2118, ISBN: 978-1-4503-2263-8, URl: http://doi.acm.org/10.1145/2505515.2505552 [retrieved: nov, 2016].

[6] A. A. Shaw and N. Gopalan, "Finding frequent trajectories by clustering and sequential pattern mining," Journal of Traffic and Transportation Engineering (English Edition), vol. 1, no. 6, 2014, pp. 393 – 403, ISSN: 2095-7564, URL: http://www.sciencedirect.com/science/article/pii/S2095756415302890 [retrieved: nov, 2016].

[7] J.-G. Lee, J. Han, and K.-Y. Whang, "Trajectory Clustering: A Partition-and-group Framework," in Proceedings of the 2007 ACM SIGMOD International Conference on Management of Data. ACM, 2007, pp. 593 – 604, ISBN: 978-1-59593-686-8, URL: http://doi.acm.org/10.1145/1247480.1247546 [retrieved: nov, 2016].

[8] H. H. Aung, L. Guo, and K.-L. Tan, Mining Sub-trajectory Cliques to Find Frequent Routes. Springer Berlin Heidelberg, 2013, pp. 92 – 109, ISBN: 978-3-642-40235-7, URL: http://dx.doi.org/10.1007/978-3-642-40235-7_6 [retrieved: nov, 2016].

[9] A. A. de Melo, G. Scheibel, F. Baldo, and F. J. Braz, "A Method for Calculating Shape Similarity among Trajectory of Moving Object Based on Statistical Correlation of Angular Deflection Vectors," in GEOProcessing 2016, The Eighth International Conference on Advanced Geographic Information Systems, Applications, and Services, IARIA, Ed., Venice, Italy, apr 2016, pp. 63 – 68, ISBN: 978-1-61208-469-5, ISSN: 2308-393X, URL: https://thinkmind.org/index.php?view=article&articleid=geoprocessing_2016_4_10_30078 [retrieved: out, 2016].

[10] Y. Zheng, L. Zhang, X. Xie, and W.-Y. Ma, "Mining Interesting Locations and Travel Sequences from GPS Trajectories," in Proceedings of the 18th International Conference on World Wide Web. ACM, 2009, pp. 791 – 800, ISBN: 978-1-60558-487-4, URL: http://doi.acm.org/10.1145/1526709.1526816 [retrieved: jan, 2017].

[11] V. C. Fontes and V. Bogorny, "Discovering Semantic Spatial and Spatio-Temporal Outliers from Moving Object Trajectories," CoRR, 2013, URL: http://arxiv.org/abs/1303.5132 [retrieved: dez, 2016].

[12] B. Morris and M. Trivedi, "Learning Trajectory Patterns by Clustering: Experimental Studies and Comparative Evaluation," in Computer Vision and Pattern Recognition, 2009. CVPR 2009. IEEE Conference on. IEEE, 2009, pp. 312 – 319, URL: http://ieeexplore.ieee.org/document/5206559/ [retrieved: jan, 2017].

[13] A. Polcyn. traclus_impl 0.999 : Python package index. [Online]. Available: https://pypi.python.org/pypi/traclus_impl [retrieved: jan, 2016]

[14] L. Schauer and M. Werner, "Clustering of Inertial Indoor Positioning Data," in 1st GI Expert Talk on Localization. Department of Computer Science of RWTH Aachen University, 2015, pp. 21 – 23, URL: http://www.cip.ifi.lmu.de/~schauer/publications/ClusteringIndoor.pdf [retrieved: jan, 2017].

[15] B. Liu. Ship Trajectory Clustering Using TraClus Algorithm. [Online]. Available: http://luborliu.me/doc/project_report_TraclusAlgorithm2014.pdf [retrieved: apr, 2014]

A Method to Identify Aggressive Driver Behaviour Based on Enriched GPS Data Analysis

Marcio Geovani Jasinski
Department of Applied Research
Senior Sistemas – SA
Blumenau, Santa Catarina – Brazil
Email: marcio.jasinski@senior.com.br

Fabiano Baldo
Computer Science Department
Santa Catarina State University – UDESC
Joinville, Santa Catarina – Brazil
Email: fabiano.baldo@udesc.br

***Abstract*—The main cause of road casualties is related to the driver behavior. The identification of unsafe driving is an important step in order to take actions to change this situation. A novel approach to address driver behavior is called naturalistic driving. This approach tries to understand drivers' behavior during everyday trips by analyzing their moving recorded data through non intrusive GPS gathering devices. Based on that premise, this paper presents a method aimed at identifying aggressive behavior in order to reduce the risk of accidents. As a consequence, it is expected to improve drivers awareness about theirs drive behaviors as well as to notify transportation and insurance companies about the driver's way of driving. The proposed method is composed of four steps, which includes data gathering, pre-processing, semantic enrichment and Trajectory Aggressivity Indicator (TAI) calculation. This indicator varies from 0 to 100 where 0 means no aggressive behavior and 100 means very aggressive behavior. The main contribution is to provide an adaptive approach that considers environmental conditions as weather and traffic to better estimate the TAI. Preliminary results pointed out that the method can identify aggressive behavior almost in a real-time manner, which might be used to notify dangerous behavior before an accident happen.**

***Keywords*–Naturalistic driving; Driver profile; Aggressive driving; GPS; Speed; Acceleration.**

I. INTRODUCTION

The number of fatal casualties on road crashes reached 1.25 million people in 2015 and it is the main cause of death among people aged 15 – 29 years old [1]. More than 95% of such accidents are caused or contributed by driver behavior factors [2]. However, even with several governmental actions devoted to reducing traffic accidents, until now there is no signal of traffic deaths declination worldwide [1].

As driver's behavior is the main cause of road casualties, the identification of unsafe driving attitudes is an important step towards taking actions to reduce them. Several methods have been studied in order to obtain a better understanding of driver behavior. However, as pointed out by Ellison et al. [3], research methods using demographic profiles, self-reported behavior and personal risk perceptions tend to assume homogeneity of behavior within groups. Moreover, self-reports and questionnaires are sensitive to user perspective, which might give a false sense of secure/insecure manners.

A novel approach to address driver behavior is called Naturalistic Driving Study (NDS). The NDS can be defined as "A study undertaken to provide insight into driver behaviour during everyday trips by recording details of the driver, the vehicle and the surroundings through nonintrusive data gathering equipment and without experimental control" [4]. This approach uses equipment like GPS device, video camera and audio recorder to obtain daily data. However, it is important to enforce the unobtrusive requirement in order to gather natural behavior for long periods of time.

The most common approaches to naturalistic behavior analysis are based on Global Positioning System (GPS) data and video recording. This work analyses naturalistic driving over data from GPS devices embedded into a smartphone. This approach has been chosen because smartphones are largely used by drivers and have all the required features to collect and transfer positioning information. In this work, these data concern the so-called trajectories.

Although GPS data already bring meaningful trajectory information, when combined with other extra information it is possible to leverage the positioning contextualization. Some of the information that can contribute to bringing context of driving movement are weather condition and road speed limits. Such information is crucial to better calculate the driver's behavior indicator. So, in this work it is assumed that the identification of drivers' behavior can be better defined when GPS trajectory data are enriched with weather and speed limit contextualization.

Based on the aforementioned assumptions, the objective of this work is to identify drivers' aggressive behavior based on the analysis of their trajectories enriched with weather and speed limit data, using a naturalistic approach. As a consequence, it is expected to contribute to improve drivers awareness about theirs driving behaviors as well as to notify transportation and insurance companies about the driver's way of driving.

This paper is structured as follows. Section II presents the related works. Section III details the proposed method and its conceptual characteristics. Section IV presents the results assessment. Finally, Section V contains conclusions and further works.

II. RELATED WORK

Driving behavior is a subject of extensive research in psychology, as stated in works like [5] and [6]. In contrast, naturalistic driving research is relatively new, but are gaining

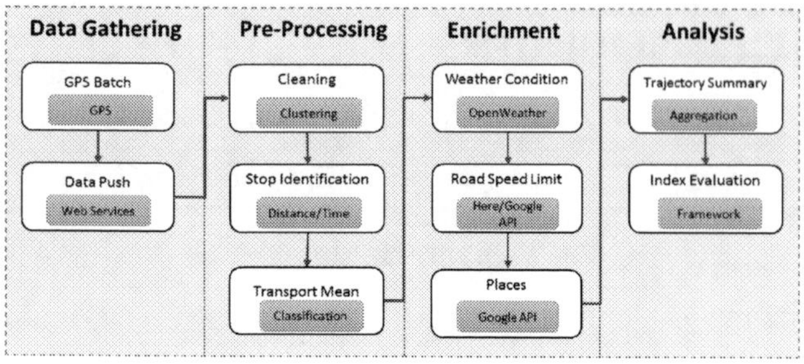

Figure 1. Proposed method to evaluate driver's trajectories

special attention due to the emerging of new technologies to data gathering. In this section, the most significant works on natural driving will be discussed.

Carboni [7] proposes a method that identifies drivers' behaviours considering three anomalies over accelerations and directions: a) abrupt movements (acceleration and deceleration); b) lane changes; c) Excessive speed. As result, the algorithm is capable of classifying drivers in the following categories: careful, distracted, dangerous and very dangerous. It was evaluated using a low number of trajectories collected from buses and cars in a very restricted area. Its main contribution is the identification of anomalous behavior, drivers classification and dangerous places.

Ellison et al. [8] propose the Driver Behavior Profile (DBP) evaluated through the Temporal and Spatial Identifiers (TSI) indicator. The temporal factors considered are purpose, date and time, the day of week and number of passengers. Behavioral factors considered are speed, acceleration and deceleration. Results indicate that different road environments elicit different behavioral responses. The authors also suggest that DBP might be used to test the effectiveness of changes to infrastructure, education campaigns or legislation proposals.

Siqueira [9] evaluates chase behavior comparing the trajectory of two objects. The proposed method considers a target and a pursuer trajectory and compares both against space and time using algorithms to identify pursuit (TRA-CHASE) and another to classify pursuit type (CLASS-CHASE). Its main contribution is the definition of the following chase patterns: a) Detective; b) Meeting; c) Capture; d) Assault; e) Hunting.

Based on the literature review, it can be seen that the assessment of drivers' behaviours using their trajectory data is a fresh and open research field. Moreover, as far as it was possible to search, it was not found any work that addresses the identification of aggressivity profiles based on weather and local speed constraints on a near real time manner as it is proposed in this work.

III. Proposed Method

As showed in Figure 1, the proposed method is composed of four phases: i) Data gathering; ii) Pre-processing; iii) Segment enrichment and iv) Aggressiveness evaluation. The following subsection describes in details each one of this phases.

The method enriches and evaluate a trajectory trough a set of a segment of 1 km long. Thus, a trajectory with 25 km will be composed of 25 segments. Every segment is enriched individually with its own speed limit, weather details and important places.

The aggressive behavior is evaluated considering speed and acceleration maneuvers. To obtain an aggressiveness index, a speed and acceleration stratification is proposed. The speed is based on the traffic violations of the Brazilian Transit Code (BTC). An incremental fine is issued to the driver accordingly the percentage of excessive speed based on the local speed limit. Table I presents the current penalties of BTC with respective fine and penalties.

TABLE I. SPEED VIOLATION AND FINES FROM BRAZILIAN TRAFFIC CODE

Violation	Severity	Fine
Up to 20%	Medium	USD 25.37 / 4 points
From 20% up to 50%	Severe	USD 37.91 / 5 points
Over 50%	Very Severe	USD 171.34 / 7 points / Suspension

Several researchers addressed acceleration limits associated with causalities and high risk of being involved in an accident. According to [10] a risk of collision starts from $-4m/s^2$. Similar conclusions were obtained by [11] with a risk of accident involvement around $-5m/s^2$. Considering mentioned works, we propose a stratification of acceleration according to Table II. A total of eight groups is considered to evaluate driver speeding up and breaking.

TABLE II. ACCELERATION DISTRIBUTION BY SEVERITY

Severity	Acceleration m/s^2
Dangerous	[-9.0 a -14.0]
Aggressive	[-5.5 a -9.0)
Normal	[-3.0 a -5.5)
Safe	[0 a -3.0)
Safe	[0 a 1.5)
Normal	[1.5 a 3.5)
Aggressive	[3.5 a 7.0)
Dangerous	[7.0 a 12.0]

A. *Data Gathering*

The data gathering is enabled by an Android application that periodically collects the driver's current geo-positioning and time. The application was developed to collect data as a background service using one second time interval to request the GPS sensor as well as the clock. This strategy enforces the approach to register the driving behavior as more naturalistic as possible because the driver does not need to open the application on every journey since it is always tracking the smartphone position. The collected data is sent as a stream over Internet, or mobile communication like 3G or 4G, to the server periodically within intervals of 60 seconds.

B. *Pre-processing*

The pre-processing phase includes trajectory cleaning, segmentation and transportation mean identification. The trajectory cleaning is performed by the DBScan clustering algorithm. It is a density based algorithm proposed by Ester et al. [12], which classifies every point as CORE, BORDER or NOISE. Such classification is based on the input parameters $minPts$ and ϵ. Every point which has at least $minPts$ in a ϵ radius will be classified as CORE. A BORDER is a point which does not satisfy the CORE criteria but it is connected to a CORE. Every point which is neither a CORE nor a BORDER is classified as NOISE.

Regarding the trajectory segmentation, the proposed method considers two ways of segmenting a trajectory. The first one is a result of the absence of GPS signal, which might occur due to several situations like the impossibility of GPS device to contact enough satellites, localization service disabled or smartphone turned off. As consequence of the inability to collect GPS coordinates, the data will have a time interval without any position. Based on empirical evaluation, it was defined a number of points threshold (NPT=10) and a time frame (TF=30s) to identify time stops and thus split a trajectory into sub-trajectories. A stop is considered if the number of coordinates collected during latest TF is less or equal to NPT.

The second way of segmentation is used to find situations where the driver remains stopped in a certain place for a predefined time interval. This segmentation tries to identify whether the driver is moving or not (i.g. fueling at gas a station). Based on empirical evaluation over data previously collected, it has been defined 300 meters as distance threshold within 5 minutes of time threshold. Those values are able to identify a fast food stop and still avoid to split the trajectory in every semaphore.

The last step of the pre-processing is the identification and distinction of transportation mean between Motorized Transport (MT) and Non-Motorised Transport (NMT). This is necessary since the data gathering is performed by smartphone and thus several means of transportation are presented in the trajectories. The proposed method applies a classifier in order to identify the transport mean splitting trajectory accordingly. The classifier was trained with 55% of the Geolife dataset[13] using the J48 algorithm from Weka [14]. The output from J48 is a decision tree which indicates that motorized movements usually will present speed over 15 km/h. However, during a heavy traffic, semaphores and crossings it is possible that an MT coordinates might be confused as an NMT. To ensure that trajectory will not be split on every crossing, a threshold for MT and NMT was defined based on data gathered during real experiments. A minimum of 5 coordinates over 15 km/h is enough to identify a MT while a minimum of 15 is necessary to detect an NMT.

C. Semantic Enrichment

The semantic enrichment intends to attach additional information in the trajectory in order to help the calculation of more accurate driver's aggressive behaviour. There are several external factors that affect traffic safety and that can not be extracted by GPS device itself. Some of the currently supported ones are road speed limit, weather conditions and important places surrounding. These factors impact in the aggressiveness analysis over speed and acceleration limits.

There are three types of trajectory semantic enrichment currently supported: weather, road speed limit and important place. Every semantic element impacts the aggressiveness analysis over speed and acceleration.

During a trajectory, the driver may travel through different roads with different speed limits. To gather this information the method makes requests to external APIs of services like Google Maps. However, as the speed limit of certain roads would not be available through an API service, several strategies are applied in order to define to speed limit:

- Speed limit API – Consists of requesting to a specialized web service the speed limit of a specific road;
- Inverse geocoding and database query – The road name is obtained through inverse geocoding. Thus, a query is performed against an internal database of registered roads and its respective speed limit is retrieved.
- Inverse geocoding and road type definition – Roads which are not registered in the internal database have the speed limit defined accordingly to its prefixes. In Brazil, there are five type of roads formerly defined by national authorities as shown in Table III.
- Average speed evaluation – This approach guess the maximum speed based on previous segment speed average. The speed will be limited according to Table III, which means that a segment with an average speed of 33 km/h will be classified as max speed of 40 km/h.

TABLE III. SPEED LIMIT BASED ON BRAZILIAN TRAFFIC CODE

Road Type	Speed Limit
Highway	110 km/h
Roadway	80 km/h
Arterial roadway	60 km/h
Municipal streets	40 km/h
Local streets	30 km/h

Although there is not formal law defining the impact of weather conditions on the road, the public authorities are allowed to issue a fine in case of driver conducts the vehicle in a dangerous manner. The BTC stands that "a fine is applicable if the driver is driving with incompatible speed considering the road conditions". Weather is one of the aspects that affects the road conditions and hence the driving safety. In order to consider the weather in driver's behaviour, every segment is enriched with weather conditions through calls to Weather API. Depending on the weather condition, a reduction over speed limit and acceleration is applied according to Table IV and Table V.

TABLE IV. WEATHER IMPACT OVER ROAD SPEED LIMIT

Weather	Speed Reduction factor
Drizzle	10%
Light rain	15%
Moderate rain	20%
Heavy intensity rain	25%
Very heavy rain	30%

The speed reduction is based on the principle that traveling at 95 km/h on a sunny day is secure considering a highway with speed limit of 110 km/h. However, such speed might be dangerous under heavy rain. Since it has not been found specific reduction values in the literature, Table IV has been defined based on automotive specialists recommendations [15].

The wet road also has an important impact on the car friction to gain speed and mainly to reduce speed. Hence, the same acceleration intensity for the dry road will be more dangerous if applied to the wet road. To obtain the reduction factors presented on Table V a model based on Newtonian classical physics was designed. This model considered a well

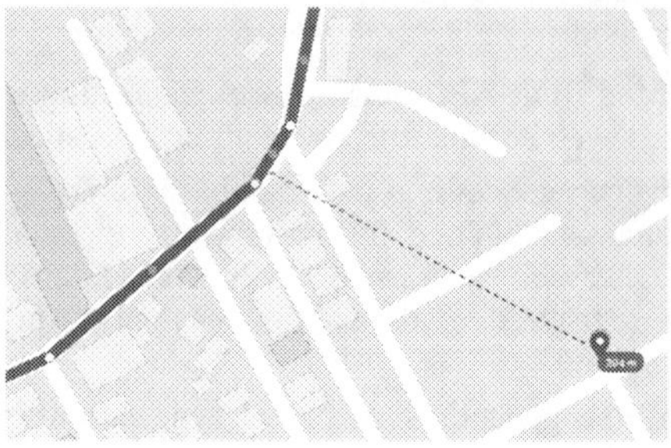

Figure 2. Important place mismatch by street name

balanced car and a simple friction model between the road and the car tires. As result, the relationship of acceleration and road friction was obtained according to (1), where a is the acceleration, μ is the road friction and g is the gravity of earth. Applying a road friction coefficient for each weather condition (1) it was possible to obtain the acceleration reduction factor for each one of them, respectively.

TABLE V. WEATHER IMPACT OVER DRIVER ACCELERATION

Weather	Friction	Reduction factor
Dry weather	0.85	-
Drizzle	0.80	6%
Light rain	0.7	18%
Moderate rain	0.6	29%
Heavy intensity rain	0.5	41%
Very heavy rain	0.4	53%

$$a = g\mu/2 \tag{1}$$

Finally, as last semantic enrichment, a search for important places is performed in order to identify buildings which require speed reduction. An external service from Google [16] is used to retrieve important places near to a specific coordinate. These important places include schools, universities, hospitals, and health care institutions. Once an important place is found within a circular area of 1 km radius distance from driver's current position, the maximum speed is reduced to 30 km/h ever.

To indeed consider a found important place as a speed limit reducer, the important place must be on the same road where the driver is traveling. One example of such situation is presented in Figure 2. This is ensured by matching the driver's current street name and the name of the street where each one of the found important places is located.

D. Aggressiveness Evaluation

The evaluation phase calculates the aggressiveness indicator using speed and acceleration values combined with the semantic enrichment done previously. The indicator varies from 0 to 100 where 0 means no aggressivety and 100 high aggressivety. Currently, the method considers BTC definitions to obtain the indicator, but it can be configured to any other country and laws. In the same way, BTC increases the fine according to the level of the transit violation, the method applies stronger weights to highlight the driver aggressiveness. Those weights were defined considering BTC rules and adjusted using hit and try over real trajectories. Table VI presents weights for speed violations and Table VII presents weights to acceleration categories.

TABLE VI. WEIGHT ACCORDING TO SPEED BEHAVIOR

	Speed behavior	Weight
1	Under speed limit	0
2	Up to 20% over the limit	1.5
3	From 20% to 50% over the limit	3.0
4	Over 50% over the limit	5.0

TABLE VII. WEIGHT ACCORDING TO ACCELERATION BEHAVIOR

	Acceleration Type	Weight
1	Safe	0
2	Normal	1.5
3	Aggressive	3.0
4	Dangerous	5.0

During a full trajectory, the aggressive behavior might appear occasionally. However, those specific moments are the most common situations of accidents. So, a segment indicator is obtained by the composition of two sub-indexes: exclusive aggressive index and mean index. A segment is evaluated considering speed and acceleration by calculating Segment Aggressiveness Indicator (SAI) accordingly to (2).

$$SAI = \frac{((ASEI * p_{as}) + (MSI * p_{ms}))}{2} + \frac{((AAEI * p_{aa}) + (MAI * p_{ma}))}{2} \tag{2}$$

$ASEI$ = Aggressive speed exclusive index
MSI = Mean speed index
$AAEI$ = Aggressive acceleration exclusive index
MAI = Mean acceleration index
p_{as} = Aggressive speed percentage
p_{ms} = Non aggressive speed percentage
p_{aa} = Aggressive acceleration percentage
p_{ma} = Non aggressive acceleration percentage

Every coordinate of a segment is evaluated individually to be classified according to speed and acceleration using classification presented in Table I and Table II.

The ASEI and MSI indexes are obtained accordingly to (3) and (4). Equation 3 discard safe values, so pa_k is the percentage k class considering only aggressive behavior, w_k is the weight of class k and avg_k the average speed of k class aggressive coordinates. On the order hand, Equation 4 considers all coordinates, so pm_k is the percentage k class and avg_k the average speed of k class coordinates.

$$ASEI = \sum_{k=2}^{4} w_k * pa_k * avg_k \tag{3}$$

$$MSI = \sum_{k=1}^{4} w_k * pm_k * avg_k \tag{4}$$

The acceleration indexes are obtained in the same way as speed. The Exclusively Acceleration Index (AAEI) is obtained by (5). The equation is composed of the sum of aggressive acceleration evaluation and the sum of aggressive deceleration. The w_k is the weight, pa_k is the percentage and avg_k is the acceleration average for class k. Similarly, (6) gives the mean acceleration evaluation.

$$AAEI = \sum_{k=1}^{3}(w_k * pa_k * avg_k) + \sum_{k=6}^{8}(w_k * pa_k * avg_k) \quad (5)$$

$$MAI = \sum_{k=1}^{8} w_k * p_k * avg_k \quad (6)$$

The Trajectory Aggressiveness Indicator (TAI), presented in (7), is composed of all segment indicators and it reflects the general behavior of a driver in a specific trajectory.

$$TAI = \frac{\sum_{i=1}^{n} SAI_i}{n} \quad (7)$$

IV. Assessment

In order to assess the proposed method, it has been collected a set of trajectories surrounding the city of Blumenau, in the so-called Itajai River Valley Area, Brazil, from February to October 2016, summing up 7.911 kilometers. Currently, the data set contains more than 2.000 hours of 10 drivers performing daily activities, such as going to work, to the gym, to restaurants and to home. However, there are also several trips in highways like BR-101 and BR-470.

Results indicate aggressiveness tendency once drivers join the roadways (max speed of 80km/h) and highways (max speed of 110km/h) with an average TAI of 36.87. Urban trajectories resulted in a lower TAI average of 17.98. This can be explained by the fact that urban roads usually prevent drivers of speeding with semaphores, heavy traffic, pedestrians and radar speeds.

The method is able to correctly identify driver aggressiveness considering external conditions like weather conditions and important places closeness. This result could be analyzed in the scenario of a trip from Governador Celso Ramos/SC/Brazil to Blumenau/SC/Brazil during a rainy day between 08:21:15 PM - 9:57:36 PM comprising 106.26km.

The trip starts at a highway limited by 110 km/h in a light rain night. Since light rain was identified, the method applies a speed reduction factor of 18% resulting in 90.2 km/h max speed. Later, the driver join the SC-412 roadway, which is limited to 80 km/h, and thus the speed limit was reduced to 65,6 km/h. Finally, an urban area is reached and so the speed limit was reduced from 50 km/h to 41 km/h. In the same way, the acceleration limits were also reduced accordingly to Table VIII for all segments.

The aggressiveness evaluation results to a TAI of $29,91$, which can be described as a moderate aggressive driving. However, such indicator was only obtained due to the weather conditions. Otherwise, in a sunny day, the TAI would be $18,96$. So, without the weather condition enrichment, the driver would be considered a safe conductor one during this trajectory.

Table IX and Table X show in details the speed distribution and acceleration distribution, respectively. Table IX shows that without semantic enrichment 86.34% of speed coordinates would be considered safe, however considering the weather

TABLE VIII. ACCELERATION LIMITS CHANGED BY REDUCTION FACTOR (18%)

Classification	Standard Limit	Reduced Limit (18%)
Dangerous	[-9,0 a -14,0]	[-7,38 a -11,48]
Aggressive	[-5,5 a -9,0)	[-4,51 a -7,38)
Intermediate	[-3,0 a -5,5)	[-2,46 a -4,51)
Safe	[0 a -3,0)	[0 a -2,46)
Safe	[0 a 1,5)	[0 a 1,14)
Normal	[1,5 a 3,5)	[1,23 a 2,87)
Intermediate	[3,5 a 7,0)	[2,87 a 5,74)
Dangerous	[7,0 a 12,0]	[5,74 a 9,84]

condition the safe speed coordinates reduce to 46.50%. A similar effect can be seen over acceleration, Table X presents that intermediate accelerations increased 0.62%, as well as aggressive accelerations appeared in wet road.

TABLE IX. SPEED DISTRIBUTION CONSIDERING WET AND DRY ROAD

Classification	% Wet road	% Dry Road
Under limit	46,50%	86,34%
Up to 10%	27,13%	8,25%
From 10% to 20%	14,78%	1,67%
From 20% to 50%	8,28%	1,31%
Over 50%	3,32%	2,43%

TABLE X. ACCELERATION DISTRIBUTION CONSIDERING WET AND DRY ROAD

Classification	% Wet Road	% Dry Road
Safe	97,65%	98,40%
Intermediate	2,22%	1,60%
Aggressive	0,13%	0%
Dangerous	0%	0%

The aggressiveness evaluation indicates that the driver rarely applies abrupt movements. However, the majority of the trajectory is performed using a considerable dangerous speed. During the trip, a maximum speed of 120.71 km/h was registered while the speed average was 75.37 km/h. Also, few accelerations associated with risk of accidents were registered mainly on deceleration with the max of -5.03 m/s^2.

Several scenarios were evaluated in details in order to assess the method accuracy in a qualitative approach. Due to space limitation, it was not possible to present all of them, but the method obtained satisfactory results considering urban trajectories, roadway trajectories and also hybrid ones.

During the assessment, it was identified some improvements and limitations that need to be addressed in further works. For instance, the road speed limit is susceptible to errors due to the lack of GPS accuracy. The impact of such errors is considerable when the algorithm has to define the speed limit by inverse geocoding. Figure 3 presents a speed limit changed from 80 km/h to 50 km/h due to an incorrect inverse geocoding query. As consequence, the segment 53 evaluated the driver behavior as very aggressive (limited at 50 km/h), although he/she was not driving aggressively in the correct street (limited at 80 km/h).

Some scenarios indicate that the segment size of 1 km should be reduced in order to obtain more accurate results. Otherwise, the verification of the important place street does not match with the driver's current street due to road changes.

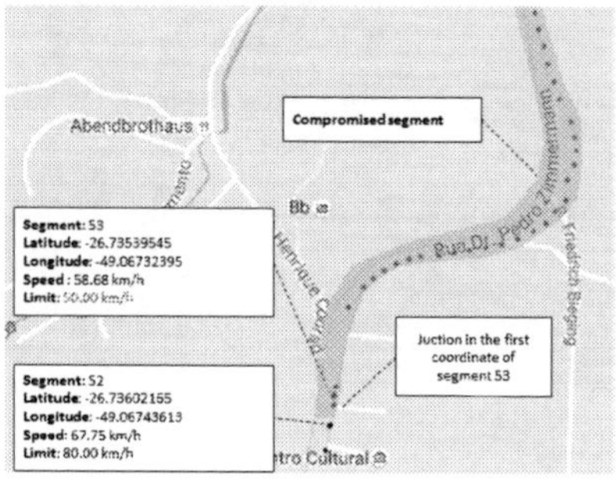

Figure 3. Junction compromising speed limit of a segment

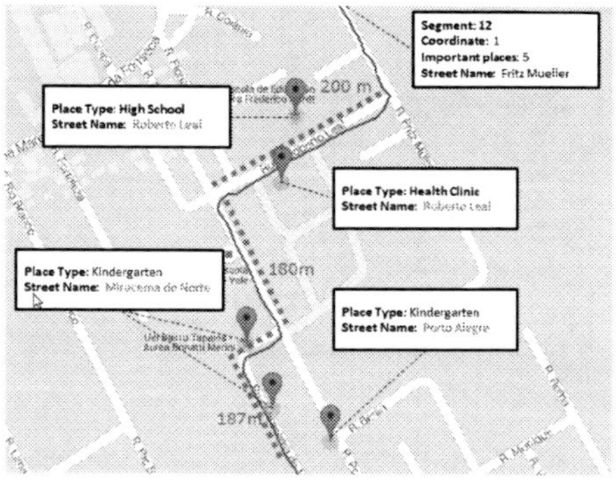

Figure 4. Five important places missed by 1 km segment using first coordinate street name

Figure 4 present this situation where the segment street name is defined by its first coordinate. However, the driver changes streets passing in front of an important place, which is placed in a different street name. The situation is ignored by the method since the segment street name and important place street name do not match.

Finally, the pre-processing phase seems to be effective but has several improvements that may be done. The DBScan cleaner is able to remove noises distant 30 meters from the core, but this is not sufficient to clean noises under such limit. To solve this situation another approach must be used since the noise under 30 meters are common on GPS devices.

V. CONCLUSION

This paper has presented a naturalistic driver method to identify driver's aggressive behavior. The method is composed of four steps that are capable of gather, clean, enrich and analysis the drivers' trajectories in order to identify aggressive behaviours in a near real time response. The main advantage of such method is its adaptive approach that considers environmental conditions as weather and road speed limits to better estimate the driver aggressivity indicator. This indicator varies between 0 and 100 where 0 means no aggressivity while 100 means the highest aggressivity possible. Moreover, the method can bring fast feedback to the drivers about their aggressive behaviours on specific situations and can help them to change habits in order to avoid accidents.

Another contribution is that the aggressivity indicator might be adapted according to every demand. This approach might be useful to transportation companies willing to improve the safety of their drivers. Moreover, identifying aggressive drivers allow insurance companies to offer discounts accordingly to every driver profile.

Although the proposed method is already under experimental usage, several improvements are possible. For instance, abrupt movements like passing or crossing lanes are no considered yet and can be added in future works. Another improvement might be explored information available for other sensors from the smartphone such as accelerometer. Finally, it is also important to conduct a massive evaluation to improve weather reduction values based on real data.

REFERENCES

[1] "Global status report on road safety 2015," 2015, [Retrieved: Feb., 2017]. [Online]. Available: http://www.who.int

[2] E. Petridou and M. Moustaki, "Human factors in the causation of road traffic crashes," European Journal of Epidemiology, vol. 16, no. 9, 2000, pp. 819–826, [Retrieved: Jan., 2017]. [Online]. Available: http://www.jstor.org/stable/3581952

[3] A. B. Ellison, S. P. Greaves, and M. C. Bliemer, "Driver behaviour profiles for road safety analysis," Accident Analysis & Prevention, vol. 76, 2015, pp. 118 – 132, [Retrieved: Jan., 2017]. [Online]. Available: http://www.sciencedirect.com/science/article/pii/S0001457515000202

[4] "Naturalistic driving: observing everyday driving behaviour," 2010, [Retrieved: Feb., 2017]. [Online]. Available: http://www.udrive.eu

[5] G. Underwood, C. P., S. Wright, and D. Crundall, "Anger while driving," Transportation Research, vol. 2, no. 1, 1999, pp. 55–68.

[6] E. Gulian, G. Matthews, A. I. Glendon, D. R. Davies, and L. M. Debney, "Dimensions of driver stress," Ergonomics, vol. 32, no. 6, 1989, pp. 585–602.

[7] E. M. Carboni, "Analysis of drivers behaviour through moving object trajectories," Master's thesis, Universidade Federal de Santa Catarina, 2014, dissertao de Mestrado - Universidade Federal de Santa Catarina - UFSC.

[8] A. B. Ellison, M. C. Bliemer, and S. P. Greaves, "Evaluating changes in driver behaviour: A risk profiling approach," Accident Analysis & Prevention, vol. 75, 2015, pp. 298 – 309, [Retrieved: Feb., 2017]. [Online]. Available: http://www.sciencedirect.com/science/article/pii/S0001457514003972

[9] F. de Lucca Siqueira, "Discover of pursue patterns in moving object trajectories," Master's thesis, Universidade Federal de Santa Catarina, 2012, dissertao de Mestrado - Universidade Federal de Santa Catarina - UFSC.

[10] O. Bagdadi and A. Vrhelyi, "Jerky drivingan indicator of accident proneness?" Accident Analysis & Prevention, vol. 43, no. 4, 2011, pp. 1359 – 1363, [Retrieved: Feb., 2017]. [Online]. Available: http://www.sciencedirect.com/science/article/pii/S0001457511000236

[11] T. A. Dingus, S. Klauer, V. Neale, A. Petersen, S. Lee, J. Sudweeks, M. Perez, J. Hankey, D. Ramsey, and S. Gupta, "The 100-car naturalistic driving study, phase ii-results of the 100-car field experiment," Virginia Tech Transportation Institute, Tech. Rep., 2006.

[12] M. Ester, H. Kriegel, J. Sander, and X. Xu, "A density-based algorithm for discovering clusters in large spatial databases with noise," in Proceedings of the Second International Conference on Knowledge Discovery and Data Mining. AAAI Press, 1996, pp. 226–231.

[13] Y. Zheng, X. Xie, and W.-Y. Ma, "Geolife: A collaborative social networking service among user, location and trajectory," IEEE Database Engineering Bulletin, June 2010, [Retrieved: Feb., 2017]. [Online]. Available: http://research.microsoft.com/apps/pubs/default.aspx?id=131038

[14] M. Hall, E. Frank, G. Holmes, B. Pfahringer, P. Reutemann, and I. H. Witten, "The weka data mining software: An update," SIGKDD Explorations, vol. 11, no. 1, 2009.

[15] R. Jenkins, "Driving in rain," http://www.driving-test-success.com/driving-articles/driving-in-rain.htm, 2015, [Retrieved: Jan., 2017].

[16] "Google places api," 2017, [Retrieved: Feb., 2017]. [Online]. Available: https://developers.google.com/places

Methodology and Integrated Knowledge for Complex Knowledge Mining: Natural Sciences and Archaeology Case Study Results

Claus-Peter Rückemann
Westfälische Wilhelms-Universität Münster (WWU),
Leibniz Universität Hannover,
North-German Supercomputing Alliance (HLRN), Germany
Email: ruckema@uni-muenster.de

Abstract—**This paper presents a new methodology for advanced knowledge mining, improving complex discovery and decision making results and providing potential for creating new insights. The paper provides the results of the present research and from an implementation and a case study. The case study utilises topics, techniques, and data from geosciences, archaeology and multi-disciplinary context. The methodology is using integrated knowledge resources for complex knowledge mining by creating workflows applying specialised tools. The resulting methodology can be applied with any disciplines and with combinations of general, as well as specialised tools. The results of the knowledge mining can be used for gaining insight and creating automated learning processes, especially with long-term knowledge resources, which are continuously in development. The goal of this research is to create new practical mining procedures, gain insight and further develop available multi-disciplinary knowledge resources.**

***Keywords*–Data-centric Knowledge Mining; Knowledge Resources; Integrative Methodology; Universal Decimal Classification; Advanced Computing.**

I. INTRODUCTION

This research is focussed on the integration of knowledge resources referring to universal classification and application components for solving complex tasks, e.g., for knowledge mining. Target of the research is a methodology integrating knowledge resources and specialised application components for a gain in knowledge, cognition, and insight. The integration of knowledge discovery and decision making processes can result in extremely challenging tasks.

The quality of results from knowledge mining is primarily connected with content and algorithms. The language or method used for expressing a 'question' and automating its translation in general is not of concern for this research. Data resources, whatever their size is, do not automatically deliver high quality results. In most cases, content and algorithms are limiting possibilities to answer complex and staggered questions in reasonable ways. Contributions to these deficiencies result from data, algorithms, and their implementations. Therefore, high quality knowledge resources, including factual, conceptual, procedural, and metacognitive knowledge, description, and documentation are increasingly important. In consequence, advancing methodologies for knowledge mining is in the focus with comparable importance.

Several disciplines contribute and specialised approaches and solutions have to be used on context for coping with any slightly complex question. Built on such in-deficit foundation, there is no direct and common practice on how to integrate specialised algorithms and applications with each other without a methodology. Appropriate methodologies will allow to integrate advanced knowledge resources and to modularise several tasks within a knowledge mining workflow.

The motivation for this research results from the unsatisfactory and non-knowledge centric instruments available. For many knowledge mining challenges, e.g., seeking good answers to complex questions, there are no solutions available for integrating complex knowledge resources and arbitrary application components. A sample question is:

Which natural events associated with the creation of crater structures with a diameter larger than 100 m could have been directly notable by human population within the last thousands of years and are still observable on-land at the area of todays' continent of Europe and which knowledge is associated with such events?

The question is quite precise but present possibilities mostly cannot achieve appropriately precise results in order to answer such questions. If one is not satisfied with arbitrary lists of hundreds of snippets of information mostly not part of an answer instead of an on-topic result then we have to find better ways. A solution is to flexibly integrate high quality data with conceptual knowledge and suitable application components with appropriate features.

This paper is organised as follows. Section II introduces the methodology applied for knowledge mining. Section III discusses implementation and case study, resulting references and associations, and the workflow implementation. Section IV discusses the results from the application of the methodology and implementation, based on previous work and re-usable components. Section V summarises the lessons learned, conclusions, and future work.

II. METHODOLOGY

With this research, a methodology is defined by a sequence of steps. The steps can be a set of procedures in order to create a result for a knowledge mining process, e.g., with a discovery process. The procedures can include data, knowledge, formal descriptions, and implementations, e.g., collecting data, retrieving information, and algorithmic specifications. The purpose can range from delivering to creating and answer to an open question, e.g., delivering knowledge for a learning or decision making process. The methodology uses a formal description of knowledge, data and information, as well as required research techniques. Content and context are represented by any knowledge objects and data available in time and space. Data may be structured and unstructured.

1a) Identification of a knowledge mining challenge.
1b) Phrasing of a problem or question.
1c) Identification of a solution or answering strategy.
1d) Context description and modeling.
1e) Mapping of sub-challenges to possible partial solutions.
1f) Interface creation for partial solutions.
2a) Creation and / or selection of cogwheel modules (modularisation into sub-challenges and partial solutions).
2b) Knowledge and information: Identification or creation and / or selection of nuclei and facets.
2c) Peeling of information-nuclei from existing evidence.
2d) Milling of nuclei.
2e) Information processing.
2f) Data selection including nuclei and facets.
2g) Information object turnaround.
3a) Workflow implementation (incl. cogwheel modules).
3b) Analysis of results.
3c) Learning process and persistent documentation.
3d) Improvement process.

We can identify three main groups within the methodology. 1a) to 1f) is a preparatory phase, 2a) to 2g) describes a gearbox of knowledge mining, and 3a) to 3d) is a consecutive phase.

The modules allow to assign specialised applications and specialised features to separate modules as will be shown in the following implementation. Options and features of specialised applications can be documented, including conceptual knowledge, with the learning process and to cope with reoccurring requirements. The methodology allows to create different approaches for a workflow.

III. Implementation and Case Study

The methodology was applied to practical situations. The following case study presents a practical workflow implementation based on the above gearbox of knowledge, including the required cogwheel modules with their mapping to important components and steps, their implementation and results.

The starting point is the above sample question. The required compositions of features and criteria can become quite complex and are commonly not implemented in any single application or component. Therefore, the integration of appropriate application components can be desireable or even required.

The plethora of information from the knowledge resources is narrowed by the conceptual knowledge, the references to classifications, e.g., to the mapping and data of:

- Craters (any, e.g., Earth and other planets),
  - volcanic features including craters,
  - impact craters including meteorites, ...
- confirmed (and non-confirmed) structures/craters,
- structures observable on-land,
- age less than (about) 9999 years old,
- larger than 100 m diameter.

The respective workflow requires a number of special calculations as well as criteria cogwheel modules for knowledge resources and spatial components.

Applying a universal classification can be used to classify the appropriate objects, the associated application components, and the respective required options for a cogwheel module, e.g., for the calculations and filters.

In this case, the two groups of components involved with creating a solution are a) advanced knowledge resources and b) knowledge mining including conceptual knowledge references, spatial data and applications.

The definition of data-centricity used is: "The term data-centric refers to a focus, in which data is most relevant in context with a purpose. Data structuring, data shaping, and long-term aspects are important concerns. Data-centricity concentrates on data-based content and is beneficial for information and knowledge and for emphasizing their value. Technical implementations need to consider distributed data, non-distributed data, and data locality and enable advanced data handling and analysis. Implementations should support separating data from technical implementations as far as possible." [1]. According to this, the implementation of the methodology is as far data-centric as possible and allows a systematic application.

The following sections describe the essentials of the cogwheel modules required, including the handling of the nuclei and information processing. The sub-challenges are presented with their mapping to applications. Relevant excerpts of data and information are discussed in anticipation of the final results. The concluding section shows the workflow implementation used for creating the final results.

A. *Multi-disciplinary knowledge resources identification*

The knowledge resources hold arbitrary multi-disciplinary knowledge (e.g., documentation of factual, conceptual, procedural, and metacognitive knowledge), in various structures as well as unstructured, objects, and references, including information on digital objects and realia objects, e.g., media objects and archived physical specimen. These resources provide the prerequisites in order to create efficient cogwheel modules and handle knowledge and information nuclei and facets for peeling and milling processes.

1) Factual knowledge: The knowledge resources also contain information on various types of crater features like volcanic craters and impact craters. Especially, the Earth's impact crater container in the knowledge resources container holds data and references for all known impact craters on Earth.

The impact features container holds the Kaali impact, represented by its major impact crater. The minor craters of this impact event are referenced from this object and form sub-objects, all of which contain their factual and referenced data.

Figure 1 shows a spatial presentation of terrestrial (meteorite) impact features resulting from the impact features container. The multi-disciplinary knowledge resources were used to create various computational views of impact craters on Earth [2]. The multi-disciplinary views, including conceptual classifications, enable an association of various characteristics common with different collection information [3].

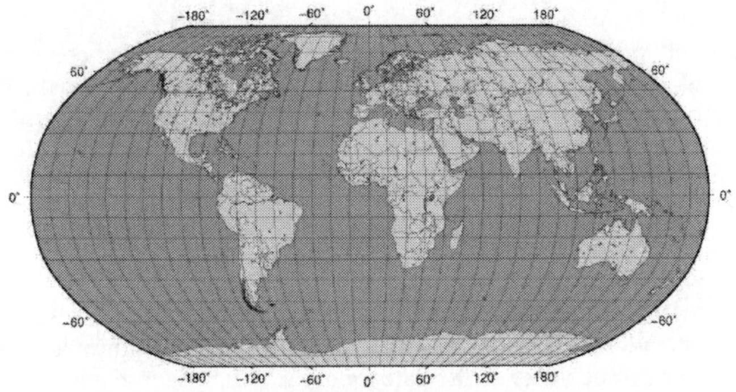

Figure 1. Impactmap – computed worldwide spatial distribution of classified terrestrial impact features (meteorite) from available object entries.

In this case, Earth surface information, georeferenced geophysical and geological factual data, have been associated.

Table I lists the factual container data used from the LX Foundation Scientific Resources [4] referenced for the Kaali crater field object and relevant with the mining challenge.

TABLE I. RESULTING FACTUAL DATA REFERENCED FOR THE KAALI CRATER FIELD (EXCERPT, LX RESOURCES).

Crater Number	*Coordinates (lat/lon)*		*Diameter (m)*	*Elevation (m)*
1	58.371270	22.664737	39	24.10
2	58.367407	22.672298	25	25.90
3	58.366556	22.677637	76	21.99
4	58.371982	22.675092	33	24.91
5	58.370815	22.675611	20	21.90
6	58.370861	22.663155	13	29.90
7	58.370306	22.671848	26	22.90
8	58.367460	22.672577	15	25.99
9	58.372715	22.669419	110	34.14

The crater field consists of 9 known craters. Crater number 9 is the major crater. Craters 1 to 8 form sub-container objects, which deliver the data.

2) Conceptual knowledge: Advanced knowledge from integration of universal classification and spatial information can provide new insights when applied with knowledge mining [5]. The use of the Universal Decimal Classification (UDC) is widely popular, e.g., in library context, geosciences [6], and mapping [7] as provided by the Natural Environment Research Council (NERC) [8] via the NERC Open Research Archive (NORA) [9]. The small excerpts of the knowledge resources objects only refer to main UDC-based classes, which for this part of the publication are taken from the Multilingual Universal Decimal Classification Summary (UDCC Publication No. 088) [10] released by the UDC Consortium under the Creative Commons Attribution Share Alike 3.0 license [11] (first release 2009, subsequent update 2012). Data in the knowledge resources carries references to classifications, e.g., UDC, for any discipline and object, e.g., natural sciences and history. Here, besides the central UDC:539.63 (impact effects) and UDC:539.8 (other physico-mechanical effects), referred top level groups for geodesy, cartography, and geography are UDC:528 [12], UDC:910 [13], and UDC:912 [14]. Tables II and III show excerpts of the conceptual data (UDC) used for geodetic / cartographic and geographic classification.

TABLE II. CLASSIFICATION WITH KNOWLEDGE RESOURCES: GEODETIC AND CARTOGRAPHIC CONCEPTUAL DATA (LX).

UDC Code	*Description (English, excerpt)*
UDC:5	MATHEMATICS. NATURAL SCIENCES
UDC:52	Astronomy. Astrophysics. Space research. Geodesy
UDC:528	Geodesy. Surveying. Photogrammetry. Remote sensing. Cartography
UDC:528.4	Field surveying. Land surveying. Cadastral survey. Topography. Engineering survey. Special fields of surveying
UDC:528.5	Geodetic instruments and equipment
UDC:528.7	Photogrammetry: aerial, terrestrial
UDC:528.8	Remote sensing
UDC:528.9	Cartography. Mapping (textual documents)

TABLE III. CLASSIFICATION WITH KNOWLEDGE RESOURCES: GEOGRAPHIC CONCEPTUAL DATA (LX).

UDC Code	*Description (English, excerpt)*
UDC:9	GEOGRAPHY. BIOGRAPHY. HISTORY
UDC:91	Geography. Exploration of the Earth and of individual countries. Travel. Regional geography
UDC:910	General questions. Geography as a science. Exploration. Travel
UDC:910.2	Kinds and techniques of geographical exploration
UDC:912	Nonliterary, nontextual representations of a region

Composite classification based on these top level classification references can refer to special items, e.g., cartographic bibliographies, historical atlases, and globes. Summarised, the classification can be used as glueing component classifying the knowledge object space and the implementation space, e.g., respective resources, objects, application components, and features of application components. This also provides the base for the creation of conceptual knowledge objects.

B. Geoscientific data and components mapping

Appropriate data was required for the topographic data related criteria. In the past, the georeferenced objects have been used with various data, e.g., with the Global Land One-kilometer Base Elevation Project (GLOBE) [15] and the 2-minute gridded global relief data (ETOPO2v2) [16].

For the required resolution of the results presented here, the knowledge resources had to be integrated with data based on the gridded ETOPO1 1 arc-minute global relief model data [17]. For special purposes data can be composed from various sources, e.g., adding Shuttle Radar Topography Mission (SRTM) data [18] from the Consultative Group on International Agricultural Research (CGIAR) [19].

The horizontal datum of ETOPO1 is World Geodetic System geographic, which was established in 1984 (WGS84) and later revised. The WGS84 specifications and references are provided by the National Geospatial-Intelligence Agency (NGA) [20] and as EPSG:4326 from the European Petroleum Survey Group Geodesy (EPSG) [21]. The vertical datum of ETOPO1 is "sea level". The source elevation data were not converted by the authors of ETOPO1 to a common vertical datum because of the large cell size of 1 arc-minute.

The Generic Mapping Tools (GMT) [22] suite application components are used for handling the spatial data, applying the related criteria, and for the visualisation.

C. *Peeling and milling of context references*

The knowledge resources provide references to multi-disciplinary knowledge, e.g., photo media objects related to an object. Examples are objects referred by conceptual knowledge and contextual knowledge references (Figure 2).

```
Photo-Object: Birgit Gersbeck-Schierholz, Hannover, Germany.
media: YES 20160629 {LXC:DETAIL--M-} {UDC:(0.034)(044)770} LXDATASTORAGE://...
 kaali2016_1.JPG ...
media: YES 20160629 {LXC:DETAIL--M-} {UDC:(0.034)(044)770} LXDATASTORAGE://...
 kaali2016_2.JPG ...
media: YES 20160629 {LXC:DETAIL--M-} {UDC:(0.034)(044)770} LXDATASTORAGE://...
 kaali2016_3.JPG ...
media: YES 20160629 {LXC:DETAIL--M-} {UDC:(0.034)(044)770} LXDATASTORAGE://...
 kaali2016_4.JPG ...
media: YES 20160629 {LXC:DETAIL--M-} {UDC:(0.034)(044)770} LXDATASTORAGE://...
 kaali2016_5.JPG ...
Object-Discoverer: Birgit Gersbeck-Schierholz, Hannover, Germany.
Photo-Object: Claus-Peter Rückemann, Minden, Germany.
media: YES 20160629 {LXC:DETAIL--M-} {UDC:(0.034)(044)770} LXDATASTORAGE://...
 img_0086.jpg
```

Figure 2. Information peeling: Media entries from knowledge resources objects (multi-disciplinary geosciences collection, LX, excerpt).

The excerpt shows referenced media for "Kaali crater" after the peeling process from the object. The excerpt of an object associated with a knowledge object is shown in Figure 3.

```
Lilium ... [Biology, Botany]:
           (lat.) Lilium martagon.
           Earth mull vegetation.
           Indicator: Eutrophic, leach enriched, clayey and loamy soils, shadow
            and penumbra location.
           ...
           Syn.: Türkenbundlilie
           Syn.: martagon lily
           Syn.: Turk's cap lily ...
```

Figure 3. Information peeling of Lilium martagon knowledge resources object (multi-disciplinary geosciences collection, LX, excerpt).

The excerpt shows an object "Lilium martagon" associated with the "Kaali crater" object after the information peeling process from this object. Figure 4 lists an excerpt of associated bibliographic references for an object.

```
cite: YES 20070000 {LXK:Kaali Kraater; Kaali crater; meteorite; impact} {UDC:
 ...} {PAGE:----..----} LXCITE://Tiirmaa:2007:Meteorite
cite: YES 20160000 {LXK:Kaali Kraater; Kaali crater; meteorite; impact} {UDC:
 ...} {PAGE:----..----} LXCITE://Tiirmaa:2016:Scars
cite: YES 20120000 {LXK:Kaali Kraater; Kaali crater; meteorite; impact;
 Excalibur; sword} {UDC:...} {PAGE:----..----} LXCITE://Faure:2012:Estonians
cite: YES 20160000 {LXK:Kaali Kraater; Kaali crater; meteorite; impact;
 Tutankhamun; dagger} {UDC:...} {PAGE:----..----} LXCITE://
 Comelli:2016:Tutankhamun
```

Figure 4. Information peeling: Citation entries from knowledge resources objects (multi-disciplinary geosciences collection, LX, excerpt).

The referenced citation entries are the result of the information peeling process from the Kaali crater object and refer to bibliographic references for meteorite craters on the island of Saaremaa [23] as well as to meteorite craters in Estonia [24].

Other references point to information for meteorite-material-usage, e.g., in context with archaeological and historical or mythical context like King Arthur's sword Excalibur ('Ex-Kali-bur') [25] directly associated with Kaali (mother goddess Kali) and its metal material and via association of sword synonyms and metal object classification to Tutankhamun's dagger [26] (made with meteorite iron from Egypt).

D. *Workflow implementation and phases*

For the case study, the required data and configuration is selected manually for the preparatory phase. The consequent modules act on base of that data, especially conceptual knowledge and factual knowledge. The central cogwheel module `cogwheel_criteria` in the knowledge mining gearbox utilises a sequence `lximpactsselect_crae_criteria` containing a number of components

1) `lximpactsselect_crae_date`
2) `lximpactsselect_crae_confirmed`
3) `lximpactsselect_crae_age_historic`
4) `lximpactsselect_crae_diameter`

for handling the criteria for the event date range, confirmed and not confirmed events, the date range, and the crater diameter. In this case the components can be considered as filter processes.

The spatial modules of the workflow (`cogwheel_world`, `cogwheel_region`) utilise the features latitude and longitude, wet / land criteria, criteria evaluation, spatial distance computation, map projection, and visualisation. The respective components are provided by GMT suite applications, especially `pscoast` and `gmtselect`. The GMT applications have to care for longitude, latitude, elevation and contribute to the applying topographical data related criteria, for topography related decision making within the information object turnaround.

The later association of knowledge objects, referenced media objects, and citation objects is supported by conceptual knowledge and discovery processes. In the consecutive phase results are analysed and persistently documented in order to improve the knowledge resources and mining algorithms.

IV. FINAL RESULTS AND DISCUSSION

Earths' impact crater objects from the classified LX factual knowledge resources are used as a factual and conceptual knowledge source for computing results, considering the respective context and selection criteria. Result can be a group of craters, fitting to all the criteria, after the mining algorithm is applied to the integrated knowledge resources and methods.

A. *Result of implemented workflow*

Figure 5 shows the resulting output, including the necessary topography (longitude, latitude, elevation), data, and information used, after the result was visualised via GMT. Criteria for decision making are the resulting target structures (meteorite craters) on land (topography and coverage), especially confirmed Earth crater groups (meteorite impact features, bullets, red, blue, and green colours), age and size of (on-land) structures, and a reasonable catchment area for Europe (blue),

A catchment center has been choosen, a circular area with a respective radius of 3000 km, automatically fitted with the map projection. The blue circle marks a reasonable area to cover the continent of Europe in this context. The blue and green bullets mark the craters inside that area. The data, items, and marks are automatically computed and visualised.

The final resulting object (bullet, green colour), which fits all criteria is the Kaali crater field, Saaremaa, Estonia. The region of positive final result of the applied knowledge mining is computed and presented via GMT, too. Figure 6 shows the region of the Kaali crater field on the island of Saaremaa, Estonia in its topographic context.

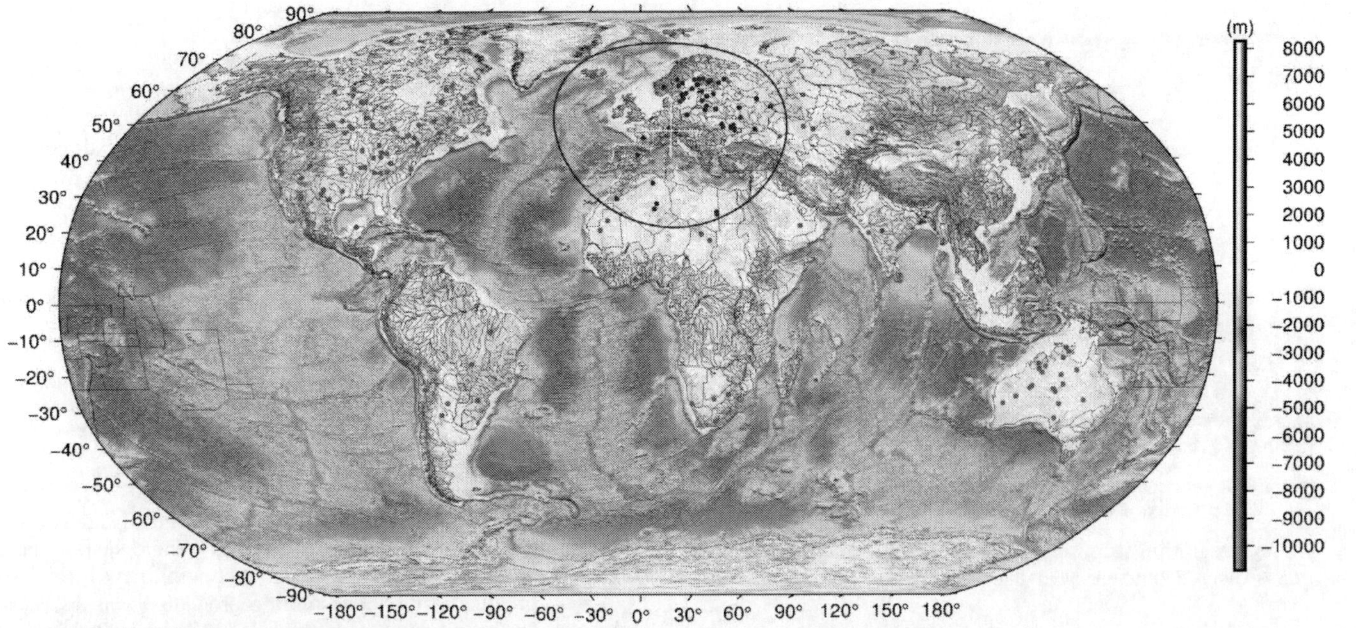

Figure 5. Knowledge mining methodology applied (LX factual and conceptual knowledge, factual data). Criteria are resulting crater groups (meteorite impacts, all coloured bullets), age and size of (on-land) structures, area, topography (all coloured bullets). Final result: Kaali crater field (green), Saaremaa, Estonia.

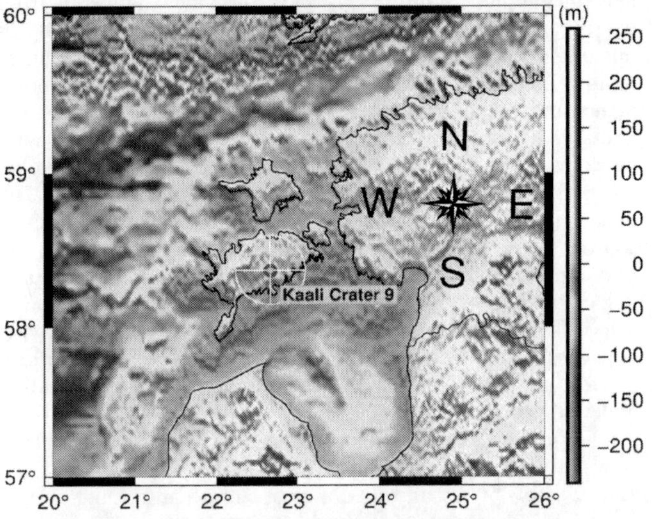

Figure 6. Detail of final result of knowledge mining in topographic context: Region around center of Kaali crater field, Saaremaa, Estonia

The bullet and the cross mark the center of the crater field (labeled Kaali Crater 9). The yellow ring marks an area of 25 km around the major crater.

B. Resulting associated information: Spatial mapping

The Keyhole Markup Language (KML) is an eXtended Markup Language (XML) based format for specifying spatial data and content. It is considered an official standard of the Open Geospatial Consortium (OGC). The KML description can be used with many spatial components and purposes, e.g., with a Google Earth or Google Maps presentation [27], with a Marble representation [28], using OpenStreetMap (OSM) [29] and national instances.

The final result from the knowledge mining with the classified LX factual knowledge can be projected onto online satellite data of the area of the Kaali crater field. The result from object and sub-objects is shown in Figure 7.

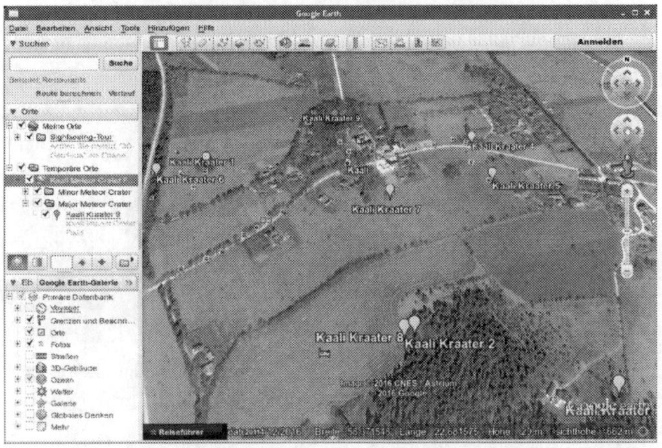

Figure 7. The resulting area of Kaali crater field, Saaremaa, Estonia, factual knowledge (craters red and green) (LX) projected onto Google Earth data.

The interactive map shows the nine craters known for the crater field. The major crater is marked in red colour, the minor craters are marked in green colour.

The the final result from the knowledge mining with the classified LX factual knowledge can be projected onto online vector and navigation data (Figure 8).

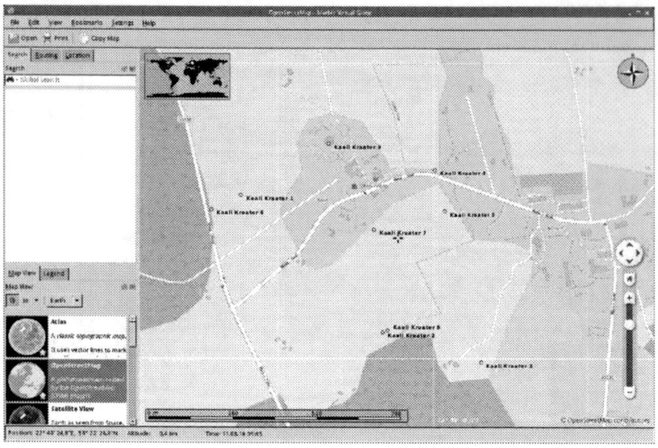

Figure 8. The resulting area of Kaali crater field, Saaremaa, Estonia, factual knowledge (craters 1 to 9) (LX) projected onto OSM data via Marble.

The integration shows craters 1 to 9 of the Kaali crater field area projected onto OSM data via Marble.

C. Resulting associated information: Media references

The integrated knowledge resources can contain references to any data, e.g., media objects. Media objects contain own references, e.g., classification, citations, documentation, and keywords and can therefore contribute in many ways to new insight – besides their intrinsic media content. The following photo data (Figure 9) from the media references for "Kaali crater" were delivered in association from the final result of the knowledge mining workflow.

Figure 9. Integrated media photo objects associated with the knowledge object "Kaali crater", Saaremaa, Estonia, referring to [30] (LX resources).

The references of these media photo objects (Figure 2) are part of objects in the knowledge resources. Media results (1–5) [30] and specimen (6) photos from the Natural Sciences Specimen Archive are dated June 29, 2016.

The photos and physical samples have been taken in 2016 by the Knowledge in Motion (KiM) natural sciences and archaeology sections at the Kaali meteorite crater field on the island of Saaremaa, Estonia, during the Geo Exploration and Information (GEXI) [31] Baltic research and studies campaign.

In detail, the resulting photo objects of the examined site (from left to right, from top to bottom) show in this sort order:

1: Major crater, view in northern direction.
2: Major crater, view in north-eastern direction.
3: Major crater, view in western direction.
4: Path towards major crater, view from southern direction.
5: Vegetation, Lilium martagon, at top of crater rim (referring to Figure 3).
6: Specimen crater pond material (quartz, melane particles, lacustrine deposits, biogenic material).

The references included in the knowledge mining workflow (Figure 4) provide the complementary information that fine particles from the Kaali crater include impactor remains (esp. significant Ni-Wüstite, Ni-Maghemite, Ni-Goethite, Hematite, Magnetite, Taenite, Kamacite), spherules and splash-forms.

V. Conclusion

This paper introduces a methodology for advanced knowledge mining, improving complex discovery and decision making results and providing potential for creating new insights.

A new practical knowledge mining procedure was successfully created based on the methodology. The mining procedure was used for efficiently integrating advanced knowledge resources and specialised application components for gaining new insight and cognition. The paper provides the results from the research and data-centric implementation of a case study of integrated knowledge and methods for answering knowledge mining challenges like complex questions. After the implementation, the case study concentrates on a context, which is derived from knowledge mining challenges associated with geosciences and archaeology. According to the methodology, the major phases were applied for the implementation. The paper presented the identification and mapping of required resources – knowledge resources and partial solutions, mapping of complementary components in their context, and excerpts of associated knowledge used for information peeling generating a base for the information processing. The resources provide conceptual and factual knowledge in integration with appropriate context data and application components for computing and visualisation.

The mapped application components – tools and filters – were used complementary for handling the complex resources, systematically peeling of information nuclei and facets, milling, and consecutive information processing, including decision making integrating spatial and conceptual criteria. The results of the knowledge mining information object turnaround, can itself become part of the knowledge resources. The methodology can be applied to many application scenarios, especially where a solution can only be gained by integration of different data and approaches. The various approaches also provide potential for optimisation for special priorities. In most cases, the optimisation can consider the individual challenges and the use of special algorithms and applications.

Future work concentrates on improving the multi-disciplinary knowledge resources and creating, utilising, and documenting advanced components for the knowledge mining cogwheel modules.

ACKNOWLEDGEMENTS

We are grateful to the "Knowledge in Motion" (KiM) long-term project, Unabhängiges Deutsches Institut für Multi-disziplinäre Forschung (DIMF), for partially funding this implementation, case study, research and studies campaign, and publication under grant D2015F1P04604, and to its senior scientific members, especially to Dipl.-Biol. Birgit Gersbeck-Schierholz, Leibniz Universität Hannover, to Dr. Friedrich Hülsmann, Gottfried Wilhelm Leibniz Bibliothek (GWLB) Hannover, and to Dipl.-Ing. Martin Hofmeister, Hannover, for fruitful discussion, inspiration, practical multi-disciplinary case studies, and the analysis of advanced concepts. We are grateful to Dipl.-Ing. Hans-Günther Müller, Cray, for his work for providing flexible practical solutions to architectural challenges and excellent technical support. We are grateful to all national and international partners in the Geo Exploration and Information cooperations for their constructive and trans-disciplinary support. We thank the Science and High Performance Supercomputing Centre (SHPSC) for long-term support for these research cooperations.

REFERENCES

[1] C.-P. Rückemann, Z. Kovacheva, L. Schubert, I. Lishchuk, B. Gersbeck-Schierholz, and F. Hülsmann, Best Practice and Definitions of Data-centric and Big Data – Science, Society, Law, Industry, and Engineering. Post-Summit Results, Sep. 19, 2016, The Sixth Symp. on Adv. Comp. and Inform. in Nat. and Appl. Sci. (SACINAS), The 14th Int. Conf. of Num. Analysis and Appl. Math. (ICNAAM), Sep. 19–25, 2016, Rhodes, Greece, 2016, URL: http://www.user.uni-hannover.de/cpr/x/publ/2016/delegatessummit2016/rueckemann_icnaam2016_summit_summary.pdf [accessed: 2016-12-22].

[2] C.-P. Rückemann, "From Multi-disciplinary Knowledge Objects to Universal Knowledge Dimensions: Creating Computational Views," International Journal On Advances in Intelligent Systems, vol. 7, no. 3&4, 2014, pp. 385–401, ISSN: 1942-2679, LCCN: 2008212456 (LoC), URL: http://www.iariajournals.org/intelligent_systems/intsys_v7_n34_2014_paged.pdf [accessed: 2016-08-28].

[3] C.-P. Rückemann, "Long-term Sustainable Knowledge Classification with Scientific Computing: The Multi-disciplinary View on Natural Sciences and Humanities," International Journal on Advances in Software, vol. 7, no. 1&2, 2014, pp. 302–317, ISSN: 1942-2628.

[4] "LX-Project," 2016, URL: http://www.user.uni-hannover.de/cpr/x/rprojs/en/#LX [accessed: 2016-06-18].

[5] F. Hülsmann and C.-P. Rückemann, "Advanced Knowledge from Universal Classification and Spatial Information," KiMrise, KiM Meeting, August 8, 2016, Knowledge in Motion, Hannover, Germany, 2016.

[6] T. V. Loudon, "Geoscience after IT: Part N, Cumulated References," Computers and Geosciences, vol. 26, no. 3, 2000, ISSN: 0098-3004, British Geological Survey, Natural Environment Research Council (NERC), UK, URL: http://nora.nerc.ac.uk/2410/1/Part_N.pdf [acc.: 2016-08-06].

[7] B. Stevenson, "Servicing Map Users at Aalborg University Library," LIBER Quarterly, vol. 10, 2000, pp. 454–464, ISSN: 1435-5205, DOI: 10.18352/lq.7616, URL: https://www.liberquarterly.eu/articles/10.18352/lq.7616/galley/7652/download/ [accessed: 2016-08-06].

[8] "Natural Environment Research Council (NERC)," UK, URL: http://www.nerc.ac.uk/ [accessed: 2016-08-06].

[9] "NERC Open Research Archive (NORA)," Natural Environment Research Council (NERC), UK, URL: http://nora.nerc.ac.uk [accessed: 2016-08-06].

[10] "Multilingual Universal Decimal Classification Summary," 2012, UDC Consortium, 2012, Web resource, v. 1.1. The Hague: UDC Consortium (UDCC Publication No. 088), URL: http://www.udcc.org/udcsummary/php/index.php [accessed: 2016-01-01].

[11] "Creative Commons Attribution Share Alike 3.0 license," 2012, URL: http://creativecommons.org/licenses/by-sa/3.0/ [accessed: 2016-01-01].

[12] "UDC 528: Geodesy. Surveying. Photogrammetry. Remote sensing. Cartography," 2016, Universal Decimal Classification (UDC), URL: http://udcdata.info/027504 [accessed: 2016-08-06].

[13] "UDC 910: General questions. Geography as a science. Exploration. Travel," 2016, Universal Decimal Classification (UDC), URL: http://udcdata.info/068129 [accessed: 2016-08-06].

[14] "UDC 912: Nonliterary, nontextual representations of a region," 2016, Universal Decimal Classification (UDC), URL: http://udcdata.info/068183 [accessed: 2016-08-06].

[15] "Global Land One-kilometer Base Elevation Project (GLOBE)," National Geophysical Data Center (NGDC), National Centers for Environmental Information (NCEI), National Oceanic and Atmospheric Administration (NOAA), NOAA Satellite and Information Service (NESDIS), U.S. Department of Commerce (DOC), URL: http://www.ngdc.noaa.gov/mgg/topo/globe.html [accessed: 2016-08-06].

[16] "2-Minute Gridded Global Relief Data (ETOPO2v2)," 2006, June, 2006, World Data Service for Geophysics, Boulder, USA, National Geophysical Data Center, National Centers for Environmental Information (NCEI), National Oceanic and Atmospheric Administration (NOAA), URL: http://www.ngdc.noaa.gov/mgg/fliers/06mgg01.html [accessed: 2016-08-06].

[17] C. Amante and B. W. Eakins, "ETOPO1 1 Arc-Minute Global Relief Model: Procedures, Data Sources and Analysis," 2009, NOAA Technical Memorandum NESDIS NGDC-24. National Geophysical Data Center, NOAA. DOI: 10.7289/V5C8276M, World Data Service for Geophysics, Boulder, USA, Nat. Geophysical Data Center, Nat. Centers for Env. Inf. (NCEI), Nat. Oceanic and Atmospheric Admin. (NOAA).

[18] "CGIAR Consortium for Spatial Information (CGIAR-CSI)," 2016, URL: http://www.cgiar-csi.org [accessed: 2016-08-06].

[19] "Consultative Group on International Agricultural Research (CGIAR)," 2016, URL: http://www.cgiar.org [accessed: 2016-08-06].

[20] "World Geodetic System (WGS)," 2012, National Geospatial-Intelligence Agency (NGA), URL: http://earth-info.nga.mil/GandG/wgs84/index.html [accessed: 2016-08-06].

[21] "Spatial reference for EPSG:4326," European Petroleum Survey Group Geodesy (EPSG), URL: https://epsg.io/4326 [accessed: 2016-08-06].

[22] "GMT - Generic Mapping Tools," 2016, URL: http://gmt.soest.hawaii.edu/ [accessed: 2016-08-06].

[23] R. Tiirmaa, Scars of Stars on the Island of Saaremaa. Commission of Meteoritics of Estonian Academy of Sciences, (post 2005), Kaali Kraater, Saaremaa, Estland.

[24] R. Tiirmaa, V. Puura, A. Soesoo, and S. Suuroja, Estonian Meteorite Craters, 2007, MTÜ GEOGuide Baltoscandia. Tallinn (ed.), Inst. of Geology at Tallinn Univ. of Technology; University of Turku, Dept. of Geology; ISBN: 978-9985-9834-1-6, URL: http://www.gi.ee/geoturism/MetCraters_ENG_062011_100dpiS.pdf [accessed: 2016-08-27].

[25] G. Faure and T. M. Mensing, The Estonians; The long road to independence. Lulu.com, 2012, ISBN: 978-1-105-53003-6, URL: https://books.google.ru/books?id=hnq7AwAAQBAJ [accessed: 2016-08-27].

[26] D. Comelli, M. D'orazio, L. Folco, M. El-Halwagy, T. Frizzi, R. Alberti, V. Capogrosso, A. Elnaggar, H. Hassan, A. Nevin, F. Porcelli, M. G. Rashed, and G. Valentini, "The meteoritic origin of Tutankhamun's iron dagger blade," Meteoritics & Planetary Science, vol. 51, no. 7, Jul. 2016, pp. 1301–1309, the Meteoritical Society, DOI: 10.1111/maps.12664.

[27] "Google Maps," URL: http://www.google.com/maps [acc.: 2016-08-06].

[28] "Marble," 2016, URL: https://marble.kde.org/ [accessed: 2016-08-06].

[29] "OpenStreetMap (OSM)," 2016, URL: http://www.openstreetmap.org [accessed: 2016-08-06].

[30] B. Gersbeck-Schierholz, "Where the Sun has Taken a Rest: The Kaali Meteorite Crater," KiM On-site Summit, Knowledge in Motion, June 29, 2016, On-Site Summit Meeting, Knowledge in Motion Baltic Research and Studies Campaign 2016, "Unabhängiges Deutsches Institut für Multi-disziplinäre Forschung (DIMF)", Saaremaa, Estonia, 2016.

[31] "Geo Exploration and Information (GEXI)," 1996, 1999, 2010, 2016, URL: http://www.user.uni-hannover.de/cpr/x/rprojs/en/index.html#GEXI [accessed: 2016-08-28].

Specifying the Engineering Viewpoint of ICA's Formal Model in a Corporate Spatial Data Infrastructure

Rubens Moraes Torres, Jugurta Lisboa-Filho
Departamento de Informática
Universidade Federal de Viçosa
Viçosa, MG, Brazil
e-mail: rubens.torres@ufv.br, jugurta@ufv.br

Italo Lopes Oliveira
Departamento de Informática e Estatística
Universidade Federal de Santa Catarina
Florianópolis – SC - Brazil
e-mail: italo.oliveira@posgrad.ufsc.br

Carlos Alberto Moura, Alexander Gonçalves da Silva
Companhia Energética de Minas Gerais (Cemig)
Belo Horizonte – MG – Brazil
e-mail: camoura@cemig.com.br, ags@cemig.com.br

Abstract— **The International Cartographic Association (ICA) proposed a formal model to describe Spatial Data Infrastructure (SDI) regardless of technologies or implementations using the Reference Model of Open Distributed Processing (RM-ODP) framework. The framework consists of five viewpoints. ICA's model specified the Enterprise, Computational, and Information viewpoints, but not the Engineering and Technology viewpoints. The Companhia Energética de Minas Gerais (Cemig) has developed an SDI, called SDI-Cemig, aiming to facilitate the discovery, sharing, and use of geospatial data among employees and consumers. This paper presents a specification of the SDI-Cemig components using the Engineering viewpoint based on ICA's formal model.**

Keywords- ICA Model; SDI; RM-ODP; Engineering Viewpoint.

I. INTRODUCTION

Users access a Spatial Data Infrastructure (SDI) aiming to recover and carry out operations on geospatial data for spatial-temporal analyses and to use decision-making support mechanisms in those systems [1]. The growth in SDI creation and use derives from the increase in geospatial data available. Currently, geospatial data are generated daily by people using devices (e.g., cameras, tablets, smartphones), web systems, sensors (e.g., Global Positioning System trackers and cameras), and by initiatives of businesses and corporations to map data on Earth's surface [2]. According to Harvey et al. [3], SDIs improve the sharing and use of geospatial data and services, which helps different users of a given community.

The Companhia Energética de Minas Gerais (Minas Gerais Power Company - Cemig), a corporation comprising over 200 companies, is developing SDI-Cemig in order to help its employees and clients share and discover geospatial data. The research & development project called "Geoportal Cemig – SDI-Based Corporate GIS" is funded by a partnership between Cemig and the Fundação de Amparo à Pesquisa do Estado de Minas Gerais (Research Support Foundation of the State of Minas Gerais - Fapemig). One of the goals of this project consists in creating a method to develop corporate SDIs.

The International Cartographic Association (ICA) has proposed a model to describe SDIs by specifying three of the five viewpoints of the Reference Model for Open Distributed Processing (RM-ODP), namely the Enterprise, Information, and Computational viewpoints [4]. The other viewpoints of the RM-ODP framework, i.e., Engineering and Technology, were not described in the ICA's model.

The ICA's formal model for SDI was later extended by other researchers to describe more properly the actors and policies in the SDI [5]-[9]. According to Oliveira et al. [7], the ICA's formal model can be adapted to describe corporate SDIs, with the open possibility of creating the Engineering and Technology viewpoints.

This study presents the specification of the Engineering viewpoint for SDI-Cemig, based on the adapted formal SDI model by the ICA. The paper is structured as follows. The Section II details, briefly, studies that specify SDI through the use of the RM-ODP. Section III describes the ICA's formal SDI model. Section IV presents the specification of the Engineering viewpoint for SDI-Cemig. Section V discusses the results presented in this study and Section VI reports final considerations and possible future works.

II. RELATED WORKS

Several studies have used the RM-ODP to specify an SDI [10]-[13]. The research in [10] specifies only the stakeholders of the Namibian SDI using as model the actors specified in [4]. The proposal in [11] aims to improve the urban planning and management through the use of an SDI. The authors specify the RM-ODP Information viewpoint of an SDI, considering the inherent requirements of the urban planning. The remaining viewpoints of the RM-ODP are not specified. The framework developed in [12] specifies semantic SDI (SSDI) using the RM-ODP. Only the Enterprise, Information and Computation viewpoints are detailed. At last, [13], as [4], proposes a reference model for the marine SDI of Germany (MDI-DE) using the RM-ODP. However, in [13], only the Enterprise viewpoint is presented.

Differently from the studies cited in this section, our study presents the specification of the Engineering viewpoint from an SDI that, at the best of knowledge, has not been detailed in the SDI literature. Moreover, our specification is based on a formal model which, with exception of [10], is not presented in the studies detailed.

III. ICA'S FORMAL MODEL FOR SDI SPECIFICATION

The RM-ODP framework results from a partnership among the International Organization for Standardization (ISO), the International Electrotechnical Commission (IEC), and the Telecommunication Standardization Sector [14]. It consists of a framework to specify heterogeneous distributed systems, enabling the distribution, interoperability, portability, platform independence, and technology [15].

In Hjelmager et al. [4], the ICA proposed the use of the RM-ODP model as a reference to design and create an SDI. Its use allows modeling actors, policies [4], data semantics, objects, and features [6] required for an SDI. One advantage of using the model is the great independence of technology and implementation [4]. For example, two companies may use the same modeling to implement their respective SDIs while using different sets of technologies with no need to change the modeling.

RM-ODP comprises five viewpoints, where each represents an architectural viewpoint of the system [16]. The viewpoints do not show isolated parts of a system, but rather describe a different viewpoint of the same system. By using viewpoints, the model is specified as five smaller models, with each viewpoint accounting for specific relevant issues [14][17]. Fig. 1 illustrates a diagram representing those five viewpoints.

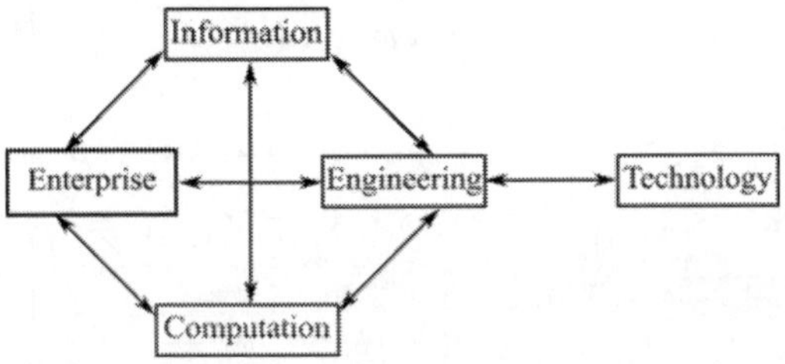

Figure 1. Viewpoints of the RM-ODP framework [4].

According to Linington et al. [17], the Enterprise viewpoint defines the scope and policies of the system, where the system requirements are defined. The Information viewpoint works with information semantics and its processing, describing the structures and types of data used. The Computational viewpoint defines a distribution by functionally breaking down the system into objects that interact in interfaces. It describes the features provided by the system and objects are built based on its features. The Engineering viewpoint is built based on the mechanisms and features required, supporting interactions distributed among the objects that make up the system. It describes the distribution of processing and communication among its several objects. The Technology viewpoint is related to the needs of the system regarding technology, describing the technologies required for processing, features, and information visualization.

This study approaches only the Engineering viewpoint of SDI-Cemig. The detailed definitions of the Enterprise, Information, and Computational viewpoints can be found in [8][9]. The Technology viewpoint is beyond the scope of this study and shall be specified in future works.

A. *Engineering Viewpoint*

The Engineering viewpoint aims to identify and specify interactions among distributed objects, focusing on their communication, organization, and distribution. It comprehends the distribution of compounds and the connections among them, besides defining common roles to support the distribution of components [18].

One advantage of using the Engineering viewpoint is creating a neutral and independent model not bound to specific technologies. That provides freedom in the choice of available and preferred technologies in an organization wishing to implement a given project. Along with the idea of a neutral model, a certain technology may be more easily replaced in case the organization decides to change it for private internal reasons [19].

Below, there are some components that are part of the Engineering viewpoint, according to [17], which were used to model SDI-Cemig in Section IV.

Basic Engineering Object (BEO) corresponds to the smallest representation when specifying the modeling. It is a special type of object in the Engineering viewpoint that represents a computational object defined in the Computational viewpoint that may also represent an actor, human or not, in the system. BEOs represent abstractions of elements that make up the system.

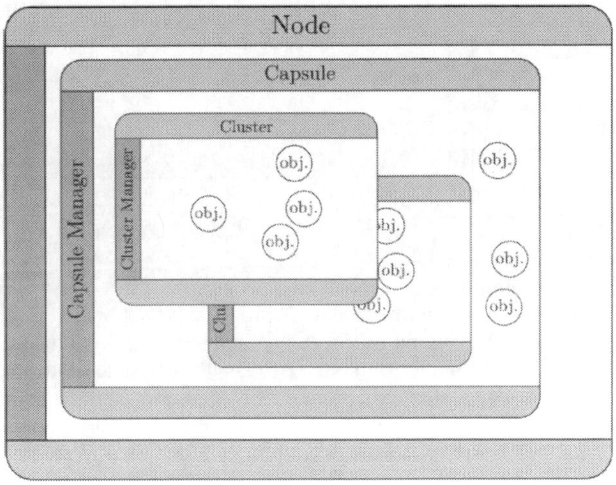

Figure 2. Viewpoints of the RM-ODP framework [4].

Fig. 2 illustrates the organization of objects in the Engineering viewpoint. A hierarchy can be seen among objects in the viewpoint. For example, within a Node there are Capsules, within a Capsule there are Clusters, and within a Cluster there are BEOs.

A cluster consists in a collection of BEOs grouped into similar functions and having lifecycles in the system [18]. A capsule represents a unit independent of processing or storage that is able to support an object collection. They are isolated from each other so as to ensure a capsule does not directly interfere with another. The node represents a physical or virtual object capable of processing, communication, and storage. It may represent a computer, the assembly of several devices that together determine a unit, a virtual machine in a computer, as long as the element has the capabilities mentioned above. They also have a high degree of isolation [17].

The structure of components in the Engineering viewpoint is split into components isolated from the capsule element. Therefore, mechanisms must be used in the communication among elements in distant structures. To that end, a communication channel structure is employed [19].

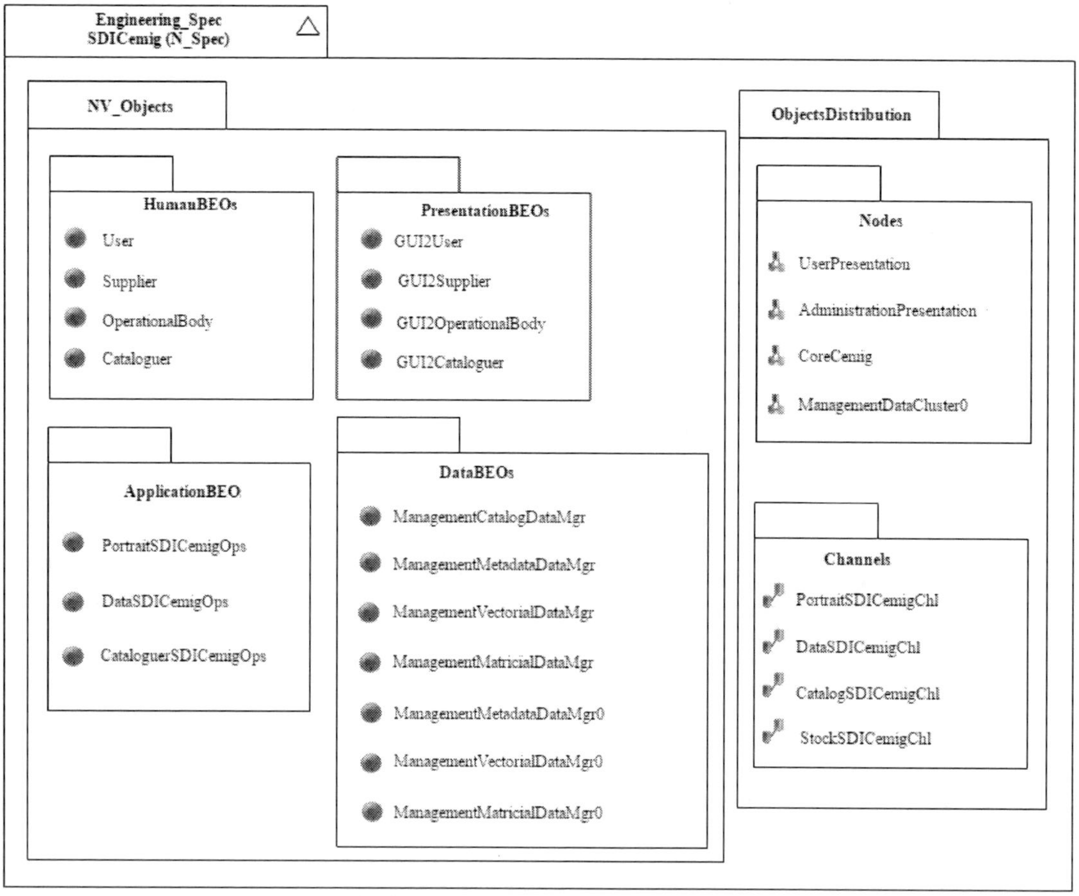

Figure 3. Overall organization of Engineering objects in SDI-Cemig.

Communication channels represent a transparent communication infrastructure, which allows objects in the Engineering viewpoint to interact, and are commonly used in the communication among BEOs of different nodes. A channel often does not need to be specified in detail since they are implemented at a lower level and the goal of the channel is to represent a communication among elements [17].

IV. ENGINEERING VIEWPOINT OF THE SDI-CEMIG

As described in Section I, Cemig seeks to develop an SDI, called SDI-Cemig, to help its employees and clients discover, share, and use geospatial data and services. This Section describes the Engineering viewpoint of SDI-Cemig. The Technology viewpoint is beyond the scope of this study, thus, it will not be detailed, while the Enterprise, Information, and Computational viewpoints of SDI-Cemig have already been described in [8][9].

The modeling of SDI-Cemig used ICA's adapted formal model for SDI. In order to create and name the elements, the examples provided by [17] when detailing the Engineering viewpoint were used as reference. The notation used terms that had meaning closer to their functionality. Names begin with a capital letter and the next words are never separated with spaces, also beginning with a capital letter. Since some components would have similar or even the same names, prefixes and suffixes were used in the nomenclature to differentiate their functionalities.

The overall organization of the specification of the Engineering viewpoint for SDI-Cemig is shown in Fig. 3. That figure represents the elements of the viewpoint grouped according to the functionalities of their objects. The overall organization represents a global view of the components of the Engineering viewpoint and is organized into two divisions: *ObjectsDistribution* and *NV_Objects*.

The division *NV_Objects* groups objects represent the basic elements, represented by BEOs, which are grouped into packages of similar functions. The objects were grouped into four packages: *HumanBEOs*, *ApplicationBEOs*, *PresentationBEOs*, and *DataBEO*.

The package *HumanBEOs* includes the actors that take part in the application, defined as: *User*, *Supplier*, *OperationalBody*, and *Cataloguer*. In the package *PresentationBEOs*, the BEOs represent the interfaces for the actors included in the package *HumanBEOs*. In its nomenclature, the prefix GUI2 (graphical user interface to) is added to the corresponding name in the package *HumanBEOs*. Therefore, the components of the package *PresentationBEOs* were described as: *GUI2User*; *GUI2Supplier*; *GUI2OperationalBody*; and *GUI2Cataloguer*.

The package *ApplicationBEOs* represents the features actors in SDI-Cemig may use in its functioning and administration. They represent three roles found by [9] that are required for the functioning of SDI-Cemig. The suffix Ops (Operations) is added to its nomenclature in each of its components. The components created were: *PortraitSDICemigOps*; *DataSDICemigOps*; and *CataloguerSDICemigOps*.

Finally, the package *DataBEOs* has BEOs related to information of the database. The package has components with roles in data storage and management. The suffix DataMgr (Data manager) was adopted in its nomenclature.

One way of improving the performance of information processing is to use object replication in a seamless way [16]. It can be seen that some elements have the number zero after the DataMgr suffix. This number indicates that the component is a replication of the component of analogous name and its goal is to reach better performance in the use of the application. The following objects of the *DataBEO* package were duplicated: *ManagementMetadataDataMgr*, *ManagementVectorialDataMgr*, and *ManagementMatricial-DataMgr*. It can be seen that the component *ManagementCatalogDataMgr* was not replicated since it is a component with catalog functionality and does not deal with large information volumes.

The second division, *ObjectsDistribution*, has components that represent the logical distribution and communication. It is made up of two packages: Nodes and Channels. The package Nodes represents a set of Node elements defined for the system, whose definition can be found in Subsection 3.*A*. For SDI-Cemig, four Nodes were defined: *UserPresentation*; *AdministrationPresentation*; *CoreCemig*; and *ManagementDataCluster0*.

The package *Channels* used the suffix Chl (Channel) in its nomenclature. The package aims to perform the communication of the components since the Nodes are isolated and need a means to communicate. The following channels were defined: *PortraitSDICemigChl*; *DataSDICemigChl*; *CataloguerSDICemigChl*; and *StockSDICemigChlDistribution* of Engineering Objects of SDI-Cemig.

According to Becerra et al. [19], the Engineering viewpoint specifies a communication infrastructure that must support the distribution of objects of the Computational viewpoint with no regard for the choice of technologies to implement it. Fig. 4 presents a version of the distribution of compounds of the Engineering viewpoint in SDI-Cemig grouped according to their interactions with other computational objects and packages grouping them. According to Linington et al. [17] Engineering objects represent in an abstract way the distribution and organization of the system, enabling a technology-independent modeling.

The administration of Engineering objects in SDI-Cemig were grouped into five groups: *HumanBEOs*, representing actors specified in the Enterprise [8] and Computational [9] viewpoints, namely: *UserPresentation* - represents the interfaces used by the actor *User*; *AdministrationPresentation* - represents the interfaces among the actors that manage the system; *ManagementDataCluster* - represents performance functionalities with the use of data replication; and *CoreCemig* - represents the system's processing core. *CoreCemig* is subdivided into *ApplicationCluster* - responsible for the system's features, *ManagementCatalogCluster* - responsible for a catalog of information available in the application, and *ManagementDataCluster* - responsible for the storage of data in the system.

The Engineering objects of the group *HumanBEOs* represent objects defined in the Enterprise viewpoint, each with its own access interface. Each client of the system has its own presentation layer with an analogous name. For instance, for the object Supplier of SDI-Cemig, there is an object in the presentation with the name GUI2Supplier.

The communication among the objects in the clusters *UserPresentation*, *AdministrationPresenttion*, and *ApplicationCluster*, the latter representing the system features, is performed through channels since they are in different Nodes. As shown in Fig. 4, there are three communication channels among the presentation clusters and feature cluster. *PortraitSDICemigOps*, *DataSDICemigOps*, and *CataloguerSDICemigOps*.

The channels are responsible for the communication between the presentation and feature layers contained in the application cluster. The link of each component to a given object and its required interfaces is based on the Computational viewpoint created by Oliveira et al. [9].

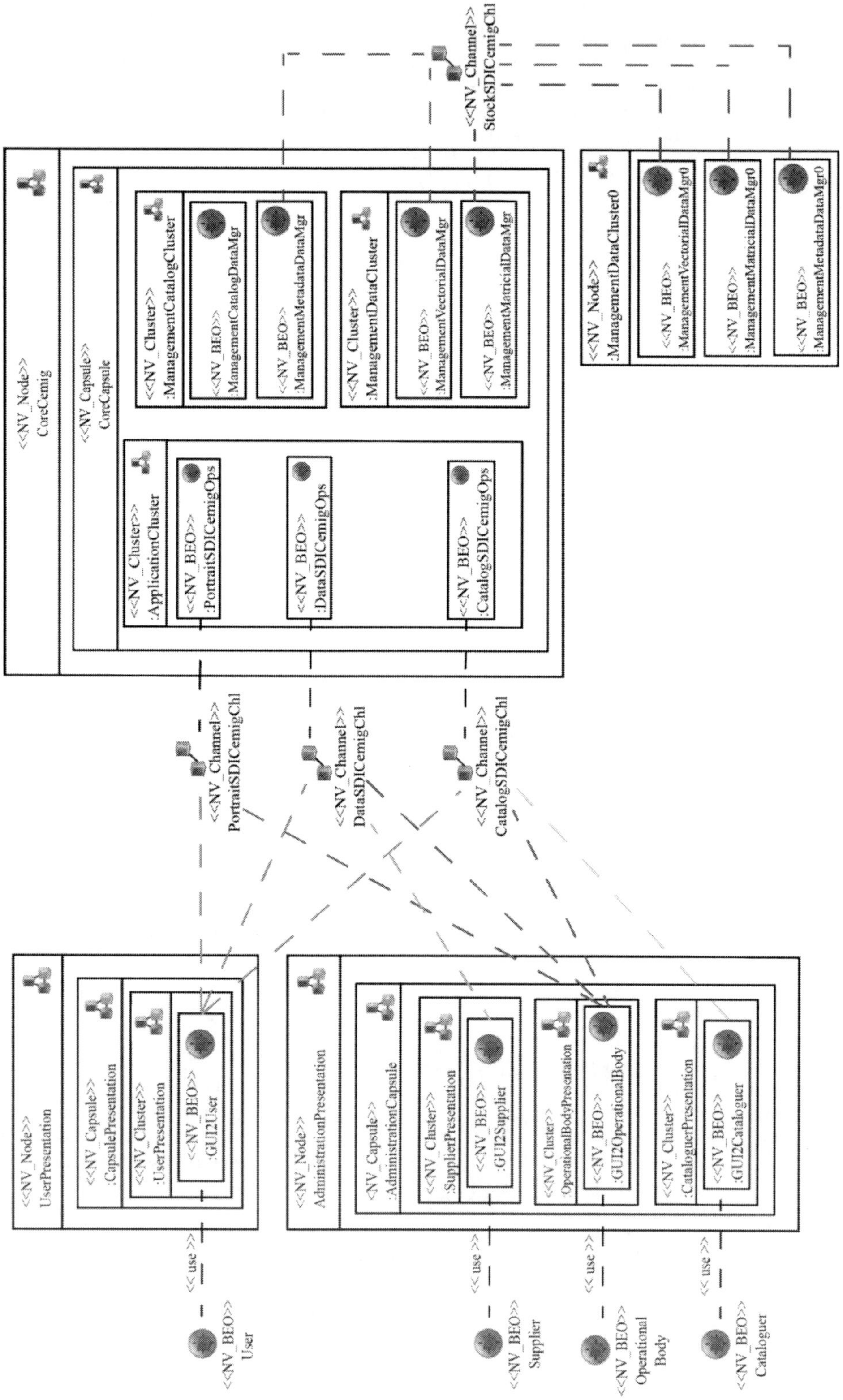

Figure 4. Engineering viewpoint of SDI-Cemig.

The channel *PortraitSDICemigChl* is responsible for performing the communication targeted at *PortraitSDICemigOps*. It fulfills requests coming from *GUI2User* and *GUI2OperationalBody* for map visualization and comprises the following interfaces: *GetMap_WMS*, *GetFeatureinfo_WMS*, and *GetCapabilities_WMS*.

The channel *DataSDICemigChl* performs the communication to *DataSDICemigOps* serving the interfaces *GUI2User*, *GUI2OperationalBody*, and *GUI2Supplier*. It plays a role in transmitting geographic information. Interfaces included: *GetPropertyValue_WFS*, *DescribeCoverage_WCS*, *GetCoverage_WCS*, *GetFeature_WFS-G*, *DescribeFeatureType_WFS*, *DescribeFeatureType_WFS-G*, *GetCapabilities_**, and *Transaction_**. The channel *CatalogSDICemigChl* fulfills the requests of *GUI2User*, *GUI2OperationalBody*, *GUI2Supplier*, and *GUI2Cataloguer*. The channel fulfills requests related to the SDI catalog. It serves the interfaces *GetRecords_CS*, *GetRecordbyID_CS*, *GetCapabilities_CS*, *GetRecords_CS*, *Transaction_CS*, and *Harvest_CS*.

V. Discussion of Results

ICA's model brings together a set of basic concepts that an SDI requires to work. The creation of the Engineering viewpoint for SDI-Cemig is a continuation and extension of the studies by Oliveira et al. [8][9] on the specification of the Enterprise, Information, and Computational viewpoints for a corporate SDI. As in the cited studies, the Engineering viewpoint described in the present study meets the basic requirements (e.g., enabling the discovery, recovery, sharing of geospatial data) of an SDI.

The Engineering viewpoint comprises structurally isolated nodes, i.e., nodes that work independently. Therefore, a failure in one component does not directly lead to a failure in another component. In case of a component being restructured, the others do not need to be adapted, since the communication is performed through channels and the new structure only needs to use the same communication structure of existing channels. Regarding the components, the system may receive new features through the creation of new objects and communication channels.

According to Oliveira et al. [9], the model applied in the specification of the SDI-Cemig can be used to build others corporate SDIs. It is observed that the SDI-Cemig has a restriction in the proposed specification, that is, it does not have geoprocessing services for a production of new geospatial data.

The viewpoint proposed in this work constitutes a continuation of this specification, maintaining the proposal for widespread use. The specification is proposed in such way that the new corporate SDIs implementations fit with the above-mentioned restriction. If there is the need to include new geoprocessing services or modifying existing one in the SDI, the model allows the expansion of functionality in the specification through the creation of new components.

This study, together with [8] and [9], present, at the best of our knowledge, the most complete specification of an SDI existing in the literature, approaching 4 of 5 of the RM-ODP viewpoints. Furthermore, our case study is based on a corporate SDI, whose kind is not sufficiently discussed in the literature.

VI. Conclusion and Futurework

By specifying the fourth viewpoint of the ICA's model, SDI-Cemig now has four viewpoints specified: Enterprise; Information; Computational; and Engineering. Since the RM-ODP framework comprises five viewpoints, only the Technology viewpoint still has to be specified, which, as the Engineering viewpoint, is not approached by ICA's SDI formal model. It must meet the requirements of the viewpoints already created and the company's technological availability.

The specification of the Engineering viewpoint for SDI-Cemig suggests that a similar specification may be used in other corporate SDIs, particularly of companies in the power sector. In case changes are required, the construction of the specification in modules enables the required adaptation to include new features. The specification of SDI-Cemig using ICA's adapted SDI formal model may help researchers and designers who wish to model SDIs based on the ICA's model even if they comprise a different SDI level.

Intended future works include specifying the Technology viewpoint of SDI-Cemig while checking it fits the viewpoints already created. After its specification, the specification will contemplate the five viewpoints of the RM-ODP model.

Acknowledgment

This research project was partially funded by Fapemig and CAPES, along with Cemig.

References

[1] A. Jhummarwala, M. D. Potdar, and P. Chauhan, "Parallel and distributed gis for processing geo-data: An overview", International Journal of Computer Applications, v. 106, n. 16, pp. 9–16, 2014.

[2] J. Carpenter and J. Snell, "Future trends in geospatial information management: The five to ten year vision". UN-GGIM, pp. 11–16, 2013.

[3] F. Harvey, A. Iwaniak, S. Coetzee, and A. Cooper, "SDI past, present and future: a review and status assessment", Spatially Enabling Government, Industry and Citizens, 2012.

[4] J. Hjelmager et al.,"An Initial Formal model for Spatial Data Infrastructure", International Journal of Geographic Information Science, v. 22, n. 11-12, pp. 1295-1309, 2008.

[5] R. Béjar, M. A. Latre, J. Nogueras-Iso, P. R. Muro-Medrano, and F. J. Zarazaga-Soria, "An RM-ODP enterprise view for spatial data infrastructures", Computer Standards & Interfaces, v. 34, pp. 263-272, 2012.

[6] A. Cooper et al.,"A Spatial Data Infrastructure Model from the Computational Viewpoint", International Journal of Geographical Information Science, v. 27, n. 6, pp. 1133-1151, 2013.

[7] I. L. Oliveira and J. Lisboa-Filho, "A Spatial Data Infrastructure Review – Sorting the Actors and Policies from Enterprise Viewpoint, Proceedings of the 17th International Conference on Enterprise Information Systems", vol. 17, pp. 287-294, 2014.

[8] I. L. Oliveira, J. Lisboa-Filho, C. A. Moura and A. G. Silva, "Especifying the Enterprise and Information Viewpoints for a

Corporate Spatial Data Infrastructure using ICA's Formal Model", In: 18th International Conference on Enterprise Information Systems, 2016, Rome. Proceedings of the 18th International Conference on Enterprise Information Systems, 2016.

[9] I. L. Oliveira, J. Lisboa-Filho, C. A. Moura, and A. G. Silva, "Specifying the Computation Viewpoints for a Corporate Spatial Data Infrastructure Using ICA's Formal Model", International Conference on Computational Science and Its Applications, Springer International Publishing, 2016.

[10] K. M. Sinvula, S. Coetzee, A. K. Cooper, E. Nangolo, W. Owusu-Banahene, V. Rautenbach and M. Hipondoka, "A Contextual ICA Stakeholder Model Approach for the Namibian Spatial Data Infrastructure (NamSDI)", In Cartography from Pole to Pole, pp. 381-394, Springer Berlin Heidelberg, 2014.

[11] F. M. Qureshi, A. Rajabifard and H. Olfat, "Facilitating urban planning and management at local level through the development of SDI (case study of Lahore-Pakistan)", 2009.

[12] T. D. Fernández and J. L. C. Fernández, "Towards semantic spatial data infrastructures: a framework for sustainable development", In Proc. GSDI 10th Conference, 2008.

[13] C. Rüh, P. Korduan and R. Bill, "Development of the reference model for the marine spatial data infrastructure Germany (MDI-DE)", EnviroInfo 2011: Innovations in Sharing Environmental Observations and Information, 419-425, 2011.

[14] K. Raymond, "Reference Model for Open Distributed Processing (RM-ODP): Introduction", Open Distributed Processing, pp. 3-14, 1998.

[15] K. Farooqui, L. Logrippo, and J. De Meer, "The ISO Reference Model for Open Distributed Processing: an introduction", Computer Networks and ISDN Systems, v. 27, n. 8, pp. 1215-1229, 1995.

[16] C. Egyhazy, and R. Mukherji, "Interoperability Architecture Using RM-ODP", Communications of ACM, vol.47, n. 2, 2004.

[17] P. F. Linington, Z. Milosevic, A. Tanaka, and A. Vallecilo, "Building Enterprise Systems with ODP: An Introduction to Open Distributed Processing", CRC Press, 2011.

[18] J. R. Putman, "Architecting with RM-ODP", Prentice Hall, New Jersey, 2000.

[19] J. L. R. Becerra, E. Garcia-Jr, N. Tanomaru, D. N. Moraes et al. (2003) "Arquitetura de um Middleware Corporativo na Companhia de Transmissão de Energia Elétrica Paulista", Polytechnic School USP, São Paulo, 2003.